'Past explorers and pioneers found and exploited "new worlds". Humanity will need multiple planets this century to meet its growing agricultural, industrial and consumer needs, but we only have one. So we have to build a new world on the one planet we have. Tania Ellis shows how new breeds of social innovators and entrepreneurs are leading the charge.'
John Elkington, Co-Founder and Executive Chairman of Volans, Co-Founder and Non-Executive Director of SustainAbility, and co-author of *The Power of Unreasonable People*

'If you are joining the social entrepreneurship revolution, or seeking to apply its principles in a mainstream business setting, this insightful and incredibly well researched book sets out the rules of the road ahead.'
John Grant, author of *Co-opportunity* **and** *The Green Marketing Manifesto*

'Plan A is central to the future competitive success of Marks & Spencer, and to our future relationship with customers and suppliers alike. It is a powerful example that "sustainable development" is making its way into the core of business strategy. It is no longer a nice-to-have, but a need-to-have. *The New Pioneers* – packed with case studies and guided by the principles which inform them – shows how companies are leveraging their competitive advantage and building innovative business models by putting sustainability into the core of their thinking and practice.'
Richard S. Gillies, Director, Plan A, CSR & Sustainable Business, Marks & Spencer

'Like James Cameron with his movie *Avatar* is changing the film industry from two dimensions to three dimensions, Tania Ellis's new book shows the changing face of business from a one dimensional profit focus to capitalism in three dimensions. *The New Pioneers* takes the reader on a step-by-step journey through the evolution of business and its stakeholders providing new insights, lessons learned and roads to walk for creating a future where business globally will play an important part of creating a better world today and tomorrow.'
Mads Kjaer, founder of MYC4

'. . ."*The New Pioneers*" is a very timely arrival that talks about developing future leaders and talent as businesses begin to recognize more and more that corporate sustainability is stretching the bandwidth of both current business models as well as their leadership profiles.'
Anant G. Nadkarni, Vice President – Group Corporate Sustainability, Tata

'In meticulous, convincing and heartening detail, Tania Ellis rolls out persuasive evidence that a "responsibility revolution" is well underway in the relationship between consumers and corporations. It is empowered by global communications networks the market revolutionaries of past generations – from Henry Ford to Ralph Nader – could never have conceived. It is inspired by indisputable proof – from climate change to the Great Recession – that we are indeed one world and that conscience is the best business model. Today, with governments having difficulty addressing some of the world's most perplexing problems, consumers, corporations and civil society must take the lead. As Ms Ellis documents so skillfully, that is precisely what they are doing.'
William Becker, Presidential Climate Action Project

Praise for *The New Pioneers*

'[Tania Ellis's] book shows the spectrum of thinking and concrete action around social
ecologically responsible business that has emerged in the last decade. This spectrum i
wider than any label such as Corporate Social Responsibility, Corporate Global Citizen
Social Investment, Social Entrepreneurship or Social Business would suggest, and her
aggregating this information will go a long way to inspiring others to lead further into
the future. It comprises exciting opportunities of engaging new actors and forging nev
partnerships to "improve the state of the world".'
Professor Klaus Schwab (from the foreword), Founder and Executive Chairman,
World Economic Forum; Founder, Schwab Foundation for Social Entrepreneurship

'*The New Pioneers* needs to be not only read – but more importantly acted on – by all
at the frontiers of building and giving life to the new economy. As we enter the Age o
Sustainability, it will be the abundancy of our talents that will drive innovation which
opportunity in extreme resource scarcity. To harness these talents across the globe, er
different cultures on the basis of shared equity, we need to know what works and wh
what, framed by a challenge to current mindsets. *The New Pioneers* provides all that –
much more.'
Tony Manwaring, Chief Executive, Tomorrow's Company

'The world is changing and the new pioneers are the ones changing it. If you want to
sense of what's happening – or even better, if you want to help make it happen – rea
book. It's a handbook for the global revolution!'
**Alan M. Webber, Co-founding Editor, Fast Company magazine and author of *Rules o*
*52 Truths for Winning at Business Without Losing Your Self***

'We are living through one of history's great transitions – from the Age of Greed to t
Responsibility – and Tania Ellis's "new pioneers" are at the leading edge of the revol
This is a book that informs and inspires, reminding us that a better world is not only
but is already being created. It is an insightful window on a remarkable movement –
to action for us all.'
Dr Wayne Visser, Director of CSR International and author of *The Age of Responsibili*

'I welcome *The New Pioneers*, as a contribution to moving forward the vision of more
and sustainable businesses, reforming markets and growing "greener" economies w
Tania Ellis has performed a great service and we hope this book is widely-read!'
Hazel Henderson, author of *Ethical Markets: Growing the Green Economy* (2006) and
Ethical Markets Media (USA and Brazil)

'For 150 years we have directed companies on two false assumptions, viz. that planet
infinite resources and an infinite capacity to absorb waste. The consequence is an ec
crisis which has driven companies into a new economy – business as unusual and le
make more with less. *The New Pioneers* illustrates that the stakeholder inclusive gove
approach now prevails and everyone has a role to play to make the new face of capit:
work.'
Mervyn King, Chairman of the Global Reporting Initiative

THE NEW PIONEERS

THE NEW PIONEERS

SUSTAINABLE BUSINESS SUCCESS

THROUGH SOCIAL INNOVATION AND

SOCIAL ENTREPRENEURSHIP

TANIA ELLIS

A John Wiley & Sons, Ltd., Publication

Library of Congress Cataloging-in-Publication Data

Ellis, Tania.
　　The new pioneers : sustainable business success through social innovation and social entrepreneurship / Tania Ellis.
　　　　p. cm.
　　Summary: "The chief purpose of the book is to show that the concept and principles of social entrepreneurship and sustainable business have potential everywhere, not just among the idealistic few"– Provided by publisher.
　　Includes bibliographical references and index.
　　ISBN 978-0-470-74842-8
　1. Social entrepreneurship and social innovation,　2. Social responsibility of business.
3. Twenty first century business–Forecasting.　I. Title.
　　HD60.E55 2010
　　658.4′08—dc22
　　　　　　　　　　　　　　　　　　　　　　　　　　　　　2010022096

A catalogue record for this book is available from the British Library.

ISBN 978-0-470-74842-8 (hardback), ISBN 978-0-470-97367-7 (ebk),
ISBN 978-0-470-97130-7 (ebk), ISBN 978-0-470-97131-4 (ebk)

Typeset in 10/14.5pt FF Scala by Best-set Premedia Limited, Hong Kong
Printed in Great Britain by TJ International Ltd, Padstow, Cornwall, UK

[

Pioneer/ ˌpaɪə'nɪə (r)/ *n*

1. a person who is the first to study and develop a new area of knowledge, culture, etc.
2. a person who is among the first to go into an area or a country to settle or work there.

]

Advanced Learner's Oxford Dictionary

CONTENTS

FOREWORD

Forty years ago, I founded the World Economic Forum, then named the European Management Forum. In 1971, the first meeting was held in Davos, bringing together a group of European business leaders under the patronage of the European Commission and industrial associations. Over the last decades, the name has changed to reflect the much more global nature of the organization. Our motto is 'entrepreneurship in the global public interest'.

Since the beginning, the 'stakeholder' management approach has been the core concept guiding our activities – it forms the philosophical basis of the World Economic Forum and led to its creation. The main idea is that leadership is meant to serve all stakeholders of a company – and at a higher level, serve the global community. Leaders must act as the trustees for the long-term prosperity of the community. This concept must be revitalized in the form of stakeholder capitalism in which the creative and entrepreneurial forces of capitalism are made to work in the interests of all stakeholders. And we must expand the concept to include true global citizenship where all stakeholders of our global community work together to improve the state of the world.

Today, the Forum is the foremost global multistakeholder organization, convening and integrating communities of leaders from all walks of life – particularly from business, government and civil society. In this capacity, the sense of 'community' is underscored by a collaborative spirit, where each individual is not only aware of his or her rights, but also his or her responsibilities. Currently, the Forum manages over 25 different communities such as our Partners, Members, industry-related communities and Global Growth Companies (the New Champions). But the Forum also develops communities of the key figures among globally active NGOs, Trade Unions, and Faith Leaders – not to mention our Women Leaders, Young Global Leaders and Social Entrepreneurs. All of these communities are selected and invited to ensure the highest level of quality, relevance and representation. The fundamental value that the Forum provides to all of these communities lies not only in the interaction stimulated within each community, but also in stimulating interaction among all our communities.

The purpose of the World Economic Forum is to act as a force for reflection and connection – bridging ideas, proposals, stakeholders, countries and cultures. The Forum provides a new way to integrate the world's top leaders into processes of joint problem definition, joint search for solutions and – whenever possible – joint action. We can look back on a long list of major achievements catalyzed by the Forum. These include the announcement of the 'Global Compact' by then UN Secretary-General Kofi Annan in 1999, to "give a human face to the global market", the announcement for a Global Alliance for Vaccines and Immunization (GAVI) a year later and the informal meetings that took place between political leaders from Greece and Turkey, East and West Germany and South Africa which shaped the future of their countries.

While the World Economic Forum has demonstrated the power of convening the world's leaders from all walks of life, we found that we also needed to find a way to identify people who have discovered innovative and practical solutions to social, economic and environmental problems at the local level. My belief has always been that, in the end, economic and social progress can best be achieved through entrepreneurship of all kinds. With that philosophy, ten years ago, my wife Hilde and I created the Schwab Foundation for Social Entrepreneurship because we recognized that the most promising and innovative solutions to our world's problems were often spearheaded by rather unknown individuals working tirelessly in the shadows of the market and the public sector. The Schwab Foundation encourages and develops entrepreneurs working for the public interest – supporting them and providing an unprecedented opportunity to further legitimacy and make strategic contacts.

Over the past decade, social entrepreneurs have become highly sought after contributors to the initiatives and industry conversations among business leaders in the Forum on topics such as climate change, health, housing, education, financial inclusion, mobile services, just to name a few. Today, I cannot imagine an annual or regional meeting without including the grounded and pragmatic voices of the social entrepreneurs. They exemplify that a more sustainable form of capitalism that serves society overall is possible and they provide inspiration for others to follow and build on their approaches.

Overall, it is clear that the basis of any progress made in the complex and fast moving world of the 21st century lies in the ability to understand the motivations of all different stakeholders of global society. We will build a better world not just by formulating well-considered policies or reforming institutions, but rather by renewing our value systems to integrate a true individual and collective approach to our common future. And in this context, Tania Ellis makes a clear case for how the 'New Pioneers' are playing an integral role. Her book shows the spectrum of thinking and concrete action around socially and ecologically responsible business that has emerged in the last decade. This spectrum is much wider than any label such as Corporate Social Responsibility, Corporate Global Citizenship, Social Investment, Social Entrepreneurship or Social Business would suggest, and her work in aggregating this information will go a long way to inspiring others to lead further into the future. It comprises exciting opportunities of engaging new actors and forging new partnerships to "improve the state of the world".

Professor Klaus Schwab
Founder and Executive Chairman, World Economic Forum
Founder, Schwab Foundation for Social Entrepreneurship

INTRODUCTION

Welcome to the 'age of globalization', 'the turnaround society', 'the era of compassionate capitalism', 'the new era of creativity and growth', 'the era of innovation', 'the age of sustainability', 'the era of globality', 'the entrepreneurial society' or 'the era of co-creation' – the 21st century already has many names. In other words, welcome to a world of profound changes that will affect our way of thinking, living and working for the next many years to come.

Welcome to a world of possibilities – but also to a new world of disorder with financial, social and environmental crises that have left their mark, globally and nationally, on organizations and individuals. This world of disorder is giving rise to new needs. And new needs require new solutions.

Einstein's famous quote: 'No problem can be solved from the same level of consciousness that created it', says it all: the financial, environmental and social challenges of the 21st century cannot be met with solutions based on 20th century mindsets, models and designs. In short, social innovation has become more important than ever.

With crises come breakdowns and fear, which makes it tempting to tell a story of doom and gloom. But crises need not be negative. They are helpful signs that we need to reorientate and change our way of thinking. In fact, the Greek word *krisis* means 'decisive moment'. Because with each crisis also comes a window of opportunity to manifest new actions. In this case an opportunity to innovate for the world that is emerging rather than the one we are leaving behind.

The world is changing – and so is mankind. The combined effects of globalization, technologization and changing priorities have led to a burgeoning awareness of the fact that we cannot keep on consuming and developing at the expense of the environment, social commitments and our inner values.

These outer and inner pressures are already blurring the borders between business and society, work and life, making money and doing good. And they are driving revolutionary reconceptions of prosperity and growth.

We do not know exactly what the future will look like, but everywhere there are glimpses of a new, emerging economic world order which builds on sustainable development and a blend of social and financial values. And this is what this book is all about.

It is a story about us and about business. It is about the internal and external dimensions of change shaping our lives in new ways and creating a new face of capitalism. It is about the challenges and new rules that are paving the way for business unusual. And it is about the opportunities and new solutions that are making it possible for us to solve some of society's critical problems. It is about a new wave of innovations that are bridging humanism and economics. And it is about the New Pioneers that are paving the way: the social business innovators of our time.

A global movement

The New Pioneers are part of a global consciousness movement – a social megatrend – that is based on values such as ethics, responsibility, meaning and the conviction that we are all part of the same greater whole. It is a movement carried forward by a vision of sustainable development as the future foundation for growth, innovation and value creation – a vision which is already becoming a reality.

The global consciousness movement has been working just like an underground seed which no one really notices until it is in full bloom. We started to see the first signs of the current transformation back in the 1960s and 1970s in the shape of flower children and hippies, who were part of a peaceful cultural protest movement as a counter reaction to political conservatism and war.

It was also in these decades that many grassroot movements and NGOs were established. People got involved in charity, human rights and environmental organizations, which became catalysts for anything from anti-nuclear and peace movements to the struggle for women's lib and gay rights. Likewise, the New Age movement, humanist psychology and alternative treatment also saw the light of day.

This was the kick-off to what was later to be coined by social scientists *the silent revolution* – a gradual values shift as a counter reaction to the one-sided emphasis on material and financial gain that has ruled Western society for decades. As a result, inner-oriented, immaterial values like individualism, autonomy and self-actualization are today gradually taking the place of the outer-oriented, material values like prestige, power and wealth that have predominated in Western society for the past 25–50 years.

Because of its underground nature, this movement has been under the public radar for years. But in 2002 the silent revolution was given a voice in the groundbreaking book *The Cultural Creatives* by sociologist Paul H. Ray and professor of psychology Sherry R. Anderson.

For the first time, quantitative data and research on American values and lifestyles from the mid-1980s to the 2000s were compared, analysed and verified. Out of it came a living picture of a subculture with people characterized by awareness of the environment, ecology, of spiritual and personal development and a self-imposed simple way of living. A culture with quality of life and sustainable development at its core.

In the 1960s the Cultural Creatives constituted less than 5% of the American population, but in little more than the span of a generation this 'cultural virus' of sustainability and higher purpose has become more like a global social epidemic with an emerging international community.

In 1999 26% of the US population – 50 million people – and a similar percentage of the population in 15 European Union countries were already affecting business and society as employees, managers, consumers, investors and entrepreneurs in the name of enlightened self-interest.[1] And ever since the numbers appear to be growing, with millions of 'deserters' from other subcultures that have become disillusioned with the values of money, status and 'bigger is better'.[2]

What was once a collection of niche movements has now developed into a critical mass of people that are aware of the consequences of humanity's unsustainable growth – and they want to make a difference in each their own way. It is an underground movement that has evolved into a gradual, collective awakening – a global mind shift that is marking a change in survival strategies: from maximising economic growth to maximising survival and wellbeing through lifestyle changes.[3]

But unlike conventional definitions of a movement, this one does not have a leader or an ideology. It has no manifesto or doctrine. Instead, it is driven bottom-up by millions of individuals, groups and organizations that are unified by ideas and actions to protect and save humanity and the environment. It is what has been characterized 'the largest movement on Earth' and a 'creative expression of people's needs worldwide'.[4]

The silent revolution has become a visible force for good that is transforming the (business) world at this very moment. And thanks to the Internet and the emergence of new social media, it has now been given an even more powerful voice. These technological accelerators of change are, at this very moment, driving new expressions of responsibility, democracy, transparency, self-organization and cooperation, which in effect are creating global communities of problem solvers, co-creators, activists and change-makers of all shapes and sizes – both inside and outside organizations. Personal initiative and collaborative innovation are at the heart of the 21st century transformation game.

In the midst of a paradigm shift

The World Values Survey, conducted since 1981 in more than 80 societies on six continents, shows that the current values shift has been growing particularly in countries like Denmark, Finland, Sweden, Norway, Iceland, the Netherlands, Switzerland, the UK, Canada and the USA.[3] Some of the characteristics of this post-modern shift are:

- A tendency for economic growth to be subordinate to concerns for environmental sustainability.

- A general questioning of authority and declining trust in science and technology to solve problems.
- More emphasis on personal authority, i.e. what comes from an inner sense of what is appropriate.
- Growing interest in discovering personal meaning and purpose in life.
- Desire for meaningful work and the quality of the work experience.
- New roles for women that allow for greater self-realization.

Researchers from the World Values Survey predict that these new values will form the predominant values system in Western Europe some time after the year 2020.[5] Western society is therefore currently in a period of transition towards a new world view of what society, business and the economy are really for.

A paradigm shift is a change of mindset, a new set of assumptions, concepts, values and practices shared by a community of people. The shift happens – and crises come to life – when the existing frameworks create problems or no longer fulfil current needs. It marks the evolution of mankind and development in society as we have seen it during times of transition from the hunter-gatherer era to the agricultural era, on to the industrial era and now to the era-of-already-many-names.

The new 21st century paradigm described in this book is based on the need to bring all the key relationships in our lives into balance: intuitive and rational, masculine and feminine, inner and outer, personal and global. It aims at bridging differences, connecting people, celebrating diversity, harmonising efforts and looking for higher common ground.[6] And, like in the preceding eras, this requires new mindsets, systems, tools and skills. It is sustainability made manifest at all levels.

This is why we now need to re-evaluate, adjust and possibly fundamentally change our basic assumptions about how to live, work, learn, cooperate, conduct politics, manage economies and technologies, solve problems and do business.

The acclaimed business thinker Peter Drucker, who coined the term 'knowledge society', put it this way: 'Within a few short decades, society rearranges itself – its worldview; its basic values; its social and political structure; its arts; its key institutions. Fifty years later, there is a new world. And the people born then cannot even imagine the world in which their grandparents lived and into which their own parents were born.'[7] It is no coincidence that the title of the World Economic Forum's annual meeting in Davos in 2010 was *Improve the State of the World: Rethink, Redesign, Rebuild.*

The current development is not just a Western fad. We see traces of it around the world in different shapes and sizes, and the vision of sustainable development is already shared by many – although countervailing trends also exist. This is why we are also living in a world of apparent paradoxes: countries use economic growth as the measure of social progress although citizens are slowing down to advance wellbeing; consumers are both price conscious and ethically aware; employees search for both material wealth and spiritual growth; public institutions deliver welfare solutions and are run like businesses; non-profit organizations use market methods to create social value; and companies are socially responsible while making a profit. But paradoxes are better than none – they may even lay the foundation for new solutions.

On a personal level, I have experienced the current transition. 'Do you want to save the world, or do you want to make money?' was the choice that many of my generation had to make when we entered the labour market in the 1980s. This was a time when most companies operated with one bottom line and acknowledged only a single obligation: to make money – and left the rest for others to deal with. And it was a time when employees went to work to make a living – and realized themselves in their spare time.

But as I soon came to discover as a business manager throughout the 1990s with responsibility for hundreds of service employees: the times they are a-changin'. Along with the influence of Generation Y (born 1976–1991) came new expectations of feedback, involvement and development. Today's employees want influence on their daily work routines. They want to understand how their efforts are contributing to the larger picture. And professional development must go hand in hand with personal growth and fulfilment. Today, it is all about creating the good (work) life.

At the same time, in the wake of conflicts like the Greenpeace–Shell confrontation when environmentalists occupied the oil platform Brent Spar to prevent Shell from disposing of it in the deep Atlantic waters off the west coast of Scotland, and the later Enron and Worldcom accounting scandals, issues of business and society, profit making and ethics were also starting to emerge.

Along with these developments came discussions and new questions. Why are these changes happening? Is it possible to meet people's needs and business needs at the same time? Can companies make money while being positive contributors to society? And if so, how?

Social innovations

When the old answers no longer fit the new questions, significant changes happen. And the changes are often driven by catalytic events such as climate change or the recent credit crunch. Or by the intervention of social innovators.

Social innovation stems from people's unfulfilled needs. It creates social value or change and thereby drives social development and renewal in society. It is society's hidden growth and value maker and an expression of our social evolution. It is an expression of how we think, learn, live and work. And it is about new solutions that solve societal problems or meet people's unfulfilled needs in new ways that improve their lives.

The co-operative movement, legislation, tax, therapy, insurance, stenography, labour unions, social welfare centres, kindergartens, management concepts, pedagogical methods and e-learning are all examples of social innovations that have emerged in the context of a particular period in history to meet the needs of their time. As we evolve as a species, new social innovations are consequently coming to light. In fact, some of the most fruitful periods for social innovation have been in times of transition. And so, once again, social innovation is now proving to be a significant driver of creating value in benefit of society.

Social innovation is not reserved for one particular sector in society. It is found in the public sector, in the civil sector, in the private sector – and in the cross-section between the three. And although social innovation creates social value, it can be used both commercially and non-commercially. In fact, the concept of money as a means of transaction between people is a social innovation that can be traced back to around 3200 B.C. and is consequently also being developed and adapted in support of a sustainable future.

Local Exchange Trading Systems (LETS) and other local currencies, venture philanthropy, microcredit, CSR (corporate social responsibility), the triple bottom line, SRI (socially responsible investing), the market-based Fairtrade system, the Cradle-to-Cradle or BOP (bottom of the pyramid) concepts, Gross Company Happiness measures, emissions trading and indeed hybrid social business models are all examples of recent concepts that have been born from permeating traditional borders between economics and humanism as answers to some of the vital sustainability questions that are being asked right now.

This blending of economic and social values is, in other words, generating new social innovations that are creating wealth and welfare for the benefit of society, the environment, people's wellbeing and the health of the bottom line.

Similarly, social movements now include movements like the Slow Movement, which aims at a cultural shift toward slowing down life's pace, the Green Belt Movement International, which aims at empowering communities worldwide to protect the environment and to promote good governance and cultures of peace, and – most recently – Transition Towns, which aim at equipping communities for the dual challenges of climate change and peak oil by seeking out community-led initiatives to reduce energy usage as well as to increase their own self-reliance and wellbeing.

Just like these movements, many other social innovations have come to life as a result of the commitment, enthusiasm and perseverance of individuals before they eventually became commonly known concepts.

Sparked by a protest against the opening of a McDonald's restaurant in Rome in 1986, Carlo Petrini started the Slow Food movement, which quickly expanded to other areas. Today the broader Slow Movement includes Slow Management, Slow Cities and Slow Trade, and has over 100 000 members in 132 countries.[8]

The Green Belt Movement was founded in the 1970s by Wangari Maathai, a Kenyan environmentalist and women's rights activist, whose efforts on reforestation were later acknowledged with the 2004 Nobel Peace Prize and a membership of the Kenyan Parliament. The Movement has already educated thousands of low-income women about forestry, has created about 3000 part-time jobs and is now operating in other parts of the world, including Japan, West India and South America.

Likewise, the Transition Town movement was created by Louise Rooney in Kinsale, Ireland and popularized by Rob Hobkins in Totnes, England in 2005, and already now has member communities in other parts of Ireland, England, Wales, Scotland, Australia, Chile, Japan, New Zealand and the USA.

Social innovations are, in other words, often born with the initiative from committed citizens with social visions, will and drive. They are driven by passionate pioneers and grassroots activists rather than from political environments and government-owned research and development laboratories. They are driven from within and from below. For often it is those who have the social problems or unsatisfied needs closest to them who also have the solutions.

Society teems with thousands of ideas for social innovation, often where the problems occur and where the needs arise. The great challenge is, however, to systematize the ideas and to find the resources for turning them into action, so they can be widely distributed and achieve full effect. This is why many social innovators are becoming social business entrepreneurs.

The pioneers of our time

30 years ago nobody had heard about Bangladeshi economist Muhammad Yunus, who conceived the idea of microcredit – a system of extending small loans to the poor so they could start their own businesses as an instrument to eradicate poverty. Today the concepts of microcredit and Grameen Bank's social business model – for which Yunus was awarded a Nobel Prize in 2006 – have become textbook examples of social innovation and social entrepreneurship, terms which only a few people had heard of a decade ago but which the world is now starting to embrace.

The social entrepreneurship potential of solving social problems in innovative ways is attracting both politicians and businesspeople. In the case of Grameen Bank, its commercial success has convinced large commercial banks to get involved with microfinancing – not only in poor countries but also in wealthy Western nations. And in addition to the many distinguished accolades Muhammad Yunus has already received, he was most recently awarded the American Presidential Medal of Freedom – the nation's highest civilian award to people who have made a difference in the nation or the world.

'They remind us that we each have it within our power to fulfill dreams, to advance the dreams of others, and to remake the world for our children,' US President Barack Obama stated at the ceremony that marked Muhammad Yunus's pioneering efforts as one of the world's most effective champions of Obama's 'yes we can' spirit.[9] The White House now even has an Office of Social Innovation and Civic Participation, which is in charge of a first-of-its-kind $50 million fund to boost the efforts of the country's most cutting-edge non-profits and social entrepreneurs.

Just like Muhammad Yunus, other New Pioneers are paving the way for responsible and sustainable business one innovative step at a time. And just as the settlers and explorers of the past were the first to enter a new land and settle, the New Pioneers are discovering and cultivating new areas of knowledge, new cultures, new insights, new thoughts and new solutions that bridge economy and humanism – that pave the way for heartcore business.

In this book you will be introduced to New Pioneers that have navigated the current paradoxes and challenged 20th century business logics. By doing so, they have discovered new solutions in the shape of new partnerships, new ways to use resources, new organizational forms, new systems, processes and work methods, new products and services, and indeed new designs and business models that address some of the world's most pressing social and environmental challenges.

The New Pioneers are this century's generation of visionary leaders, social entrepreneurs and social intrapreneurs that are turning the doom and gloom of current global challenges into new business opportunities and sustainable ways of creating value. They are continuously setting foot on new land and charting the contours of new paths for the benefit and inspiration of others in society. They are showing us glints of the new economic world order where social responsibility and innovation drive good business. And they are doing it in a wide range of industries from media, food, agriculture and banking to medicine, cosmetics, IT and design.

The New Pioneers are creating new hybrids of doing business and solving society's problems. They are showing old world companies and organizations how to tackle new world challenges for the benefit of both humanity and the bottom line.

A wave of creative destruction

The Austrian economist Joseph Schumpeter (1883–1950) was perhaps the most powerful thinker ever on innovation, entrepreneurship and capitalism, and to this very day his ideas still have great resonance.

Schumpeter introduced the term 'creative destruction' in economics to describe the process of transformation that accompanies radical innovation. In his vision of capitalism, innovative entry by entrepreneurs was the force that sustained long-term economic growth, even as it destroyed the value of established companies that enjoyed some degree of monopoly power.[10] And he championed the role of the entrepreneur in both start-ups and in established companies.

'Without innovations, no entrepreneurs; without entrepreneurial achievement, no capitalist returns and no capitalist propulsion,' Schumpeter wrote during the Great Depression of the 1930s.[11]

The recent downturn, which some economists have labelled the worst financial crisis in seven decades, is reinforcing a new wave of creative destruction to counter the current economic, social and environmental imbalances that are putting their negative mark on both businesses and nations alike.

Innovative sustainability initiatives by large commercial companies and the emergence of hybrid social business models created by social entrepreneurs are some of the testimonials to the fact that it is possible – and necessary – to create a new industrial revolution that rejects unsustainable business models and embraces value creation for the bottom line as well as the common good. They represent the new global mindset that will transform business and society.

There are still a wide number of yet unexploited opportunities in the interface between social entrepreneurship, commercial companies and the social missions of public and civil organizations. New opportunities with the potential to solve many of society's yet unsolved problems – but also new opportunities to create sustainable business solutions with an economic growth potential in both million and billion dollar categories.

No wonder several economists have claimed that the 21st century is going to be 'the century of Schumpeter' in yet unprecedented ways.[11]

A guide to the 'new business revolution'

We are the first generation of global citizens. And the choices we will be making now and in the next decade will affect the next many generations to come. Thomas Jefferson's claim more than four centuries ago that 'every generation needs a new revolution' still holds true. But the revolution for the current generation is an entrepreneurial one, in which the combination of individual creativity and economic dynamism is spreading all over the world.[12]

With business being one of the most dominant institutions of this century, understanding the implications of the current changes is just as important for future generations as it is for the future survival and growth of businesses' bottom line.

This is the reason why I have, for the past seven years, specialized in working with social business trends with the purpose of guiding and inspiring individuals and organizations to explore and engage in innovative and sustainable practices that generate both human and economic growth.

This has led to exciting work on committees and boards, involvement in grassroots projects and social ventures, the development of new business strategies for corporations as well as speaking engagements for thousands of people from ministries, companies, NGOs, unions, public institutions, business schools and universities.

Business school students, for example, want to develop their professional skills to serve a higher purpose. Ministries want to develop new policies that encourage companies to integrate corporate responsibility and social innovation as part of their core business. NGOs want to partner with corporations to create more social value. And businesses want to create a workplace that can attract the new generation on the labour market as well as products and services that meet their customers' needs in new, sustainable ways.

In short, they want to understand the implications of the current changes in business and society – and they want to develop solutions to meet the new needs that follow in the wake of these changes without compromising the needs of future generations.

The purpose of this book is to give you an overview of the powerful drivers of the current paradigm shift, and to introduce you to some of the many social innovations and New Pioneers that are paving the way forward. To provide you with an inspirational guide and roadmap of how to build or maintain a sustainable business, big or small, in the new economic world order. To present glimpses of what the emerging future may look like.

The book builds on thoughts and findings from my past seven years of field research including conversations and consultations with business executives, civil servants, academics, consultants, entrepreneurs, innovators and activists as well as ploughing through hundreds of articles, books and surveys. To guide you, the book has been divided into two major themes:

I: *New times – new needs*

The 'why?' and 'what?' – the framework for sustainable business. Why is the operating environment of business changing? What are the flaws of capitalism in its current form? And what does all this imply for companies now and in the future? This part of the book provides snapshots of the outer and inner globalization drivers of the new business paradigm. It presents three global imbalances that are giving rise to three sustainable growth principles as well as five needs which are creating five new markets of change that companies must take into account in their strategic planning. Read this part to gain insight into the new rules of business in the new economic world order.

II: *New needs – new solutions*

The 'how?' and 'who?' – the routes to sustainable business success. How are companies leveraging their competitive advantage, building new business models and creating blended value for the benefit of society and the bottom line? And who are the travellers on the sustainability journey that are creating a new face of capitalism? This part of the book provides a wide range of examples of how sustainable business strategies are put into practice, including the benefits and paradoxes. It presents three dimensions of the new business paradigm, seven growth strategies, four enabling cornerstones as well as some of the future next steps required to turn pioneering ideas into sustainable business actions. Read this part to gain insight into how to navigate on the roads to sustainability by following the trails of the New Pioneers.

By the time you have read the book, you will have been introduced to many different perspectives on the pioneering force for good, and you will have heard the voices of many different people from around the world. But the story of the New Pioneers is still half told and many voices are as yet unheard, so I invite you to meet more change-makers, tell your own stories and learn more about sustainable business at **www.thenewpioneers.biz**

Part I

New Times – New Needs

Chapter 1

Globalization has made the world smaller and business opportunities bigger. But nations and corporations alike must adapt their growth strategies to the current megacrises and disruptions that are creating a new world of disorder. Pioneering entrepreneurs and companies are developing innovative solutions and applying sustainable growth principles to address issues like climate change, resource scarcity, poverty, labour rights and health threats. New rules for future economic growth are paving the way for business unusual.

A business world of disorder
– the new business paradigm

'Future generations are likely to view the current times as a pivot point, when old frameworks were discarded and new ones began to emerge. They might describe that pivot point as a "reset", when business as usual was no longer possible, and new ways of thinking and acting were needed.'[1]
Business for Social Responsibility (BSR)

'Values have shrunken to fantastic levels; taxes have risen; our ability to pay has fallen; ... the means of exchange are frozen in the currents of trade; the withered leaves of industrial enterprise lie on every side; ... the savings of many years in thousands of families are gone ... Practices of the unscrupulous money changers stand indicted

in the court of public opinion, rejected by the hearts and minds of men
... Faced by failure of credit they have proposed only the lending of more
money ... They know only the rules of a generation of self-seekers ...
The measure of the restoration lies in the extent to which we apply
social values more noble than mere monetary profit ... Restoration calls,
however, not for changes in ethics alone. This Nation asks for action,
and action now.'[2]

This quote could well have been a present-day description of the current
state of the world in the wake of the recent financial crisis. But these are the
words of Franklin D. Roosevelt, when he assumed the office of President of
the United States in the midst of a deep financial and economic crisis in 1933.

Unlike previous financial crises, this one has, however, not only showed
us that the market is a good servant but a terrible master when it comes to
sustainable outcomes. It has also showed us how vulnerable and interconnected the world is today.

What started as an American financial crisis – triggered by easy credit
conditions, sub-prime lending and a short-term focus on profiting from a
booming property market which led to a massive housing bubble that burst
in the US, bringing down major financial institutions like Lehman Brothers,
Merrill Lynch and Fannie Mae – within a year turned into an economic
tsunami that flooded the rest of the world.

The rippling effect on global stock markets led to a global credit crisis that
has resulted in the failure of key businesses, declines in consumer wealth, an
increase in unemployment rates and a significant decline in economic
activities.

For the small island republic of Iceland, which only a few years earlier
was ranked as one of the wealthiest and most developed nations in the world,
the economic crisis has resulted in the collapse of all three of the country's
major banks, and led to – relative to the size of its economy – the largest
suffering by any country in economic history with a national currency in free
fall and the bankruptcy of its people, for many of whom the previous eight
years had been one long party on the crest of the worldwide credit boom.[3]

For those where the party was only getting started – the developing countries – it has put foreign direct investments (FDI), commercial lending and

aid budgets under pressure, with the risk of weaker export revenues, lower investment and growth rates, lost employment and negative social effects like higher poverty, more crime and weaker health systems.[4]

Roosevelt's call for ethics and application of social values as a part of successful market systems is the same call that politicians, economists, the general public and even CEOs are voicing today. It is also the basis of the key messages which will be discussed in this chapter:

1. The economic crisis has shown us that the current version of capitalism is based on a fundamentally flawed design and that it must be revised and renewed – that there is a need for responsible and sustainable financial systems and business models.
2. But it is not a mere economic but rather a systemic crisis that is forming a new social contract between business and society – because when the context of business is changing, business must also change.
3. This is why 21st century business builds on an alliance between economic and humanistic values – not necessarily driven by morals or ethics but just as much by necessity. Enter: the new business paradigm.

Goodbye to an era of greed?

'*Shame*' and '*Cap Greed*' were some of the slogans on home-made signs of an angry crowd that met Richard S. Fuld Jr., the former chief executive of the bankrupted Lehman Brothers, when he appeared before the American Congress to account for the remunerations of $350 million that he had received during his time as CEO, even while he was pleading for a federal rescue of his company.

The immoral aspects of greed, selfishness and short-term profit thinking are just some of the causes that have been proposed as the root core of the crisis. A systems failure of governments to regulate is another.

As a result, tougher rules that force the financial services industry to take a responsible and long-term approach to remuneration were agreed in 2009 at the G20 summit in Pittsburgh where the world's 20 most powerful national leaders met to coordinate their positions to ensure a Framework for Strong, Sustainable and Balanced Growth.

But, as German Chancellor Angela Merkel pointed out at the World Economic Forum in Davos that same year, if governments 'are not in a position to show that we can create a social order for the world in which such crises do not take place, then we'll face stronger questions as to whether this is really the right economic system.'[5]

Merkel's concern is shared by many others, who propose the root cause of the economic crisis to be the insufficiency of the fundamental financial and economic systems because of their in-built goals for continuous growth to which there are natural limits.

For even though it would be tempting to put the blame on our dark sides of desire, greed and selfishness, the economic system itself also engenders problems. Businesses operating on the classic formula are simply doing what they have been designed to do: maximize short-term profits and create economic growth.

As Frank Dixon, managing director of financial services firm Innovest Strategic Value Investors, which helps financial sector clients develop socially responsible investment products, argues: 'There is no shortage of good intentions among business leaders. No CEO wants to hurt children or leave a legacy of environmental destruction. The problem is not bad intentions. In nearly all cases, the situation is good business leaders wanting to do the right thing in a system that often forces them to do the wrong thing. We have a system problem, not a people problem.'[6]

This is the reason why economists like Belgian professor of international finance and former banker at the Belgian Central Bank, Bernard Lietaer, who was involved in the establishment of the 'ECU' or European Currency Unit, argue that the current design of our monetary system as well as our understanding of and agreements around money are at the root of most problems in our society. According to Lietaer it has a limited functionality and architecture, because it is programmed to meet industrial values and goals of economic growth at the expense of environmental and social sustainability by undervaluing care, education and other tasks crucial to maintaining a society.

Another economist who is rethinking economics along similar lines is microcredit pioneer and social innovator Muhammad Yunus. Like Lietaer, Yunus believes that capitalism as a system is only half developed, and that it is based on the assumption that people are one-dimensional beings concerned only with the pursuit of maximizing profit.

The limitations of relying entirely on the market economy and the profit motive, if the race for wealth is at the expense of justice and compassion, was something that the father of capitalism, Adam Smith, already warned about in the 18th century. He was, in fact, both a defender and critic of capitalism, who on the one hand advocated a self-interest-based economic exchange, but on the other hand also talked about the importance of broader values that go beyond profits like humanity, generosity and public spirit.[7]

This is also what French President Nicolas Sarkozy called for in a speech in 2007, in the light of outsized corporate pay packages and golden handshakes for fired executives: 'I believe in the creative force of capitalism, but I am convinced that capitalism cannot survive without an ethic, without respect for a number of spiritual values, without humanism, without respect for people,' he said and emphasized a greater sense of social and personal responsibility on the part of businesses as well as a renewed emphasis on entrepreneurship and work as the keys to the 'moralization of capitalism'.[5]

From a spiritual point of view, the crisis has not only shed new light on the greed culture made broadly acceptable by the housing boom. It is also an expression of a stage in the evolution of humanity where the present financial and economic systems are outdated because humanity is moving to the next level of evolution with new needs and demands as a result.[8] Capitalism in its classic form is now even threatened because people are losing interest in working hard and making money.

Supporters of this perspective therefore believe that the goal of economic growth must be replaced by an even higher goal, which serves human needs in a broader way by including the immaterial values that are starting to predominate, particularly in the Western part of the world, now that all reasonable material needs have been covered.

Whichever view you take, however, the bottom line remains the same: the global effect of the economic tsunami is a tough after-party wakeup call. Markets have failed and have destroyed conventional wisdom about how to run an efficient economy in a sustainable way. It is time for a new version of capitalism which matches 21st century needs and demands.

The 21st century social contract

The Social Contract was the title of a book by 18th century French philosopher Jean-Jacques Rousseau, who theorized about the best way to set up a political community in the face of the problems of commercial society.

Three centuries later these problems have intensified to a degree that is challenging fundamental, classic business logics about how and why to run a business. Today, companies operate in a business world of disorder with an increasingly complex web of systems that are all under stress. And it is difficult to have a balanced business in an unbalanced world – or, as the World Business Council for Sustainable Development puts it: business cannot succeed in societies that fail.

Global megacrises ranging from security threats, global warming and the depletion of natural resources to food shortage and the growing gap between the rich and the poor as well as higher personal levels of stress and other serious health threats are already making their mark in all sections of society, including business. And the crises are all closely interlinked, which is why they cannot be understood in isolation.

Hundreds of reports, analyses and books from the past decade all point in the direction of a new global risk pattern that constitutes a complex systemic crisis where the lack of solutions to one imbalance leads to the acceleration of another. A collapse in any one of the systems triggers critical issues in another.

Economic imbalances, natural disasters or energy and food crises, for example, are triggers of social inequality, extreme poverty or regional disputes over resources, which again may accelerate security threats like political or religious radicalism, terrorism and war.

Or take the economic crisis, which can lead to postponing the development of solutions to the global climate crisis, which in turn will worsen, for example, health issues, food and resource availability and the number of climate refugees that are forced to relocate because of global warming-related environmental disasters.

Many businesses are affected directly or indirectly by these societal trends. For they are not only making it more difficult for companies to sustain their operations in locations where resource scarcity, natural disasters or social instability either raise costs or endanger their operations. They are also changing stakeholder demands and public policies.

Companies are expected to share responsibility with governments for tackling issues which, in the old world economy, they would have ignored in their pursuit of profit. As a result, old world companies who were traditionally agents of wealth creation now see their role being expanded to also include the role of problem-solving contributors to society. Rationale: having moved unsustainably through the natural world system for decades, businesses constitute a significant part of the current problems – and must therefore naturally be a part of the solutions. The pursuit of economic growth can, in other words, no longer be at any price.

On this point, it is worth noting that, although government and civil society still play a crucial role, business has indeed emerged as this century's most powerful institution on the planet.

When it comes to the count of multinationals, for example, it has risen ten-fold, from a modest 7258 in 1970 to 63 000 in 2000 and nearly 79 000 by 2006.[10] Along with their 821 000 subsidiaries spread all over the world, these multinational corporations directly employ 90 million people (of whom some 20 million in the developing countries) and produce 25% of the world's gross product. The top 1000 of them account for 80% of the world's industrial output.[11] Of the 100 largest economies in the world today, 51 are therefore corporations and 49 are countries, and the combined annual turnover of the world's ten largest multinational corporations surpasses the gross domestic product for 100 of the world's poorest nations.[12]

In some countries, legislative measures are already having an impact on responsible business practices.[13] In France, for example, the 'new economic regulations' law, *nouvelles regulations économiques* (NRE), requires publicly quoted companies to disclose social and environmental, in addition to financial indicators. In Denmark, the Danish Financial Statements Act has recently upped the ante with a 'comply or explain' amendment with statutory requirements of corporate social responsibility reporting for all large businesses. In the UK the general duties of directors in the Companies Act 2006 include promoting the success of the company by regarding, among other things, the interests of its employees and the impact of the company's operations on the community and the environment. The UK Government even has a Minister for Corporate Social Responsibility (CSR).

But voluntary actions around the world also illustrate the fact that this is a new business parameter that is gaining ground. For example, the number of the world's largest companies in countries as diverse as South Africa, Brazil and Norway that include non-financial reporting in their annual reports has almost tripled in just a decade.[13]

Many voluntary guidelines, principles and standards have also been designed to help companies operate responsibly, e.g. the Global Reporting Initiative (GRI), the OECD Guidelines for Multinational Enterprises, AccountAbility's AA1000 guidelines, Goldman Sachs's ESG framework, Social Accountability International's (SAI) SA8000 certification and the International Organization for Standardization's ISO26000 Guidance Standard on Social Responsibility and ISO14001 Environmental Management Standard. Even within industries the companies themselves are launching collaborative, self-regulating initiatives like The Global Social Compliance Programme (GSCP), The Marine Stewardship Council and The Electronic Industry Code of Conduct.[14]

On top of this, recent governmental responses to the economic crisis in the USA and Europe have been likened to the US's 1930s New Deal, a package of economic programmes to give relief to the unemployed, reform business and financial practices and promote recovery of the economy. This time, however, its reach is on a global scale, and business leaders can expect more scrutiny and more intrusive regulation, and will therefore need to understand and respond to political developments of this kind.[15]

There has also been a general decline of trust in business overall in the wake of the economic crisis. The gap between the needs and expectations of society on the one hand and the objectives and practices of many businesses on the other has, in fact, widened dramatically.

According to the 2009 Edelman Trust Barometer, nearly two-thirds of the public reported less trust in businesses than the year before. And since an economy can only operate effectively on the basis of trust among the parties involved, the task for business leaders now is to rebuild trust by re-establishing connections with society and consumers, by making business meet sustainability challenges and act in the broader interest of society.

This is at least the recommendation of Business for Social Responsibility (BSR), an international organization which works with a global network of more than 250 member companies to develop sustainable business strategies and solutions. In their 2008 report, *Meeting the Challenge of a Reset World*, they sum up the sustainable business way forward as to:

1. Develop business strategies based on long-term trends;
2. Innovate for sustainability and value;
3. Think big – develop systemic answers;
4. Refocus on partnerships with governments;
5. Rebuild trust.

In short, the social contract between business and society is in the course of being reformulated, making it more extensive and complex than ever.

Business as unusual

While businesses throughout time have contributed positively to society by creating jobs, raising living standards and increasing wealth, many have also directly or indirectly had a negative impact on – or even accelerated – the current imbalances through their practices.

Pollution, unsustainable manufacturing, unsafe products, destruction of natural habitat, disruption of indigenous cultures and degradation of cultural values by overemphasising materialism are just a few examples of the by-products of activities that affect the wellbeing of people or the environment – the so-called negative externalities.

In fact, one of the great flaws in the classic version of capitalism is the failure to incorporate externalities into the market price of goods and services, e.g. the costs of restoring the environment or treating people who have become ill because of pollution caused by industries. Result: the cheap, unsustainable product may actually end up being the most expensive choice. But to remedy the environmental and social problems caused by companies, the price is often paid by taxpayers.

The reason why? Throughout time companies have profited from the historic privilege of *limited liability*, where a firm's liability is no more than the sum of its investment. Consequently, the responsibility for possible negative impacts on society is limited. It is only the company – not its owners or investors – that can be sued.

This is why corporate critics like Joel Bakan, Canadian professor of law and creator of book and documentary *The Corporation*, argue that companies are legally bound to act like psychopaths who are charming but egocentric, narcissistic and willing to eliminate all obstacles to their pursuit of profit and power.

Today there are still economists and businesspeople who argue that companies are only amoral instruments of commerce and extensions of their shareholders' property rights, and consequently that it makes no sense to talk about corporate responsibility because – as the liberal the-business-of-business-is-business economist Milton Friedman argued in the 1970s – only people can have responsibilities, and the social responsibility of business is to increase its profits. So there are still private equity funds and companies that operate with one bottom line and have their sole focus on creating shareholder value.

This one-legged business logic originates from what one of the world's leading authorities on sustainable development in business, US professor of management Stuart L. Hart, has dubbed *The Great Trade-Off Illusion*, where an entire generation of business leaders has been reared to believe that corporations wishing to incorporate corporate responsibility must sacrifice financial performance in order to do so.[12]

Arguments against Corporate Social Responsibility

Mallen Baker, writer, speaker and strategic advisor on corporate social responsibility, goes about it tongue-in-cheek when listing some of the common arguments against including social responsibility in business practices:

continued on next page...

- Businesses are owned by their shareholders – money spent on CSR by managers is theft of the rightful property of the owners.
- The leading companies who report on their social responsibility are basket cases – the most effective business leaders don't waste time with this stuff.
- Our company is too busy surviving hard times to do this. We can't afford to take our eye off the ball – we have to focus on core business.
- It's the responsibility of the politicians to deal with all this stuff. It's not our role to get involved.
- I have no time for this. I've got to get out and sell more to make our profit line.

Source: www.mallenbaker.net [16]

But today, companies that 20 years ago were held accountable only for direct or regulated consequences of their actions find themselves held accountable for the consequences of their actions in areas that go way beyond their immediate field of business.

Today's business 'licence to operate' is dependent on how well companies meet expectations of a broad range of stakeholders, including regulators, investors, employees, local communities and society at large. And in a globalized world, these expectations are growing, so conduct that would have been ethically acceptable in the industrial era is becoming unacceptable now.

This was reflected in a 2007 GlobeScan poll on corporate citizenship, where the pollsters found that large majorities of citizens in 25 countries hold companies completely responsible for the safety of their products, fair treatment of employees, responsible management of their supply chain and for not harming the environment.

This may not come as a big surprise, but more surprising was that, in addition to these operational aspects of business, a significant number of citizens also held companies completely responsible for improving education and skills in communities, responding to public concerns, increasing global economic stability, reducing human rights abuses and reducing the rich–poor gap.[7]

Lawsuits have already been filed against car companies for the costs of their alleged diminution of ecosystems, against tobacco companies for their alleged misleading of smokers about the dangers and addictiveness of cigarettes and against fast food companies for the alleged responsibility for their customers' obesity.

In 2006, for example, California's Governor Schwarzenegger filed a lawsuit against car companies Toyota, General Motors, Ford, Chrysler, Honda and Nissan for their vehicles' alleged diminution of its beaches, ozone layer and endangered animals, and has now signed a bill to put a cap on California's greenhouse gas emissions.

And in Japan the government is beginning to recognize the extent of responsibility that companies bear in overworking employees. Here courts have already awarded damages to relatives in cases of work overload. In one case a company was ordered to pay 200 million yen (the equivalent of $2.5 million) to a man overworked into a coma.[8]

All this has implications for companies' freedom to operate, their reputation and brand value, the cost of capital and perceived investor risk. To meet these kinds of anticipated changes, externalities need to be internalized.

Carbon trading, payment for ecosystem services like water and cap-and-trade systems for pollutant reduction are just some of the economic instruments and market-based approaches where externalities are already being incorporated into business practices.

As Tony Manwaring, CEO of the influential UK-based think-and-do-tank, Tomorrow's Company, explains: 'In the past, companies conducted "PEST" analyses (political, economic, social, technological issues) to monitor their externalities and to develop alternative scenarios for planning purposes. But today these externalities have become business-critical, and so companies have to be proactive in managing them in order to be effective. The question of whether they are doing it to look good or to be good becomes secondary because they simply *have* to work that way.'

In other words, business as usual is no longer an option.

Social investors

Investors of capital are starting to steer away from sectors and companies within sectors whose risks and potential liabilities are not well understood. Their calculus is increasingly reflecting the uncertainties of potential costs and liabilities associated with externalities, future regulatory constraints or restricted access to natural resources.[19] The rationale: there is no point in having investments in a system that is failing.

According to the Washington DC-based Social Investment Forum, so-called *socially responsible investing* (*SRI*) has soared 5000% in less than two decades (in 1984 SRI was a $40 billion market, by 2003 it had morphed into a $2.16 trillion industry).[20] In 2005 almost one dollar in ten under management in the US – $2.3 trillion – was invested in SRI funds. And global investment banking firm Goldman Sachs anticipates that additional professional managers, although not necessarily adopting a pure SRI mandate, will increasingly incorporate environmental issues into their analyses.[21]

Large pension funds around the world are already using screening agencies like Ethical Investment Service (EIRIS) to assess how companies tackle so-called ESG (environmental, social, governance) issues like eco-friendly practices, human rights and corruption. 475 large institutional investors around the world representing more than $55 trillion of funds (2009 figures) investigate the emissions strategy of companies through The Carbon Disclosure Project (CDP). And stock market indexes like the FTSE4Good Index Series and the Dow Jones Sustainability Index are tracking the financial performance of companies that focus on creating long-term shareholder value by embracing opportunities and managing risks derived from economic, environmental and social developments.

Several SRI-related initiatives have already been launched to help finance providers screen projects for risks, e.g. the Equator Principles, a benchmark for the financial industry to manage social and environmental issues in project financing; the CERES network of investors, environmental organizations and other public interest groups who initiated the Global Reporting Initiative (GRI), a de facto international standard for corporate reporting on environmental, social and economic performance; and the Principles for Responsible Investment (PRI), an investor-led and UN-backed initiative.

The Principles for Responsible Investment (PRI)

1. We will incorporate ESG (environmental, social and corporate governance) issues into investment analysis and decision-making processes.
2. We will be active owners and incorporate ESG issues into our ownership policies and practices.
3. We will seek appropriate disclosure on ESG issues by the entitites in which we invest.
4. We will promote acceptance and implementation of the Principles within the investment industry.
5. We will work together to enhance our effectiveness in implementing the Principles.
6. We will each report on our activities and progress towards implementing the Principles.

Source: www.unpri.org

Interestingly, corporate scandals and the recent economic crisis have only proven beneficial to this trend: during 2008, when the crisis seriously started making its mark, the number of signatories to the PRI more than doubled to 381 as a response to the crisis, and has since then increased to 560 investors managing a total of $18 trillion in assets, including private equity firms.[22] And when investment firm Good Capital launched its conference Social Capital Markets in 2008, two-thirds of the participants signed up after the collapse of Lehman Brothers, constituting what the conference organizer called 'a new asset class'.[23]

All these trends point in the direction of companies that are starting to address business risks in a proactive manner in order to preserve future freedoms and to seek first-mover advantages over their competitors. They have realized that turning a profit is no longer enough. Instead, they need new strategic and operational business practices which also take society's interests into account.

A survey from McKinsey & Co captured this shift very clearly back in 2006. Of more than 4000 executives in 116 countries, only 16% adopted the view that business should 'focus solely on providing highest possible returns to investors while obeying all laws and regulations', whereas the other 84% agreed that business should 'generate high returns to investors but balance that with contributing to the broader public good'.[17] And apparently action is following words: more than nine out of ten of 400 surveyed CEOs told McKinsey that their companies were addressing more environmental, social and governance issues than in the previous five years. Not for moral reasons but to improve competitiveness.[24]

So while the 20th century business paradigm is based on the conviction that profit is both a means and an end, visionary corporate leaders and social business entrepreneurs are proving that corporate success and social welfare is not a zero-sum game – a hierarchical either/or way of prioritising the relationship between business and society. They are paving the way for a new business logic founded on the belief that social responsibility can go hand in hand with economic growth.

Today, industrial society's traditional one-legged business logic is being challenged by strategic businessmen and businesswomen that are using corporate responsibility as a means of making money and by activists in suits that are using market mechanisms as a means of serving society.

This does not mean that results, profit and business acumen are less relevant today. It just means that the way to make business is changing. Today, the commercial drive for finding new business opportunities can be a vehicle for positive change that benefits both business and society. And the idealistic drive to find new ways to address social and environmental needs can result in new products and services – even new business models and industries.

In other words, we are in the midst of a shift to a new business paradigm that rests on principles of responsibility, reciprocity, sustainability and long-term thinking. As CEO of Tomorrow's Company, Tony Manwaring, reasons, 'companies need to move beyond the narrow view that this is business and this is community. It is in the company's self-interest to strategically and proactively take a role in managing these issues by operating in the intersection points of the triple context of economic, social and environmental issues.

It would be a fundamental mistake to believe that business as usual will work in tomorrow's markets.'

In conclusion, the choice is no longer between *either* the capitalist *or* the socialist model. Instead a new version of capitalism – social capitalism if you will – which integrates *both* humanistic *and* economic values will form corporate agendas and sow the seeds of future business models that create both commercial competitiveness and sustainable social change.

With the increasing number of companies that are following this new path of value creation the future is already here.

The great globalization race
– how nations compete

> 'Global competitiveness in the era of globality – where the new rules are no rules – requires new ways, new thinking. This is a battle that any nation dares not lose.'[25]
>
> *Harold Sirkin*

What unique strengths and competences should we focus on and advance to ensure our global competitiveness? How do we ensure continuous growth and welfare? These and similar key questions occupy policy-makers and business leaders today, because the world has grown smaller and our global challenges have grown bigger and more complex than ever.

'Growth, growth, growth' is still the mantra of most nations and companies. With the damaging effects of the recent financial crisis, reviving economic growth has, in fact, become *the* most important priority for policy-makers and business leaders, who share the basic assumption that the continued liberalization of trade and finance will generate employment and raise living standards across the globe. International competition is the way forward. The great globalization race is on.

The purpose of this and the remaining sections of Chapter 1 is to take a closer look at why the new 'both/and' business paradigm, where commercial interests are integrated with society's, must be linked to a new way of perceiving growth. Why?

- Globalization is creating a new economic world order with new players and new rules – and this is opening up a world of new business opportunities.
- For nations and companies alike this means a change in their competitive strategies – although the end goal is still the same: to create quantitative economic growth.
- The relentless pursuit of limitless, one-dimensional growth is, however, the root cause of the current megacrises. The corporate world will therefore be playing a significant role as a problem-solving contributor to society.
- Future wealth and welfare creation will be based on social innovations as well as new sustainable growth principles.

Nothing new under the sun – and yet ...

While the term 'globalization' was coined in the late 1970s, the concept has been part of human history from the very beginning. From the central Asian caravan linking Europe, the Middle East and China as early as 206 B.C. over the Silk Road of the early 16th century to the era of colonial trade, the history of human civilisation is one of growing interconnectedness.

Now, however, technological development has made the world more interconnected than ever. Changes are happening at a scale and pace that is historically unique. Globalization may be old news, but the visibility and speed of changes brought on by globalization are unlike anything ever seen before.

In 1453 it took 40 days for the pope to learn that Constantinople had fallen to the Turks. In 2001 the World Trade Center twin towers fell in real time on live television with the whole world watching.[26] And in 2008 a crisis that started in a small segment of the US housing market developed into a global credit crisis within the same year, putting most of the advanced economies in a simultaneous recession for the first time since World War II.

Just like the traders of yesterday, today's businesses are both affected by and are active contributors to globalization. For many, today's globalization is therefore associated with corporatization and free trade.

But globalization has changed the rules of competition for everybody in the business of creating value. As Harold Sirkin, co-author of the book *Globality*, concludes: 'In the new world of globality, the new rule is that there are no rules.' [25] Competitive parameters are changing for companies and nations alike, with a new economic world order as a result.

The new economic world order

When the Iron Curtain fell in 1989, markets previously limited by national borders and high customs barriers were replaced with free trade, expanding from one billion workers and consumers in the Western world to three billion in countries like China, India, Russia and Eastern Europe.[27]

Since then, the world's population has increased by almost 34%, consumption has grown even more, trade has almost tripled and the average income per head has gone up by about 40%.[28]

At the same time, technological inventions like satellites, telecommunications and the Internet have opened up a world of new insights – and a world of new business opportunities. New technology has made it possible to share knowledge virtually and to trade across borders. This seemingly borderless world is often referred to as *the global village* – a village where distance and national borders no longer really matter. (The interviews for this book, for instance, have been transcribed by Flatworldsolutions.com, an Indian company I found on the Internet.)

The forces of globalization have, in other words, built economic and societal ties across the world. They have opened up new markets, generated employment and fuelled economic growth.

But there are new twists to the competitive landscape in the globalized economy, which for decades has been dominated by Western countries. As a result, we are witnessing the emergence of new corporate entities, new global leaders and new growth strategies.

The globally integrated company

One of the traits of the new economic world order is the outsourcing of jobs and production processes from industrialized countries to low-wage countries like China and India that have access to a larger pool of both talented and cheaper labour. Another is the relocation of whole company departments.

One 2006 analysis assessed that 3.3 million American service jobs will be relocated within the period 2000–2015.[29] The multinational communications company Cisco Systems, for example, has planned to move 20% of its leaders to India by 2010, and electronics mogul L G Philips is already filling 12 000 jobs in Poland as well as investing $1.1bn there.[15] The global technology company IBM expects to more than double its Indian operations by 2010, adding more than 50 000 employees[15] and recently offered laid-off workers in the USA the chance to keep their jobs if they were willing to move abroad.

Well into the 21st century corporations will continue to add more links to their supply chains, stretching across the globe for cheaper materials and labour. Soon, we will no longer be able unambiguously to define a car as 'American' or a tool as 'Japanese', when their raw materials, production and assembly in an increasing number of cases will be taking place in several different countries.[30] Just like other processes such as research and development are also starting to be outsourced.

IBM's CEO, Samuel Palmisano, refers to this new emerging business model as 'the globally integrated enterprise' – a new corporate entity based on collaborative innovation, integrated production and outsourcing to specialists.[31] It treats its functions and operations as component pieces, and it can pull the pieces apart and put them back in new combinations, depending on which operations the company wants to excel at and which are best suited to its partners.

Contrary to the traditional multinational company which was designed to deal with the 'protection and nationalism' that dominated the 20th century by building plants and establishing local workforce policies in Europe and Asia, but kept research and development and product design principally in the home country, the globally integrated enterprise spreads its strategies, production capacity and management around the world in order to be close to markets and customers.

It is, in other words, a trend that is changing business structurally, operationally and culturally. In the future, companies of all sizes will be less defined by national identity and will think of the world as their home markets.

New global leaders

In the new economic world order Western businesses are not only extending their operations to other parts of the world. They are also being taken over by companies from the large emerging economies led by the so-called BRIC countries (Brazil, Russia, India, China).

Who would have thought that some of the world's top Western brands like Jaguar, Land Rover and Hummer would end up being acquired by emerging market corporate giants like Indian Tata and Chinese Tengzhong? Nevertheless, this is the reality that many established brands and multinationals will be facing over the coming decades.

Among the new global challengers Russian gas company Gazprom already provides 25% of Europe's natural gas while Turkish Vestel is the largest supplier of televisions in Europe. Mexico-based CEMEX has fast become one of the largest cement producers in the world and India's Suzlon Energy ranges among the world's top manufacturers of wind turbines.

These are not one-off examples. So far, 100 companies from 14 countries including Mexico, Turkey and the BRIC countries have already been identified with the near potential to become global leaders. In 2006, these 14 countries accounted for 17.3% of the world's total economic output, or gross domestic product,[25] and according to Boston Consulting Group, the top 100 companies from the rapidly developing economies (RDEs) are together growing ten times faster than the USA's GDP, 24 times faster than Japan's and 34 times faster than Germany's.[32]

Already by now, as *Newsweek*'s senior editor Rana Foroohar illustrated vividly when she gave a talk at the annual Confederation of Danish Industry's Business Summit in September 2009, the world's tallest building is in Taipei (since Foroohar's speech it is now in Dubai!), the world's richest man is Mexican, the world's largest publicly traded corporations are Chinese, the world's largest mall is in China, the biggest plane is built in Russia, the largest refinery is being constructed in India, where Bollywood has overtaken Hollywood, and the biggest investment fund is located in the United Arab Emirates.

No wonder the global investment banking and securities firm Goldman Sachs as far back as 2003 estimated that by 2041, China will be the world's largest economy, outranking the USA, and that together the BRIC countries could economically outgrow the USA, Japan, the UK, Germany, France and Italy.[33] In fact, growth has accelerated at such a rate that Goldman Sachs now predicts that these major emerging markets will overtake the combined

GDP of the G7 nations – Canada, France, Germany, Italy, Japan, the UK and the USA – by 2027, slightly more than a decade sooner than originally forecast.

With emerging powerhouses like that, analysts believe that the world's future economic growth will be taking place in developing nations, that the growth of Europe, Japan and the USA will be largely based on theirs, and that this power shift will most probably be reflected in future versions of the World Economic Forum's Global Competitiveness Index.[34]

World Economic Forum's Global Competitiveness Index

	2009	2008	2007
1	Switzerland	United States	United States
2	United States	Switzerland	Switzerland
3	Singapore	Denmark	Denmark
4	Sweden	Sweden	Sweden
5	Denmark	Singapore	Germany
6	Finland	Finland	Finland
7	Germany	Germany	Singapore
8	Japan	Netherlands	Japan
9	Canada	Japan	United Kingdom
10	Netherlands	Canada	Netherlands

Source: World Economic Forum's *Global Competitiveness Report 2008–2009*.

Together all these factors are contributing to a world of hyper-competition where – quoting words from the book *Globality* – 'everyone from everywhere is competing for everything' right from customers and market shares to raw materials, energy, skilled and unskilled workers and knowledge.

New growth strategies

Just as in most businesses, growth is a cornerstone of the globalization race for nations around the world. And the strategic key to growth is the development and efficient use of resources – human, natural, technological and capital resources – depending on the respective countries' social, economic, political and historical context.

Some of these resources are, however, already scarce and the need to access new resources is therefore necessary in order to drive and sustain continuous growth.

China, for example, which has historically relied heavily on natural resources like domestic coal to power its industry and electric utilities, now faces severe problems with air pollution and public health. On top of this, China has only a limited amount of arable land for a populaton of more than one billion. If this land is deforested, overfertilized or allowed to erode it will constitute a major challenge in the near future.[35]

Already the second largest energy consumer in the world after the USA, China is now facing an unprecedented need for resources, which has led to its *Clean Revolution* with stronger governmental energy policies that are not only driving innovation in low-carbon technologies but also diverting billions of dollars of investment into energy efficiency and renewable energy.[36] Worried by its reliance on coal, China's goal is to have 15% of its total energy needs met by renewables by the year 2020, and it has imposed a requirement on power companies to generate a fifth of their electricity from renewable resources by then.[37]

All this has already resulted in Chinese 'green-collar' jobs and a global leadership position as a renewable energy producer: the energy-consuming giant is one of the world's top three countries manufacturing solar photo-voltaics, and China has installed more solar heating systems than the rest of the world put together.[38]

For the USA, abundance in almost every resource has been immensely beneficial to economic growth. Fossil fuels, for example, have been so readily available that they have been underpriced and overused. Consequently, the country's domestic petroleum reserves are now declining sharply, forcing significantly higher prices and greater reliance on imports.[35]

The current Obama administration has responded by putting cleaner energy at the heart of its domestic agenda with the economic stimulus plan, *American Recovery and Reinvestment Act* of 2009, which includes more than $80 billion for clean energy investments that are expected to jump-start the nation's economy and create new jobs on a large scale.[39]

Just like China and the USA, other nations have started to develop strate-gies which will move them to low-carbon economies that are resilient to the effects of climate change. At the same time most industrialized countries are developing into knowledge economies where growth and value creation are driven by new technologies, know-how, speed, creativity and innovation. Competitive production today is, in other words, not only dependent on natural resources. More than ever it is about producing new knowledge, using it quickly and in new ways.

The European Union (EU) countries, for example, have launched the *Lisbon Strategy* with the objective to make the EU 'the most dynamic and competitive knowledge-based economy in the world capable of sustainable economic growth'.

In the UK where natural resources are relatively scarce, the nation has already abandoned heavy industries including coal mining and the automobile industry in favour of human and technological resources, and knowledge-based industries (high to medium tech manufacturing, finance, telecommunications, business services, education and health) already generate about 40% of the UK's GDP.[40]

This is also the case for one of the five most competitive nations in the world, Denmark. With a population of five million people and limited natural resources, this small Scandinavian country has, over the past 200 years, transformed from an agrarian and later industrial society to a primarily service society. Today knowledge-intensive service trades like banking, insurance, design and information and communication technologies (ICT) are among the most job and growth-creating trades in the Danish economy.[41]

In a knowledge economy, where the production tools are located in the mind of each member of staff, the individual worker has gained new importance and value. Human competence is the new raw material, and just as precious as financial capital, technology and natural resources. And just as scarce – at least in some parts of the world. By the year 2050, the median age in countries like Italy, Japan and Singapore is expected to exceed 50 years, and the elderly will be supported by a diminishing number of young people.[42] At the same time, the US Census Bureau estimates that by that time about 85% of the world's population will live in the so-called developing countries.[42]

Consequently, in about 50 years' time, the economic map of the world will be very different from what it is today. The developing countries will have almost endless human resources to fuel the global economy. In the West the retirement of the *Baby Boomer* generation (born 1946–1961) and the newly arriving scarce workforce of *Generation Y* (born 1976–1991) and *Millenniums* (born 1991–2006) will have a negative impact on the supply of labour and talent.[43]

This means that skill shortages in one country can be addressed by transferring talent out of another country. But it also means that in the fight for human capital the ability to understand and address the motivators of future generations will be essential for businesses.

The invisible wealth and welfare driver

To combat low productivity and stagnation of economic growth most national globalization strategies tend to include essential cornerstones of investment in education, research and development, innovation, entrepreneurship, science and technology right from biotech and cleantech to ICT (information and communications technologies).

At present, however, the strategies still do not include investment in social innovation and social entrepreneurship at the same level as technological innovation and business entrepreneurship. This is not surprising though, since the 19th and 20th centuries were very much characterized by and known for technological innovations and inventions. Assembly lines, steam engines, the radio, sewing machines, washing machines and the electric light were all elements that contributed to the creation of the industrial society – with financial growth, material comfort and welfare as a result.

Nevertheless, social innovation has provided the right conditions for further technology development and economic growth. As business thinker Peter Drucker once put it: 'Social innovations – few of them owing anything to science or technology – may have had even profounder impacts on society and economy, and indeed profound impacts on science and technology themselves.'[44]

Throughout the Victorian period in the UK, for example, it was the creation of social innovations like schools, libraries, building societies and housing that supported and drove industrial growth at that time.[45]

It may also seem paradoxical that a small country like Denmark with few natural resources, high wages, high taxes, a large public sector, a relatively low level of R&D activity and a relatively low proportion of people with a higher education in science or technology has been able to top global rankings of national competitiveness.[46]

Nevertheless, it is a showcase of how social innovations can constitute a resource on a par with coal, oil and other natural materials. Because, parallel to technological innovations that modernized the then agricultural society at the end of the 19th century, social innovations like the co-operative movement, the folk high school movement and the trade union movement have been backbones in the modernization of the now knowledge and service-based welfare society.[47]

In fact, the Chief Economist and Director of the World Economic Forum's Global Competitiveness Programme, Augusto Lopez-Claro, praises the Scandinavian welfare state models that build on social innovations like tax systems, unions, a powerful public sector and a flexible job market because he believes that the Nordic countries can lend important inspiration to developing countries faced with strategic choices, which will impact their societies and economies for years to come.[48] Social innovation, technology and economic growth are tightly bound together.

Today we are again in the midst of a transition which is once more putting social innovation at the forefront of the development of our societies – and as an economic force.

Finland, for example, is engaged in large-scale 'welfare cluster' export of its social sector know-how and equipment to Japan with, among other things, the *Finnish Wellbeing Center* name and trademark of a recent Finnish innovation, which comprises a modern Finnish elderly care concept complemented by advanced Finnish technology.[49] And in Australia education is its no. 1 services export (in 2008 valued at $15.5 billion) and has in recent years become Australia's third largest export overall.[50]

One of the world's progressive centres for social innovation, the Young Foundation, in fact argues that in order to recover from the recent recession, governments need a much greater emphasis on innovation and entrepreneurship and must support the likely areas of future jobs growth (health, care, education, environmental services) rather than bailing out the failing industries (banks, cars); investing in knowledge and services rather than concrete; and mobilising the capacities of local government and voluntary organizations rather than relying solely on national institutions.[51]

The Young Foundation is now conducting a study for the policy unit of the President of the European Commission to recommend how to grow the field of social innovation in Europe. But so far, no one nation has yet made it an explicit central point of its growth or globalization strategy.

New growth paradigm wanted

The globalization race is not just about competitiveness and economic growth. It is also a race against time. Globalization has certainly made the world smaller and opened up a world of new markets and new business opportunities. But the world's almost limitless growth dynamic has also made the world more vulnerable, with adverse side effects such as resource scarcity and natural disasters, polarization and health threats. We are on a collision course with the limits of both nature and ourselves.

As early as 1987 the Brundtland Commission, which published the report *Our Common Future* with the oft-quoted definition of sustainability, warned that the world is not facing separate crises, but that they are interlinked and arise from uneven development and unsustainable economic growth that compromises the basic needs of individuals and communities as well as those of future generations.

Definition of sustainability

'Sustainable development is development that meets the needs of the present without compromising the ability of future generations to meet their own needs.'

Brundtland Commission, 1987

Ever since, there have been numerous warnings and wake-up calls to change the current course. Today the call for sustainable actions is more urgent than ever. The alternative – not taking action – may have a dramatic impact on the next generations to come, with financial, environmental and social implications and costs reaching a level not yet seen.

As Executive Director of the United Nations' Environmental Programme (UNEP), Achim Steiner, concludes in UNEP's fourth Global Environmental Outlook Report:

> 'The systematic destruction of the Earth's natural and nature-based resources has reached a point where the economic viability of economies is being challenged – and where the bill we hand on to our children may prove impossible to pay.'

Therefore, reviving or strengthening economic growth is not the only important priority. *Sustainable* growth is becoming the new development mantra.

Despite governmental efforts at climate change conferences, national globalization strategies that build on a low-carbon economy and G20 summits where some of the world's strongest nations coordinate their actions to ensure 'strong, sustainable and balanced growth', there is still one fundamental issue that needs to be addressed: our one-dimensional metric of growth in terms of material and quantitative growth.

The phrase 'sustainable growth' is, in fact, with its current interpretation an oxymoron – a self-contradictory statement – simply because nothing can grow, and therefore be sustained, forever. Everything, eventually, comes to an end either by perishing or turning into something else. Growth is neither linear nor unlimited. We cannot have infinite growth in a finite world.

If, however – as economic iconoclast Hazel Henderson and systems theorist Fridtjof Capra argue – growth is interpreted more broadly to include *qualitative* growth by including also social, ecological and spiritual dimensions, then such a multidimensional systemic process can indeed be sustainable, provided it involves a dynamic balance between growth, decline and recycling as well as learning and maturing. We need to adapt the *biological concept of development* rather than the current narrow economic concept.[52]

Nevertheless, they point out, most companies still measure growth in terms of turnover, a country's wealth is still measured in terms of its gross domestic product (GDP) and the world categorized into 'developed', 'developing' and 'less developed' countries, recognising only monetary value. All non-monetary aspects of growth and development are ignored.

So, not surprisingly, GDP measures the quantity of money-based transactions recorded in a society while omitting 'underground' cash payments like barter (exchange of products and services instead of paying money which already makes up about 15% of world trade and increases by 15% each year[53]) and unpaid work found in voluntary services within communities and families (unpaid productive work was, in 1995, estimated at $16 trillion missing from 1995's global GDP of $24 trillion[52]).

Many people are, however, oblivious to the fact that social costs like those of accidents, wars, litigation, healthcare, pollution and other externalities are actually added as *positive* contributions, i.e. as additions to the GDP, instead of deducting them. Just like a wide range of values that are not 'valued' in the economic system, from social welfare and the environment to justice and security, are absent from the calculation. This is how we measure a 'healthy economy' – GDP measures wealth and social degradation, but not progress. There is no link between economic growth and quality of life.[52,54]

So, just like old world companies throughout time have externalized social and environmental costs to taxpayers, the environment and future generations, so have governments. To measure genuine prosperity and progress there is a need to fully internalize social and environmental costs.

The goal to achieve unlimited growth also means that there is only one way forward: to stimulate consumption. This can only happen by new customers intervening in the market or by the existing ones consuming more.

The former is already being realized with the rising population of billions of people in former Third World countries, who are now starting to move from poverty to consumerism. Goldman Sachs predicts that China alone will contribute 30% of global consumption growth by 2010, more than the G3 – France, Germany and the UK – and almost double that of the USA.[55] This will pose great demands on natural resources that are already being destroyed or overexploited.

The latter is realized by creating artificial needs through, for instance, advertising and boosting disposable incomes through, for example, increased wages, returns of shares and overexpansion of financial services like bonds or loan takings – one of the very triggers of the recent economic collapse.[52]

Recognising the flaws of the current design of capitalism and the conventional concept of economic growth is therefore the first essential step to overcoming the economic crisis – indeed the systemic crisis. We need to adjust our economic systems in support of healthy development rather than maximising one part of an overall system at the expense of the other parts.

Because if the current megacrises are a systemic problem – which, on the one hand, means that the lack of solutions to one imbalance leads to the acceleration of another – this, on the other hand, also means that finding a solution to one of the problems will have a positive, synergetic effect on the other parts of the system.

No wonder the World Economic Forum, which hosts the prestigious annual meeting events between the world's most influential decision-makers in Davos, is arguing for government stimulus programmes for the short term to counter the effects of the financial crisis. And for the long term, the need for innovative technologies and new business models to transform and revitalize the global economy in a sustainable way. For example, by addressing global risks and societal concerns such as climate change, healthcare, water scarcity, ageing and food/energy security in a way that creates economic growth.[56]

Economist Joseph Schumpeter's concept of 'creative destruction', whereby companies, industries and economies are rapidly transformed by innovation, is, in other words, more called for than ever. It is time for nations and businesses alike to challenge their old world views and logics and embrace new rules and principles for future economic growth, which do not compromise the needs of either current or future generations.

Over the following sections of Chapter 1 you will be introduced to some of the mainstream companies and social entrepreneurs that are laying the trails towards a sustainable economy. The purpose is to give you an overview of some of the new business opportunities and new growth principles through the lens of the current megacrises in terms of (1) the environmental system and the principle of industrial ecology; (2) the economic system and the principle of inclusive growth; and (3) the social system and the principle of immaterial growth. In other words, we will explore three global imbalances and three sustainable growth principles in the so-called triple context.

Five planets wanted
– *environmental imbalances and growth principle 1*

> 'I sincerely believe that business is the force of change. Business is essential to solving the climate crisis, because this is what business is best at: innovating, changing, addressing risks, searching for opportunities.'[57]
>
> *Richard Branson*

Food shortage; freshwater stresses; degradation of forests, land, coasts and marine ecosystems; health hazards of indigenous peoples; pollution of earth, water and air; extinction of mammal, bird and amphibian species; natural disasters, climate change and global warming. The harmful consequences of mankind's growth and consumption over the past five decades are many, and have left a devastating mark on Mother Earth.

When the Earth's population reached 2.5 billion in 1950, it had taken humankind four billion years to get there. In 2000, only 50 years later, 6.7 billion people inhabited the world. Within half a century, the global population had grown more than during the four million years humankind had existed as a species.[58] Humanity's 'ecological footprint' (a measure of the pressure on Earth from human consumption of natural resources) has already increased to 125% of global carrying capacity. And with the prospects of a population peak of nine billion around the middle of the 21st century, it could rise even further to 170% by then.[59]

By 2025, 220 million middle-income consumer households are expected in China alone, and by 2030 the number of middle-class consumers worldwide is expected to triple, bringing almost 80% of the world's population into the middle-income bracket of purchasing power.[59] It is numbers like these which make the World Watch Institute conclude that by that time it will take an extra planet like Earth to supply the 2.5 billion consumers in India and China with the same amount of resources currently available to the inhabitants of Japan.[60] And which make the World Wildlife Fund (WWF) estimate that it will require three planets if everyone adopts the consumption patterns and lifestyles of the average citizen from the United Kingdom – five planets if they live like the average North American.[59]

Sustainable consumption challenges by type of economy

Type of economy	Example countries	Main sustainability challenges
Consumer	USA, Japan, Western Europe	Dramatically lowering resource use while maintaining economic output.
Emerging	China, South-East Asia, some countries in South America	Leapfrogging to sustainable structures of consumption and production without copying Western examples first.
Developing	Many countries in Africa, some countries in South America	Developing dedicated solutions for the 'low-income segment of the population'; providing a basis for sustainable growth.

Source: *Sustainable Consumption Facts and Trends: From a Business Perspective.* World Business Council for Sustainable Development, 2008.

No wonder 1600 of the world's most prominent scientists, and among them several Nobel Prize winners, as early as 1992 issued the following *Warning to Humanity*:

> 'We the undersigned, senior members of the world's scientific community, hereby warn all humanity of what lies ahead. A great change in our stewardship of the earth and the life on it is required, if vast human misery is to be avoided and our global home on this planet is not to be irretrievably mutilated.'[61]

Many of the industrial production impacts are being exported to the developing countries, which are carrying more than 90% of the humanitarian and economic burdens caused by climate change, although the 50 least developed countries together emit less than 1% of global carbon emissions.[62]

Among other things, this means that about 200 million people a year on average during the 1990s were affected by climate-related disasters, whereas only 1 million people in developed countries were affected,[63] and every year about 315 000 humans die because of climate-related causes – a number expected to rise to half a million in 2030 according to a report by the Global

↑ huge disparities in outcomes ? actions ? consequences

Humanitarian Forum (GHF).[62] It also means that about 1.1 billion people do not have access to clean drinking water. And that about 1.6 million people die every year from diarrhoeal diseases (including cholera) attributable to lack of access to safe drinking water and basic sanitation.[64]

There are still huge amounts of work to be done if we are to turn the current wave of environmental depletion and destruction, and the ominous warnings continue to be manifold. So, although the environmental debate has been raging for years, and environmental sceptics are still disputing whether climate change is manmade or not, the sinister bottom line remains the same: the Earth is reaching its limits.

Or, in the words of Lester R. Brown, founder of the World Watch Institute: 'Throughout history, humans have lived on the earth's sustainable yield – the interest from its natural endowment. But now we are consuming the endowment. In ecology, as in economics, we can consume principal along with interest in the short run, but in the long run it leads to bankruptcy.' [58]

In short, if economic growth is to be sustained in the future, it must be within what has been dubbed a 'one planet agenda'.

The call for business action

Concerted efforts of governments, NGOs and leading businesses to prevent further environmental damage have already had positive results like the successful outphasing of ozone-depleting substances by cutting the production of ozone-layer damaging chemicals by 95%, the reduction of acid rain in Europe and North America, falling deforestation rates in the Amazon,[28] and the access to clean drinking water that has been secured for 1.6 billion people, particularly in Eastern Asia.[65]

The United Nations Conference on Environment and Development (UNCED) in 1992 – also known as the Rio Summit – when 192 countries signed the United Nations' Framework Convention on Climate Change (UNFCCC), the Kyoto Protocol which was signed and ratified by 184 countries in 1997 and the recent follow-up at the Copenhagen Climate summit, COP15, are some of the joint actions of the world's governments to combat the issue of climate change.

Whether the outcome of the latter was a success or a failure depends on the expectations and ambitions of the beholder. But it has certainly focused collective attention on the challenges we need to resolve – and it has shown the world that solving the problems cannot be left to governments alone.

As former United Nations Secretary General Kofi Annan concluded some years ago in connection with a World Economic Forum gathering 'increasing numbers [of business leaders] are realising that they do not have to wait for governments to do the right thing – indeed, that they cannot afford to. In many cases, governments only find the courage and resources to do the right thing when business takes the lead.'[66]

The loss and degradation of Nature's ecosystems is already putting pressure on companies with expectations to corporate responsibility ranging from contributions to the development of countries in the emerging economies to maintaining competitiveness in the industrial countries. But with every challenge follows possibility, and around the world, progressive leaders are turning environmental requirements into new business opportunities instead of regarding them as liabilities.

Corporate responsibility expectations

Key areas	Expectations in industrial countries	Expectations in emerging economies
Economic development	Remain competitive and offer development opportunities to emerging economies.	Contribute to the country's development, especially structurally weak regions.
Ethics and management	Promote the adoption of environmental and social standards, throughout the value chain, especially among suppliers.	Act ethically and legally. Establish high environmental and social standards, and set an example for suppliers and competitors.
	Create transparency, regarding economic, ecological and social aspects of corporate activities, especially in emerging economies.	Help to build management competencies and institutions.

continued on next page...

Corporate responsibility expectations

Key areas	Expectations in industrial countries	Expectations in emerging economies
Employees and jobs	Promote job security through employee training and development. Proactively address challenges like equal opportunity and population ageing.	Create jobs and train employees. Ensure occupational safety and health protection. Promote and raise employee awareness of environmental protection.
Products and marketing	Ensure product safety. Offer quality products at fair prices. Promote sustainable consumption through ethically and ecologically sound products, and by informing consumers and raising their awareness.	Develop and market quality products for those at the bottom of the affluence pyramid. Ensure that products are safe and environmentally compatible. Consider the cultural and social context.
Resource efficiency and climate protection	Stronger focus on products: dematerialization of the economy by moving from product- to service-oriented business models. Help to reduce greenhouse gas emissions.	Transfer know-how and modern energy- and resource-conserving technologies. Satisfy growing consumer needs with products that use limited resources efficiently.
Social commitment	Work toward meeting the United Nations' Millennium Development Goals. Help to solve social problems, also by encouraging employee volunteering.	Support and promote, in particular, disadvantaged children and young people. Raise public awareness of environmental protection. Promote education and research for sustainable development.

Source: *Sustainable Consumption Facts and Trends: From a Business Perspective*. World Business Council for Sustainable Development, 2008.

Virgin founder, serial entrepreneur, adventurer and CEO Richard Branson is one of the business leaders who has recognized the new commercial logic, where urgent societal needs go hand in hand with new business potential.

Branson has already invested 2.6 billion dollars in a new Boeing plane, the Boeing 787-9 Dreamliner, which burns 30% less fuel than the previous generations of similar planes. He has also called for the creation of a _Carbon War Room_ (www.carbonwarroom.com) – a global initiative founded in 2008 to harness the unique influence, resources and spirit of entrepreneurs to fill the gaps in the fight against climate change. The Carbon War Room contributes to solutions within areas such as transport, electricity, built environment, industrial processes, deforestation, agriculture and waste.

In fact, several companies are already marking themselves out as leaders within the field of eco-business. They have recognized the synergies between increasing productivity and revenue and cutting greenhouse gas emissions or other eco-friendly solutions, which open up new revenue streams, new industries and radically different business models.

The total value of the carbon reduction credit market, for example, already topped $300 million in 2003 and has been growing rapidly ever since, creating significant new investment and trading opportunities.[19]

In a number of countries, 'industry clusters' are planned where the waste of one industry becomes the resource of another. In Japan, for example, recycling and take-back requirements have encouraged industrial reuse of waste. The sale of products from waste has, in fact, helped create whole new industries, including those that are developing the technologies needed to support these activities.[19]

Teijin's business model innovation

Japanese chemical company Teijin has shifted the focus of its business model on chemical solutions to global challenges. To address the challenges associated with mounting waste, Teijin has developed closed-loop recycling systems for polyester, so that polyester garments and other products can be turned back into virgin-quality polyester.

continued on next page...

> Compared with the conventional production of polyester from petro-
> leum, these systems save energy and resources and reduce CO_2 emis-
> sions and waste. Teijin manages a global network of companies that
> voluntarily collect and recycle polyester garments, and advocates the
> development and marketing of products containing these recycled
> fibres. Teijin is working with other actors in society to advocate this
> vision of the components of a sustainable product. As of May 2008,
> more than 80 manufacturers of apparel and sporting gear had joined
> the effort in Japan and overseas.
>
> Source: *Sustainable Consumption Facts and Trends*, WBCSD, 2008.

Companies are also revitalising their business models by specialising in developing world needs. Like the Swiss-based Danish company Vestergaard Frandsen, a textile business which used to produce work uniforms but now specializes in disease control textiles and other innovative life-saving products and concepts. These include PermaNet, a long-lasting mosquito bed net impregnated with insecticide; ZeroFly, a plastic sheeting that kills mosquitoes and flies; and LifeStraw, a 25 cm long water filtration straw which – at a price of less than 6 dollars for governments or international relief organizations – can be used by a person for up to a whole year to turn most dirty water into safe drinking water.

Already awarded Best Invention of the Year by *TIME* magazine and dubbed 'one of the 10 things that will change the way we live' by *Forbes* magazine, LifeStraw is expected to have a massive effect on the quality of life and health of the millions of people who do not have access to clean drinking water.

Vestergaard Frandsen's strategic shift has not only led to partnerships with governments, NGOs and international humanitarian organizations like the International Federation of the Red Cross, the United Nations' High Commission of Refugees and the World Health Organization. It has also gained them access to new markets, and the company's products are today in use in refugee camps and disaster areas all over the world.

LifeStraw. *Photo courtesy of Vestergaard Frandsen*

China's largest water company, Shenzen Water, which supplies over 7 million tons of drinking water every day, has concentrated its innovation efforts on areas including sewage treatment, decontamination of bedload and water recycling. These initiatives alone contributed over 21% of the group's sales in 2006, and its investment in process innovations for sustainable use of water resources has already led to 19 patent applications.[14]

In another fast-growing country, India, the former textile business Suzlon Energy has transformed its original business model after the purchase of a German wind turbine, which they could not keep running. And so, they decided to build and maintain turbines themselves. When Suzlon Energy was started up in 1995, the company was not even on the list of the world's top ten wind-turbine manufacturers. But with global demand for wind energy taking off, ten years later it was the fifth-largest producer in the world. Its sales and earnings tripled in the quarter ended June 30 2006, as the company earned the equivalent of $41.6 million on sales of $202.4 million, and four-fifths of Suzlon's orders now come from outside India.[37]

With the worldwide market for wind, solar, geothermal and fuel cell energy estimated at $200 billion in 2020 it is no surprise that other dynamic companies are looking to establish themselves in this and other related industries.[67]

The roster of eco-minded companies also includes iconic industrial giant, General Electric (GE) – a maker of jet engines, plastics and lighting and builder of power plants that churn large amounts of carbon dioxide into the atmosphere. In 2005 GE launched its *Ecomagination* business strategy with a pledge to improve its environmental practices by focusing technologies, production capacity and infrastructure on developing solutions such as solar energy, hybrid locomotives, fuel cells, lower-emission aircraft engines, efficient lighting and water purification technology.

GE invests $6 billion each year in research and development, of which $4 billion is allocated to solving the problems of clean energy and affordable healthcare,[68] and GE's energy-efficient technology reaped $17 billion in revenue in 2008, up 21% from the year before.[69]

Brand new players are, however, also entering the scene. Like the upcoming star within sustainable transport solutions, the California-based company Better Place, which aims to reduce global dependency on oil through the creation of a market-based transportation infrastructure for electric vehicles.

Better Place will build an electric recharge grid with mainly renewable energy generated from solar arrays and wind farms, and Renault will provide the electric vehicles by 2011 at competitive prices. The infrastructure also includes 'battery shift stations' that will enable a switch of batteries for the longer drives. The plan is to deploy the infrastructure on a country-by-country basis, and the first electric vehicle networks are already being built in Israel and Denmark as test markets in 2011.

In 2008 Deutsche Bank analysts issued a glowing report stating that Better Place's approach could be a 'paradigm shift' that causes 'massive disruption' to the auto industry and which has 'the potential to eliminate the gasoline engine altogether'.[70] One year later the company's founder, Shai Agassi, was included in *TIME* magazine's list of the world's 100 most influential people.

That it is both cost-beneficial and innovatively rewarding to incorporate sustainability principles into the company's processes is something that the world's largest manufacturer of modular carpets, Interface, quickly realized when, in 1995, it embarked on its *Mission Zero* journey to become a totally sustainable organization by 2020.

Interface is well on its way to reducing its negative environmental impacts. From its 1996 baseline the company's actual greenhouse gas emissions are down 44%, water intake per unit of production is down 80%, 100% of its electricity in Europe is renewable, 36% of the raw materials used are recycled and bio-based, and total waste sent to landfill since has been reduced by 80%, netting the company an impressive $433 million in cumulative, avoided waste costs.[71]

So when people ask Lindsey Parnell, the CEO and President of InterfaceFLOR Europe, Middle East, Africa and India, a division of US-based Interface Inc., what the costs of running a sustainable business are, he usually says: 'I don't know how much it costs, but I know how much we have saved and that more than covers any costs.'

Interface has proved how a business in a chemically-heavy industry that used to externalize its costs onto the environment within a couple of decades can become a solid business case of corporate sustainability. In 2008 the company was voted number one in Globespan's survey of environmentally sustainable businesses, marking itself as one of the front-runners of the new industrial revolution. Today Interface shares its new business model which aligns process, people, products, planet and profit with other companies around the world.

As Parnell puts it: 'Business as a force for good, as a force for nature, and as a force for sustainable growth – that's an idea worth sharing.'

Growth principle 1: industrial ecology

The formula behind the success of Interface and many other like-minded companies is the first of the three sustainable growth principles that we will be exploring: industrial ecology.

Industrial ecology is the shifting of industrial process from linear, open-loop systems in which resource and capital investments move through the system to become waste, to a circular, closed-loop system where wastes become inputs for new processes.[72]

In other words, the new business revolution evolves around designing products that are not only energy efficient but essentially also waste-free by using waste as a nutrient for new purposes.

In the case of Interface, this new growth logic has led to new service concepts like ReEntry, a scheme where the company collects used carpet tiles for reuse or redistribution to, for example, charities, schools, community groups and small businesses. Products that are not reused end up being recycled or down-cycled into other products. Likewise, the Evergreen Lease concept extends product life and recovery of carpets for repurposing by leasing rather than selling them to customers, who can then hand their carpets in when they have served their initial purpose, thereby diverting them from landfill.

In addition to creating closed-loop recycling systems that minimize negative externalization, Interface also bases a fundamental part of its design process on *biomimicry* – inspiration from Nature – the idea being that after 3.8 billion years of evolution Nature knows what works and what does not. So instead of trying to master it, people use Nature as a mentor. For Interface the 'mentoring' has certainly paid off: the result has been better products than ever, and a range of new carpet bestsellers and patents that they would never have thought of before.

The two industrial pioneers, German eco-chemist Michael Braungart and American architect William McDonough are some of the proponents of Nature's cyclical growth logic which replaces the minimising approach of eco-efficiency with an optimising approach of eco-effectiveness. They call it *Cradle-to-Cradle Design* (if you enter 'Food = Waste' on Google, you will find a link to an inspiring 15-minute documentary on their new production paradigm).

Ford Motors – an industrial ecologist

Despite tough competition from Japanese car manufacturers, massive cutbacks and advice to focus only on the financial bottom line, Ford Motors in Michigan, USA, has decided to implement Braungart and McDonough's Cradle-to-Cradle principles. So far, Ford has:

continued on next page...

- Invested $2 billion in restoration of Ford's 1100-acre Rouge River manufacturing complex in Dearborn, Michigan, turning it into a productive, life-supporting place.
- Used native plants to neutralize toxins and purify contaminated soil around the complex.
- Improved indoor work conditions for employees by installing skylight and interior arrangements that promote worker safety.
- Planted innovative vegetation roofs on its factory buildings. Among other things, it benefits birds, plants and micro organisms, filters storm water and insulates the building, reducing heating and cooling costs by up to 5%.
- Developed hybrid car model, Ford U, which is produced from materials that are later recycled or reused as biological or technological nutrients.

The Cradle-to-Cradle Design has already been adopted by companies like clothing producers Nike and Gap, chemical company BASF, energy company BP, electronics company Philips and car manufacturer Ford. But governments are also starting to embrace the concept.

In China, for example, where the plan is to move 400 million people from rural areas into urban centres by 2030, Braungart and McDonough's Cradle-to-Cradle team is working with the government to build experimental eco-village districts in six major Chinese cities with solar panels on the rooftops and local materials, all of which are either biodegradable or completely recyclable.

In summary, the common denominator for all of these different eco-based solutions is the acceptance of the need to invest in the future instead of waiting for sustainability-related issues to be embedded in legislation, or – even worse – for a time when the costs and damage of conventional practices and lifestyles will be irreversible.

The sustainability principle of industrial ecology builds on not necessarily *minimising* consumption but rather using the *right resources* in a way where waste is no longer a pollutant but a *nutrient* for a biological or technical cycle.

This is one of the innovative ways to avoid ecological bankruptcy – and to build the new sustainable business future.

More wealth and more inequality
– *economic imbalances and growth principle 2*

> 'Globalization is not just about opening up another Pizza Hut. It means distributing opportunity and the good life to all the world's population.' [73]
>
> *Iqbal Quadir*

Good news. The world is winning the fight against poverty penny by penny.

The globalization process has made us richer, tripling the global average income between 1950 and 2000,[58] and rapid economic growth has caused a historic decline in poverty: when the World Bank first published its global poverty estimates in 1990, the figure was 42%. In 2005 the figure was just over a quarter.[74]

The main reason for the decline in poverty figures is the dramatic economic boom in China, where half a billion of the Chinese population have been lifted out of poverty throughout the past three decades. In only 15 years – between 1990 and 2005 – the share of Chinese people living below the threshold of $1.25 a day fell from 60.2% to 15.9%. In India and in sub-Saharan Africa the poverty rate has also fallen, although much less.[74]

Nevertheless, the gap between the richest and the poorest on a global scale is ever-widening. In 1960 the richest 20% accounted for 70.2% of global GDP, while the poorest 20% controlled 2.3%, a ratio of 30:1. 40 years later the ratio was 80:1 with the richest quintile controlling 85% of global GDP and the poorest accounting for only 1.1%.[12]

Consequently, 1.3 billion, or roughly 20% of the world's population – predominantly in many regions of Asia and Africa – live on less than one dollar per day, the World Bank's measure for extreme poverty (based on purchasing power parity). In total, 2.7 billion people struggle to survive on less than two dollars per day.[75]

Capitalism in its current form is, in other words, still not able to cater to basic human needs in the world. And with the recent economic crisis, poverty is skyrocketing.

According to The World Bank, it has already pushed over 100 million people back into poverty, and for every percentage of decline in the global economy, 20 million people will follow.[76] The risk of a decrease in foreign direct investment and scale backs on development assistance due to lack of funds does not make future scenarios much brighter.

The global downturn has also led to a sharp increase in food shortages. In the West this has meant higher prices for food. But for billions of people who live for less than a couple of dollars a day it has led to a catastrophic halving of their buying power. In just two years, from 2006–2008, average food prices increased by 24%, thereby raising the number of chronically hungry people to one in six people worldwide.[77]

Hunger, malnutrition and infant mortality are just some of the faces of poverty. TB and HIV/AIDS-related deaths, lack of access to basic sanitation and unsafe sources of drinking water as well as women's lack of access to basic education are other manifestations of poverty. Just like lack of jobs due to lack of businesses, limited labour supplies due to poor health or malnutrition and insufficient infrastructure are factors contributing to its perpetuation.[78]

In short, poverty is about more than empty pockets. And because it, in turn, may spawn corruption, conflict, crime, security threats, undermine global public health, accelerate habitat destruction or create large-scale migration, the problems of the bottom billion are problems for us all.

In the business of poverty eradication

The closest international consensus on how to eradicate poverty so far is the United Nations' eight *Millennium Development Goals* (MDGs) with underlying specific targets to be achieved by 2015.

The Millennium Development Goals (MDGs)

Goal 1: Eradicate extreme poverty and hunger.
Goal 2: Achieve universal primary education.

continued on next page...

Goal 3: Promote gender equality and empower women.

Goal 4: Reduce child mortality.

Goal 5: Improve maternal health.

Goal 6: Combat HIV/AIDS, malaria and other diseases.

Goal 7: Ensure environmental sustainability.

Goal 8: Develop a global partnership for development.

More details at www.un.org/millenniumgoals

The World Bank, which provides loans to poorer countries for capital programmes with the goal of reducing poverty, believes that the best way for poor countries to adapt to poverty-related issues is to develop by diversifying their economies, developing health systems and strengthening their infrastructure.

To achieve the MDGs it has therefore proposed an agenda for inclusive and sustainable growth which, among other things, includes an increase in aid for trade.[63]

Fundamental shifts in food policies towards the developing world were thus recently marked at the G8 Summit in 2009, when the world's eight most powerful statesmen from the UK, the USA, Germany, France, Italy, Canada, Japan and Russia agreed to set up a $20 billion fund to support the world's poorest countries in growing and selling more of their own food, instead of providing food to aid the hungry.[79]

The notion of business-based solutions as an important factor to kick-start and sustain economic growth in low-income countries is being shared by an increasing number of people, including development experts and NGOs, who no longer believe in the effectiveness of conventional development aid programmes.

An example from The World Bank illustrates why: an internal review of just one quarter of its Africa projects launched during the 1990s showed that between 65% and 70% of these projects had failed. This included the $40 million Morogoro Shoe Factory in Tanzania, which never produced more than 4% of its planned output.[80]

It is examples like these which have made Kurt Hoffmann, director of Shell Foundation and former councillor to the United Nations, the European Union and The World Bank, join the choir of people who strongly believe that the aid industry should be reformed by applying fundamental business principles to enhance its performance and accountability in support of local job creation and entrepreneurship. Because, as Hoffman argues, poverty is about cash, and cash comes from having a job.

But this is nowhere near the centre of the aid community's strategic approach, which is why Hoffmann is calling for the private sector to contribute crucial knowledge about growth, job creation, investment and innovation. Not by engaging the external affairs representatives or Corporate Social Responsibility (CSR) specialists of mainstream businesses, but rather by engaging those inside the business who develop new commercial projects or products, manage supply chains and distribution networks or implement a regional market entry strategy.[80]

This is also the reason why the Shell Foundation – which was established as an independent registered UK charity by Shell Group in 2000 – takes an explicit 'enterprise-based' approach to developing, up-scaling and promoting solutions to the current energy, environmental and poverty challenges.

This involves applying market principles and injecting 'Business-DNA' in terms of business thinking, models and disciplines into the organization, engaging in strategic partnerships with businesses, committing funds as 'social investments' in solutions that deliver financial and social returns rather than grants and, where appropriate, leveraging the value-creating resources – the knowledge, brand and infrastructure – of the Shell Group.

Results of this approach so far include a new design of stove that emits up to 70% less CO_2, uses 60% less wood and thereby reduces the health-damaging effects of indoor smoke pollution, which is the cause of premature death for around 1.5 million people a year.[81]

The call for taking a more business-centred approach to development is not a call for privatization of the aid industry. Rather, it speaks in favour of combining the best from two worlds – although this provokes conventional ideologies about altruism and business.

So when former aid workers Martin Fisher and Nick Moon founded the non-profit organization Kickstart to develop and sell technologies like their

MoneyMaker irrigation pumps to poor African farmers, who use them to establish and run profitable small-scale enterprises, they were both branded as heretics. But experience had shown Fisher and Moon that business dynamics work. People invest more in the success of a tool they buy than in one they are given.[82]

Kickstart's impact figures speak for themselves. Since the company started in 1991 it has kickstarted the launch of more than 89 000 new businesses that have created more than 60 000 new jobs, moving almost half a million people out of poverty in Kenya, Tanzania and Mali. And with the sale of every product, Kickstart reinvests its profit to develop more new technologies.

Today The World Bank publishes regular *Doing Business* reports, which track how well nations and regions are doing in terms of creating the sorts of policy environment that let enterprise be a force for development. The global association The World Business Council for Sustainable Development (WBCSD) engages its members through the *Sustainable Livelihoods Programme*, which aims to identify business models that serve business operations in the developing world while creating opportunities for the poorest communities to prosper. And the United Nations has established the UN Global Compact, to date the world's largest voluntary network for more than 5000 companies from more than 130 countries that are committed to sustainability and responsible business practices in alignment with ten universally accepted principles that also support the Millennium Development Goals.

The UN Global Compact

Human rights	Principle 1: Businesses should support and respect the protection of internationally proclaimed human rights.
	Principle 2: Businesses should make sure that they are not complicit in human rights abuses.
Labour standards	Principle 3: Businesses should uphold the freedom of association and the effective recognition of the right to collective bargaining.
	Principle 4: The elimination of all forms of forced and compulsory labour.
	Principle 5: The effective abolition of child labour.
	Principle 6: The elimination of discrimination in respect of employment and occupation.

continued on next page...

The UN Global Compact

Environment	Principle 7: Businesses should support a precautionary approach to environmental challenges.
	Principle 8: Businesses should undertake initiatives to promote greater environmental responsibility.
	Principle 9: Businesses should encourage the development and diffusion of environmentally friendly technologies.
Anti-corruption	Principle 10: Businesses should work against corruption in all its forms, including extortion and bribery.

Source: www.unglobalcompact.org

Like the UN's Global Compact, the business organization World Business Council for Sustainable Development (WBCSD) is encouraging its members to search for more inclusive business solutions to address issues like poverty, health, labour rights and community development by working in partnerships that combine private, public and civil sector resources, skills and expertise. Not necessarily because they should feel morally obliged to do so, but simply because it makes good business sense.

But there is another good reason for these kinds of initiatives. 300 multinational corporations control 25% of the world's assets.[83] But they employ less than 1% of the world's labour force.[12]

That addressing the needs of the poorest people in the world holds huge business potential is something that has been captured in concepts like *bottom of the pyramid* – also referred to as the *Base of the Pyramid* or just BOP – coined by professor of management Stuart L. Hart and professor of corporate strategy C.K. Prahalad in 1998.

In the beginning their concept was so controversial that it took them years to find a publisher for their initial white paper, *The Fortune at the Bottom of the Pyramid*, which was eventually published in 2002.[84] Today their concept has inspired both development agencies and major corporations that have realized that although one poor citizen per definition has an increasingly low purchasing power, the sheer size of this specific socio-economic group gains access to a unique source of income, which at the same time can improve the lives of millions of people.

Economists like Peruvian Hernando de Soto, who helped inspire the World Bank's *Doing Business* initiative, Indian Amartya Sen and Bangladeshi

Muhammad Yunus have proposed similar pioneering approaches to bottom-up development based on private enterprise.

Parallel to this, multinational companies based in Europe, North America, Japan and other developed regions of the world are starting to recognize the need to move into regions with growing populations and developing economies. Thereby they can access new markets and new consumer segments, instead of relying on their traditional markets which are stagnating, shrinking or becoming intensely competitive.[42]

But many of them have not yet found the key that unlocks the gates to the huge market of the emerging 'global middle class' of low-income consumers – the four billion people who earn less than $3000 per year, the equivalent of $3.35 per day, that account for almost two-thirds of the world's population and have a combined spending power of approximately $5 trillion.[59] Which leads us to the second growth principle for a more sustainable and inclusive global economy.

Growth principle 2: inclusive growth

In 1960 the Danish businessman Erik Emborg got an idea. Why not sell milk products from dairy-rich Denmark to some of the millions of Africans who do not have access to or cannot afford to buy dairy products? And so, the Fan Milk business was born.

With recombination plants in Nigeria, Ghana, Togo and the Ivory Coast the company processes imported milk powder into milk-based products like yoghurt, chocolate milk and ice cream. The products are distributed via small depots to street merchants and bicycle vendors, who are independent entrepreneurs who, with Fan Milk funding, have access to the sales equipment like the blue distribution bikes that are found everywhere in the streets. In addition, Fan Milk provides credit to the individual entrepreneurs on a daily basis.

The market potential is huge, and in cooperation with the Danish Industrialization Fund for Developing Countries Fan Milk has now developed additional sales and distribution companies in Benin, Burkina Faso and Liberia. In total Fan Milk covers a customer base of 210 million people, employs more than 1300 staff and more than 20 000 independent sales entrepreneurs and has an annual revenue of more than $115 million. Fan Milk is, in short, both a successful business and a value-creating development effort with widespread local effect.

Since Fan Milk, the list of large corporations transforming their business models by changing price, volume or distribution of locally tailored products with the goal of giving the world's poor access to consumer goods has grown. And single-serve sachet packages, low-cost production, extended distribution and NGO partnerships are becoming new standards in these markets.[85]

Much-quoted Indian company Hindustan Lever Limited (HLL), a subdivision of the multinational corporation Unilever, is one of them. As India's largest consumer products company, HLL employs more than 15 000 employees, reaching over 700 million consumers and generating an annual turnover of more than 14 000 crores, the rough equivalent of $3 billion, as a result. To pioneer new markets among the rural poor, HLL requires all employees to spend six weeks in an Indian village to gain insight into local consumer needs and preferences. The knowledge is turned into the development of new consumer goods produced almost exclusively from local raw materials. HLL also has a rural research and development centre dedicated to developing products and technology to serve the needs of low-income villagers.

For distribution HLL uses a wide variety of local partners and supports them in developing local capabilities. And HLL has experimented with new forms of distribution such as sales via local product demonstrations, village street theatres and Project Shakti, which in 2006 enlisted around 30 000 poor and mostly illiterate women to provide them with training in selling, commercial knowledge and bookkeeping, teaching them to become fully fledged micro-entrepreneurs.The HLL strategy has not only created new jobs. It has also brought the women self-esteem, a sense of empowerment and a place in society, and has secured HLL a position as an accepted development partner among the poor.[12,86,87]

The new logic of regarding poor people as potential entrepreneurs, workers or customers who are able to improve their own situation rather than as victims or passive aid receivers is, however, no better illustrated than with the case of Muhammad Yunus's microcredit business, Grameen Bank.

With more than 23 000 employees and a recovery rate of 97%, as of January 2010, Grameen Bank has loaned more than $8.86 billion to 8.1 million borrowers, 97% of whom are women, has helped build 640 000 homes, sponsored more than 50 000 scholarships and student loans and changed the lives of 80% of Bangladeshi families.[88] These convincing results led to the United Nations designating 2005 *The International Year of Microcredit*. And commercial banks like Deutsche Bank, ABN Amro and Citigroup are now also following the microcredit path. They have realized that a billion in spare change is still a billion – and can make a huge difference.

Telecommunication companies France Telecom, Safaricom and Vodafone are also contributing to the innovations in monetary transactions with their M-PESA banking system which enables customers that do not have a bank account – typically because they do not have access to a bank or because they do not have sufficient income to justify a bank account – to complete simple payment transactions by SMS over a mobile phone. This not only provides safety from crime and helps 'un-banked' micro-entrepreneurs avoid the sky-high interest rates of loan sharks, it also gains access to a rapidly growing BOP market for information and communications technologies (ICT) in Africa that is already estimated at $2 billion (258 million people).[89]

The world's third largest cement manufacturer CEMEX, on the other hand, has developed a specific business model to address Mexican low-income needs in the do-it-yourself home-building market. Here it uses its financial strength to lend raw construction materials which are paid back with regular loan payments and applies its know-how to give technical advice and ensure efficient use of materials. As a result, home-building costs are 30% less while the construction period averages 1.5 years instead of four to six. Thereby homes are built in communities that could otherwise not afford it, and CEMEX is generating revenue from a market that did not previously exist.[14]

The Mexican giant has also invented a concrete mix with added anti-bacterial agent for flooring in low-cost housing projects in poorer communities. The treated concrete not only helps kill germs but also means that less expensive (and potentially polluting) cleaning agents need to be used.

There is, however, no 'one-size-fits-all-approach' to BOP markets, because issues such as skill levels, culture, the regulatory environment, NGO involvement and infrastructure challenges all differ from country to country. As a result, inclusive business growth often requires companies to go *beyond value chains*, i.e. to engage in broad-based education, health, enterprise development efforts, etc.[90]

The Swedish-based packaging company Tetra Pak, for example, has developed two different business models for its activities in premium and low-income markets. In both cases Tetra Pak works closely with its customers. But in low-income markets it has developed an integrated 'Cow to Consumer' value chain model from food production and food processing to food distribution and feeding programmes. Among other reasons because local food production and processing is still in its infancy, often with detrimental health effects as a result, which calls for improved food security and nutrition, promotion of education for children and fostering sustainable farming but also commercial financing of plant and equipment, market development activities and consumer information. The needs of each actor in the value chain are, in other words, addressed and integrated, creating a base for sustainable social and economic development.[14,91]

The innovation opportunities in addressing broader community needs and wants are also what lie behind Grundfos LIFELINK, an inclusive business model for sustainable supply of safe drinking water at affordable prices created by Grundfos, one of the world's leading pump manufacturers.

The Grundfos LIFELINK business model addresses the breakdown causes of many water projects: limitations of inadequate physical infrastructure for water and maintenance as well as restricted access to financial services. The model – a total solution water system with a solar-powered water pump, a water tank, a remote monitoring unit and an automatic tapping unit – also incorporates a payment facility, where the users pay for the water using smart cards and mobile banking. The payments also cover Grundfos LIFELINK's service and maintenance of the pump stations. Any surplus from the water revenue is paid back into the community's own account so it can invest in new development projects. Since 2008 Grundfos LIFELINK has been piloted in Kenya, and is expected to reach a commercial breakthrough during 2010.

Viewing BOP customers as business development partners and innovators rather than as mere buyers, suppliers or distributors who need to be developed is also an approach that is in the process of being developed and tested by Stuart Hart and his fellows at *The BOP Protocol Initiative*. By combining the engagement of local knowledge, resources, skills and needs with the resources and technologies of multinationals, the result is the co-creation of unique business models. These, in turn, create both economic value and enduring community value while establishing a foundation for long-term corporate growth and innovation.

Operating in emerging markets can, in fact, provide fertile ground for new ideas and products that may eventually also sell to consumers all over the world by serving as beta sites for what has been dubbed 'trickle-up innovation'.

The world's largest technology company, Hewlett Packard, for instance, has a 'developing country computer', an inexpensive, robust laptop designed to work in extreme climates, which is now being sold around the world. General Electric is now selling small-size, low-price handheld electrocardiogram devices and portable PC-based ultrasound machines in the USA, although these machines were originally developed for rural India and rural China.[92] And for Unilever, some 40% of the company's sales and most of its growth are now taking place in developing countries with activities ranging wider than traditional research and development.

In Ghana, for example, Unilever teaches palm oil producers to reuse plant waste while providing potable water to deprived communities. And in Brazil it provides financing to help tomato growers convert to eco-friendly drip irrigation.

For Unilever's CEO, Patrick Cescau, getting involved in issues like poverty, water scarcity and the effects of climate change is vital to staying competitive in the coming decades: 'CEOs used to frame thoughts like these in the context of moral responsibility. But now, it's also about growth and innovation. In the future, it will be the only way to do business.'[93] Unilever simply regards the (developing) world as its laboratory.

So to sum up, the principle of inclusive growth is not only blurring the borders between commercial activity and social value creation by bringing the world's poorest people into the global economy. It is also conveying new logics where public aid is transformed into private enterprise and small is turned into big. The poor are rich in resources and knowledge, and consumers, suppliers and distributors are turned into business partners. And corporate social responsibility is turned into corporate social innovation.

It is a new way out of poverty, a new way to make business and it is giving the term *developing countries* a whole new meaning.

The silent killers
– social imbalances and growth principle 3

'For the first time ever, our enemies are no longer outside us. We're quite well suited to battles with foreign powers, evil corporations or heartless states. But now we face many challenges where the enemy is us – our desires and our myopias may be what stand in the way of survival.'[45]

Geoff Mulgan

Snapshot 1: Angelina Jolie with 5-year-old starving child at a refugee camp in Darfur. Snapshot 2: Nurse Smith with 45-year-old man from Manchester with too high blood pressure. Snapshot 3: Cathy Jones calls in sick because the workload is just too much.

While credit crunch, climate change, pandemics, regional conflicts and natural disasters have dominated media headlines and attracted celebrity activism, less attention is given to the world's most lethal silent killers: lifestyle-related chronic disease and stress. And no wonder. Snapshots 2 and 3 are not as easy to sell to the population as pictures of starving refugee children in Africa or the devastating effects of tsunamis and earthquakes.

Nevertheless, these silent killers are two faces of the same coin; in fact they are, in many cases, interlinked. They are the price we are paying for valuing wealth and doing well higher than health and wellbeing.

Chronic diseases like heart disease, stroke, cancer, chronic respiratory disease and diabetes are already the cause of 60% of all annual deaths worldwide.[94] And even though 80% of these annual deaths occur in low- and middle-income countries,[94] chronic diseases are still a health threat that have not gained the same attention as other health issues like HIV/AIDS.

Nevertheless, the increasing material wealth and free trade of globalization have made stimulants like tobacco and alcohol as well as unhealthy fast food accessible and attractive to more people, spreading obesity, high blood pressure and lifestyle-related diseases from the developed countries to the rest of the world.

Tobacco production, for example, has fallen by 50% since 1960 in wealthy countries, but has increased by 300% in the low to medium-income countries.[95] In China and India alone there are more than half a billion smokers, all living with a potential risk of developing chronic diseases.

So unless we start taking fundamental precautionary measures, the World Health Organization (WHO) estimates that these kinds of lifestyle-related chronic diseases will lead to the death of an estimated 388 million people by 2015 – a number close to the entire population of Europe.[96]

The implication of this silent health threat is also an increasing financial burden. Countries like China, India and the UK, for instance, will, within the next ten years, be losing respectively 558, 237 and 33 billion US dollars in lost productivity caused by chronic diseases.[97] And in the USA the costs of employee health are already close to topping the list of company costs, exceeded only by production costs and wages.[98] Stress-related injuries alone cost American companies more than 300 billion dollars per year.[99]

Across the continent, one in four of the European Union's 41 million workers experience stress-related health problems,[100] which account for 3–4% of the annual GDP in 15 EU countries – the equivalent of about 265 billion Euros per year.[101] After-effects: low productivity, high staff turnover, loss of knowledge and competences and reduced innovation capacity.

The rise of the silent killers is no coincidence. Industrial development in the Western world has caused physical, mental and spiritual imbalances, and the dark side of material growth is evident everywhere in the shapes of workaholism, overconsumption, a sense of meaninglessness as well as symptoms like stress, exhaustion, depression and other negative mental conditions.

In ultra-efficient Japan, for example, constant pressure to perform professionally has resulted in dysfunctional families with absent fathers, juvenile delinquents and rising depression. It has also resulted in a shocking wave of murders. School children have been murdered by their friends, parents by their children and children by their parents, and strangers have been murdered in some cases only because of a feeling of frustration.[102] The Japanese even have their own word for work-related deaths, *Karoshi*, 'death from overwork', which is reported as a separate category in public statistics.

Similarly, France has recently experienced a series of work-related deaths. In only 20 months one of the world's leading telecommunications operators, France Telecom, suffered 24 deaths and 13 suicide attempts amongst its employees. Horrifying examples of a 32-year-old woman jumping from her office window, a male employee hanging himself in his office cubicle, and a 51-year-old father of two who jumped to his death from a motorway overpass have all allegedly been caused by unusually high work-related stress levels. 'I am committing suicide because of my work at France Telecom. That's the only reason' and other similar motivations were quoted in the farewell notes the telecom workers left behind.[103]

High or unreasonable work demands, low control over one's own work, low support from management or colleagues as well as psychological distress and job dissatisfaction are oft-quoted negative stress-drivers. And, as we will see in Chapter 2, intrinsic needs like purpose, meaning and self-realization are starting to influence job satisfaction and consequently business practices. Affirmation and manifestation of personal values are therefore essential to turning the tide.

Healthy people – healthy business

Utopian Change. In a nearly universal commitment to social responsibility, companies are developing products and solutions that help make life better for all. Thanks to advances in science it is now possible to stop the progression of disease in its tracks, in good part through prevention. Empowered consumers take action to form coalitions strong enough to deal with the huge healthcare and social challenges across sectors and geography. Companies and authorities collaborate to create an environment in which nutrition and physical exercise can flourish, from the design of public transportation to preferential prices on health insurance for people who maintain good weight and fitness.[104]

It may indeed sound like utopia, but *Utopian Change* is a working scenario of the world's leading diabetes care company, Novo Nordisk, who use it to help chart a path to a more equitable and healthy future. Not only is it the company's belief that this scenario is within reach, it also matches Novo Nordisk's paradoxical aspiration to defeat diabetes, the very source of its current core business.

The Triple Bottom Line principle is how Novo Nordisk has chosen to interpret its commitment to sustainable development, which implies that any decision should always seek to balance three considerations: Is it economically viable? Is it socially responsible? And is it environmentally sound? The principle is grounded in the fundamental belief that a healthy economy, environment and society are fundamental to long-term business success.

So far, this principle has led, among other things, to more than 29 600 employees, activities in 76 countries worldwide, annual billion dollar turnovers (in 2009 $9.6 billion), the development of annual sustainability reports that integrate financial and non-financial aspects of its business, top rankings on the Dow Jones Sustainability World Index, an agreement with the World Wildlife Foundation to make a substantial reduction in its CO_2 emissions as well as stakeholder involvement to stay attuned to their concerns and to explore opportunities for innovative collaboration.

Within recent years the pharmaceutical multinational has taken a major strategic shift by moving away from 'sick care' and taking a more progressive view on 'healthcare'. As Novo Nordisk's CEO, Lars Rebien Sørensen, explains: 'If you want to be a partner with society you have to engage in solving the underlying problems. As a company we have to point out – even though we don't make money on this with our current products – that prevention, naturally, is the ideal solution to diabetes, indeed that society's solution to chronic diseases overall is to change our lifestyles.'

In addition to its $255 million-funded World Diabetes Foundation, which together with the International Diabetes Federation (IDF) and the World Health Organization (WHO) has already initiated more than 230 projects to limit the diabetes epidemic in developing countries through education and capacity building, Novo Nordisk has also founded the Oxford Health Alliance (OxHA) in partnership with Oxford University in the UK.

Financed by, among others, Novo Nordisk, PepsiCo, the American Cancer Society, the Australian Department of Health and the British Medical Research Council, OxHA is working on initiatives to prevent and reduce the global impact of chronic disease, including diabetes, by raising awareness among influencers, educating critical decision-makers and rallying as many as possible to the pressing need for preventative measures.

Health authorities from six of the world's largest nations including China, Brazil, Britain and the USA have already joined OxHA along with leading academics, corporate executives, activists, doctors, nurses and many others who share a sense of urgency concerning the worldwide epidemic of chronic disease. And as a counterpart to the Bill & Melinda Gates Foundation's publication on the *Grand Challenges in Human Health,* which mainly focuses on infectious diseases in developing countries, OxHA has published the *20 Grand Challenges* with six goals to prevent and fight chronic disease with a following launch of initiatives to target, among other things, industry's role in prevention.

The Grand Challenges' six goals

1. Reorient health systems.
2. Mitigate health impacts of poverty and urbanization.
3. Engage businesses and community.
4. Modify risk factors.
5. Enhance economic, legal and environmental policies.
6. Raise public and political awareness.

Source: www.oxha.org

The Smart Choice Program is another example of how health-influential industries and their stakeholders are taking their first proactive steps towards preventative measures. It is a private–public coalition of global manufacturers, retailers, health experts and NGOs, who have created a simple label that allows consumers to make nutrition-based choices in their food purchases. The initiative is part of a global commitment to proactively fight obesity and promote healthier lifestyles in both developed and developing countries, signed by eight of the world's leading food and beverage multinationals including Coca-Cola, Unilever, Kellogg's and Nestlé.

The commitment includes developing innovations that offer healthier consumer options, promotion of physical activity and healthier lifestyles and support of public–private partnerships to accomplish the objectives of the World Health Organization (WHO) Global Strategy on Diet, Physical Activity and Health.[105]

Health insurers in the USA are going even further by experimenting with point systems, where customers are rewarded for healthy behaviour, for example, spending an hour in the gym, for which they earn points which can be used as payment to buy bicycles, organic food and preventive acupuncture treatments.[53] And insurance companies in the Netherlands and France are starting to refund their customers' expenses for cholesterol-reducing foods.[106]

At the same time, completely new, socially innovative business concepts are starting to emerge. Like the Icelandic TV series, *Lazy Town*, developed by Magnús Scheving, a well-known Icelandic athlete and public speaker on fitness, who identified the need to promote exercise and healthy food to children in a positive, motivating manner through characters like superhero Sportacus, who exposes children to a variety of entertaining situations and choices that impact their health. The series has received numerous awards and has become a huge commercial success with airtime in more than 100 countries.

Likewise, British star chef Jamie Oliver's commercial success, the TV campaign *Jamie's School Dinners*, which shed light on the disturbing effects that processed school dinners have on the pupils, is another example of how social and commercial values go hand in hand. The campaign led to newspaper headlines, a 300 000-signature petition that pressured the British Government to set new standards for school meals and to commit £280 million for proper school dinner ingredients, equipment and training.

Meanwhile, corporate responses to counter stress and burnout include an increasing emphasis on corporate purpose and awareness of the importance of work–life balance.

Japanese car manufacturer Toyota, for example, now generally limits overtime to 360 hours a year (an average of 30 hours monthly), and at some offices issues public address announcements every hour after 7 p.m. pointing out the importance of rest and urging workers to go home. At competitor Nissan, office workers are offered telecommuting to make it easier to care for children or elderly parents, and along with them dozens of large Japanese corporations have also implemented 'no overtime days', which require employees to leave the office promptly at 5:30 p.m.[107]

In Denmark, the international engineering company NNE Pharmaplan has adopted a new strategy for productivity which sets out to do more by doing less. It all started in 2003 when NNE Pharmaplan was planning the construction of a new pharmaceutical factory in Denmark, a task that usually took 36 stress-generating months. But this time, the management decided that the factory was to be built at double speed – without doubling the amount of work hours spent.

Based on knowledge about the body's reactions to strain, insufficient rest and continuous high work tempo, NNE developed a programme based on principles of interdisciplinary knowledge sharing, rest, play and insight into the best ways to optimize the body for efficient work. Among other things, this meant that employees and project managers were not allowed to work later than 3 p.m. until the last month before the opening of the factory.

Result: NNE Pharmaplan finished the factory in 18 months – half the normally prescribed time. Following the pilot project NNE continued experimenting. Today they are down to 12 months!

Growth principle 3: immaterial growth

The notion that economic growth leads to wealth, health and happiness has become an unspoken premise as the world looks today, and most companies and nations still measure progress in monetary terms. But the high costs that we are paying as employees, citizens and society call for a more sophisticated economic system, which assesses not only the wealth but also the wellbeing of society and recognizes that companies can grow in other ways than size and turnover.

In Japan, what could be called a *slowing-down-to-advance-wellbeing* counter movement is already starting to make its mark in society as well as in corporations as a way of shifting attention from economic growth to social progress. Because slowing down allows us to step back, see the whole and contemplate what is really important. Sustainable stability rather than sustainable growth could well be its mantra.

Some local governments, for example, are campaigning for a more relaxed and comfortable lifestyle by adopting *Slow Life* as their slogan and by assigning a *Slow Life Month* for special events to raise citizen awareness of slower lifestyles. Others have adopted *Take-It-Easy* or *Creating a Slow Life Community* declarations for designing communities where citizens can enjoy life to the fullest instead of nurturing the prevailing hard-work paradigm.[102]

Similar changes are also taking place in the corporate world – for example, in the Japanese paint supply company Mukouyama Painting, which strives to accomplish growth in employee happiness and customer satisfaction while maintaining a financial zero growth policy. As a result, the company no longer measures its success by sales figures or increases in profit, but by its *Gross Company Happiness* (GCH), and an increasing number of Japanese enterprises are now following suit with their own zero growth policies.[102]

Mukouyama Painting – happiness on the bottom line

Until a personal wake-up call in 1996, Mr Mukouyama was a typical Japanese executive, driving his employees hard to reach the company goals of annual growth with slogans like 'Boost sales by 20%!' The hardliner policy made his company, Mukouyama Painting, an unpopular place to work, many employees left and the available positions were difficult to fill.

Struggling with depression in 1996, Mr Mukouyama asked himself: Who am I? What is the company for? What should I do? His conclusion: 'We live in a capitalist society where people are self-centred, but I really want to live in a world full of love, peace, harmony, cooperation and self-sufficiency.'

The result was a series of reforms designed to fulfil the company's renewed purpose, and success is measured by its Gross Company Happiness (GCH) – the total happiness of all employees. In fact, the company's goal is now to decrease sales by a certain annual percentage, because Mr Mukouyama believes that focusing on customer satisfaction rather than sales will add to the happiness of his employees.

Today, the staff turnover is zero, Mr Mukouyama is happy, so are his employees, and Mukouyama Painting is famous for its dedication to corporate responsibility and its popularity in the local community.[102]

The need for metrics that measure and redefine the concept of prosperity and wellbeing is also reflected in other corporate concepts like the previously mentioned *Triple Bottom Line* – also known as *People, Planet, Profit* or the *Three Pillars of Sustainability* – which captures an expanded spectrum of economic, ecological and social values and criteria for measuring organizational (and societal) success.[108]

Novo Nordisk, for example, reports on its water and energy consumption, recycling percentages, waste volumes, CO_2 emissions, diversity in its senior management teams, frequency of work-related injuries, employee turnover rates and employee engagement levels in addition to its economic performance.

To make up for the current defect in the GDP measures of development and growth, new indicators of a country's progress have also emerged to measure the many aspects of quality of life.

The Calvert–Henderson Quality of Life Indicator, for example, measures 12 aspects and uses monetary coefficients only where appropriate. Similarly, the United Nations operates with a Human Development Index (HDI) to complement GDP by bringing in qualitative measures of poverty, gender equity, education, social inclusion, environment and health which cannot be reduced to money coefficients or aggregated into a simple number.[52]

The small nation of Bhutan has also designed the pioneering concept of gross national happiness (GNH) to supplement the more widely accepted gross domestic product (GDP) to promote sustainable development, preservation and promotion of cultural values, conservation of the natural environment and establishment of good governance. Contrary to most Western countries, Bhutan has recognized that true development in society takes place when material and immaterial development occur side by side to complement and reinforce each other.

Who would have believed that this would be recognized as more than a quaint Buddhist exercise in a small far-away country? Nevertheless, the European Commission has launched the *Beyond GDP* initiative which now works on improving our measures of progress, wealth and wellbeing of nations. Just like France's President Sarkozy has initiated a Commission on the *Measurement of Economic Performance and Social Progress.*

So to summarize, in order to counter current social imbalances we need to supplement – and ultimately fully integrate – financial growth measures with qualitative measures of health, wellbeing and other immaterial values.

The starting point is to determine what are ends and what are means. In the new paradigm economic growth – or economic stability – is the means to the ultimate end of the wellbeing of people and sustainable progress in society. In short, we need to build our future economy on real needs rather than on our desires. We need to put sustainable development in its broadest sense at the heart of our economy and our business models.

Chapter 2

The relationship between business and society is not only being changed by the external pressures of globalization. The effects of inner globalization are also making their mark on individuals who feel a sense of personal responsibility to make the world a better place, and are putting this into action as employees, activists, consumers and entrepreneurs. Web 2.0 technologies are accelerating this new wave of initiative by reinforcing international connectivity and cooperation, empowering individuals, decentralising problem solving and opening the economy to more people in innovative ways.

Generation MeWe
– conscious labour markets

> 'Our prime purpose in this life is to help others. And if you can't help them, at least don't hurt them.'[1]
>
> *Dalai Lama*

Whilst policy-makers and business leaders are operating in the old growth paradigm, looking for answers to questions about how to ensure global competitiveness and continuous economic growth, an increasing number of citizens are beginning to ask other questions such as 'who am I', 'why am I here', 'what are my talents', 'how can I make a positive difference'?

In many parts of the world, people have reached a material welfare limit and are instead turning to personal development and spiritual fulfilment as factors that top the existential barometer. As a result, there is an increasing gap between what mainstream business models and economic systems promote and nurture and what we value and need as human beings.

Over the following sections we will be exploring the link between five needs and five markets for exchange of not only products and services but also of information and knowledge. Together they are forming 'social economies' that embrace a wide range of values-based community, personal, voluntary and non-profit initiatives and informal exchanges that are blazing the trails for collaborative problem solving as well as new ways of organising and conducting business. These markets of change are, in other words, affecting the evolution of corporate social responsibility and innovation.

The effects of inner globalization

Section	Needs	Markets	Exchanges
Generation MeWe	Meaning and self-realization	Conscious labour markets	Work ↔ engagement and fulfilment
The Global Brain	Social interaction and sharing	Hybrid markets	Products and services ↔ enthusiasm and skills
Collective problem solvers	Involvement and participation	Collective intelligence markets	Problems ↔ feedback, ideas
Civil power brokers	Transparency and fairness	Activism markets	Information ↔ actions
Conscious buycotters	Ethics and responsibility	Ethical consumption markets	Values ↔ money

The quest for meaning

When Gallup asked people in China in 1994 which attitudes towards life came closest to describing their own, almost 70% said that 'to work hard and get rich' came closest.[2] These modern values of materialism co-exist with the post-modern immaterial values of the silent revolution (described in the Introduction), which is making its mark particularly – but not exclusively – in the Western part of the world.

Just like Japan's earlier mentioned *slowing-down-to-advance-wellbeing* counter movement, a 1995 Merck/Harwood survey showed that millions of Americans of all backgrounds experience a need to hit the brakes and focus on what means the most to them. They want society to move away from greed and excess and towards a way of life centred on values, community and family. They yearn for a balanced and less stressful life, and are practising the uneconomic growth principle by voluntarily scaling back their salaries and lifestyles to reflect their immaterial set of priorities. As one survey participant explained: 'I'm much more content. I may not have the extra pocket money I had before, but I'm telling you, it's worth it.'[3]

The global consciousness movement is, in other words, increasing the number of individuals who are searching for identity, wholeness, happiness and meaning. And although it may at first glance seem contradictory to these self-centred values, the sense of belonging and being connected to others as well as the value of contribution to community are today essential cornerstones of modern work and life expectations. It is a MeWe generation to which giving is the new taking and sharing is the new giving – an invisible contract based on enlightened self-interest.

Everywhere there are signs of this quest for the good (work) life and collective interest in handing over a better world to new generations.

One of the tell-tale signs is the increasing number of citizens that are following the footsteps of philanthro-celebs like Bono, Angelina Jolie, Brad Pitt and Bill Gates by actively engaging in good causes and charitable organizations. As numerous happiness surveys testify, money can certainly buy you happiness – but only as long as you spend the money on someone else.[4] And people appear to be more than willing to increase the wellbeing of both themselves and others.

Some by donating money through websites like DonorsChoose, GlobalGiving, Razoo and SmallCanBeBig, which enable direct, personal and specific donations – or by using Facebook applications like Causes.com, which, since 2007, has grown a community of over 80 million people, who have raised donations of more than $12 million in support of over 300 000 causes from breast cancer research to local parks.[5]

Others by volunteering their time – even during their holidays. 'The 1960s were all about relaxing vacations; in the 80s vacations were all about being active or seeking adventure. Now people are seeking meaningful vacations. 'People have a very quiet but desperate need to find meaning in their lives,' explains managing director, Ross Wehner, from Volunteer Adventures.[6]

During the economic crisis voluntary work has even become a way for the unemployed to showcase their talents, develop new skills, make new contacts or simply to make a positive difference until they are on a payroll again. Voluntary work is, in fact, becoming a career booster and is a factor that recruiters and human resource directors are increasingly looking at when evaluating potential new employees.[7] Just like corporate volunteering programmes that involve employees in community work are becoming an immaterial fringe benefit for those who want to make a positive difference.

The labour market is, in other words, being permeated by meaning – with new employee demands, leadership profiles and new business skills and management training as a result.

From human resource to human purpose management

> 'A career at P&G offers a chance to touch someone's life. Our people get involved – with their workplace, their community, their neighbors and each other. If you want a company whose actions reflect their ethics and whose people live their values, then you should consider a career at P&G.'[8]

This job ad from Procter & Gamble, one of the world's largest manufacturers of consumer goods, is just one of many examples of how companies are branding themselves to meet intrinsic employee needs for meaning and personal fulfilment.

Obviously, work has always had – and still has – different meanings, depending on age and work ambitions, from being 'just a job' at the daily grindstone to being 'a career' with search for self-esteem through advancement and prestige, or 'a calling' where work is morally inseparable from the individual's life.[9]

But whereas the first category was predominant in the industrial age and the second was particularly practised by the yuppies in the 1980s, the third is becoming the prevailing paradigm for 21st century employee needs, values and aspirations. Considering the amounts of hours we spend at work, it is only natural that the post-modern values shift is also reflected in work–life demands.

Maslow's pyramid of needs has been reversed: the physiological and material needs for survival and safety in terms of a steady job and a good pay cheque still count – but they can no longer stand alone. The future job psychology will increasingly be dominated by social, emotional and self-realization needs. Employees of the knowledge age have – in the words of the *Wall Street Journal* – a 'desire to shape their jobs to fit their lives rather than adapt their lives to the workplace.'[10]

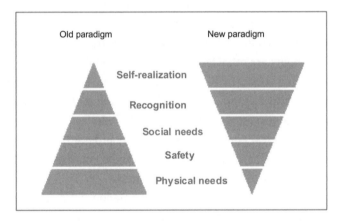

The good (work) life

So, like the millions of Americans in the above-mentioned 1995 Merck/Harwood study, future CEOs are also going down new 'downshifting' paths in their pursuit of the good (work) life. A 2006 survey, for example, among 685 global business influentials and CEOs (senior executives, financial analysts, business media and government officials in 65 countries) revealed that more than 50% would reject a position as CEO if given the choice because of (1) too little work–life balance; (2) too much focus on quarterly earnings; and (3) too much stress.[11]

Factors like corporate culture and a healthy (work) life balance have, in other words, become just as important for the next generation of managers as material incentives – a view that is shared amongst top executives from as far apart as Argentina, Australia, Belgium, Canada, France, India, The Netherlands and the USA.[12] Instead of the 'onward and upward' motto which used to characterize the classic career path, *plateauing* is therefore becoming an alternative definition of work success, simply because the price of climbing the corporate ladder is too high and activities outside work hours are given a higher priority.[13]

For the so-called Generation Y employees, on the other hand, values of freedom of choice, self-management and autonomy are reflected in their demands for regular feedback, responsibility, a career that provides a flexible transition between ideas, involvement in decision making and expectations that location and traditional working hours are irrelevant to their success.[8]

UK and US studies from the Aspen Institute Center for Business Education and McKinsey's much-quoted *War for Talent* reports also show that the best people and students are attracted to companies that fulfil the deep, personal need for meaning while making contributions to society that go beyond making a profit, and that they link brand reputation to the company's record in addressing environmental and social impacts.[8,14] In fact, employees working in companies with clear corporate responsibility programmes tend to stay in their jobs longer and be more satisfied with senior management than their peers at companies with lacklustre programmes.[15]

This is not an exclusively Western phenomenon. Studies which include African and Far Eastern students come to similar conclusions to those of McKinsey,[8] and others show that social responsibility is an even more significant driver in attracting employees in countries like Chile, India, South Africa and China than it is in the USA, UK and Japan.[16] So, even though some analysts expect Western values to move out of the mainstream as jobs and wealth drift eastward, it is just as likely that the difference between leaders in the interconnected global village may not be that great.

The next generation of employees – Generation Z or the Millennial generation – will very likely still carry the responsibility torch. Half of British teenagers today – the so-called *Greenagers* – are already concerned with issues like climate change and ethical practices. In fact, they say that they are willing to spend and invest their money with companies that behave ethically, and over 70% of them refuse – just like international business school students from the generation before them[17] – to work for unethical companies.[18]

As a fresh business school graduate once revealed to me when I asked her about her future plans: 'You know what. I am a smoker, but I could never dream of working for a tobacco company. It just isn't cool.' It is for reasons like these that companies are starting to recognize the strategic imperative of social responsibility for employee engagement.

All this is opening up a new category of job agencies on the labour market. Like GreenCareersGuide.com, the first online recruitment service focusing on green career and entrepreneurship opportunities in fields like natural building, wind power, organic farming and holistic alternative medicine. Or the British Acre Recruitment agency which specializes in jobs related to CSR, sustainability, climate change and the environment.

When immaterial values enter corporate agendas, this also has profound implications for management and leadership. 21st century human resource management is rather a case of human *purpose* management, and key leadership tasks therefore include creating and communicating, vision, values and mental models; understanding and meeting others' needs to develop; building culture and community; creating a climate of morality and ethics; and showing the way through personal actions. And this, in turn, calls for leadership characteristics like integrity, commitment, compassion, courage, humility, empathy and ethics.[9]

In other words, hard professional skills like business acumen, strategic savvy and analytical excellence are still essential but in no way sufficient to stand alone. Personal leadership and 'soft skills' are more than ever centre stage.

Up and coming executives are already being recruited as much for their soft skills in teamwork, communication, sustainability, corporate responsibility and ethics as they are for their financial and strategic skills.[19] Which is one of the reasons why the curricula of business schools worldwide are changing. When people's needs change, business must adapt.

Responsible capitalism in business schools

'As a manager, my purpose is to serve the greater good by bringing together people and resources to create value that no single individual can build alone. Therefore I will seek a course that enhances the value my enterprise can create for society over the long term.'

These were the first lines of an oath taken by 400 graduates at the world-acclaimed Harvard Business School when they received their Master's degrees in Business Administration (MBAs) at an unofficial ceremony in 2009. Similar to the ancient Hippocratic Oath recited by medical doctors to uphold a number of professional ethical standards, the graduates promised that they would guard against 'decisions and behaviour that advance my own narrow ambitions, but harm the enterprise and the societies it serves' and 'develop both myself and other managers ... so that the profession continues to grow and contribute to the wellbeing of society'.[20]

The student oath was part of a larger effort to turn management from a trade into a profession by, among other things, formalising the social contract with society and by sharing a set of values that distanced the students from earlier generations of MBAs. An effort fuelled by insider critics like acknowledged expert and professor Sumanthra Ghosal at London Business School and Canadian professor Henry Mintzberg of McGill University, who claim that the conventional MBA programmes train 'the wrong people in the wrong ways with the wrong consequences'.

The effects of the recent financial crisis have only made the MBA-critical voices even stronger, with accusations that business schools have contributed to the crisis by fostering selfish short-term thinking managers with a narrow Milton Friedman-based focus on profits and shareholder returns as the only responsibility of business.[21,22,23]

Therefore, business school insiders and analysts foresee that new economic theories will be built to replace the ones that caused the financial crisis, leading to new models, ideas and emphasis on areas like risk management, regulation, corporate governance and ethics in business textbooks and curricula.[21]

With curriculum titles like 'new economics', 'humanity and enterprise', 'globalization and the new context of business', 'leadership and innovation in complex systems' and 'responsible leadership in a globalising world', higher education institutions are already supplementing traditional management education with specialist courses to attract the new generation of conscious students, who want to balance professional success with personal and corporate responsibility. The old business school mantra *show me the money* is being replaced by the new mantra *doing good and doing well*.

The percentage of business schools worldwide that require students to take a course focused on 'business and society' has, in fact, increased dramatically over a six-year period, increasing from 34% in 2001 to 63% in 2007.[24] And the concept of social entrepreneurship and social enterprise – which we will be exploring in depth in Chapter 3 – is also pushing its way into electives, programmes and dedicated research centres at, among others, Harvard Business School, Colombia, Yale, Stanford University, Duke University, INSEAD and IESE business school.

Decisions made by globally responsible leaders rely on their awareness of outer globalization issues such as responsibility-related principles and regulations as well as the development of inner globalization issues like their own mentality, cultural understanding and personal conscience. To address these development issues business schools are starting to send out their students on field trips to other parts of the world.

For instance, IMD, a Swiss-based international business school, has, since 2002, operated with a development concept called *The Discovery Expedition*, where students spend a week in a developing country to gain insight into business climate, culture and socio-economic challenges – and to train the students in utilising empathy and relations management in unknown business territories.

And in France, The HEC School of Management has partnered with cotton producers in Senegal so that its executive MBA students can work with sustainable business at the local level in different villages to understand how to adapt operational models for future business development to local contexts and cultures.

The UNESCO prize-awarded International School of New Business Design & Social Innovation, Kaospilots in Denmark, which in 2007 was nominated by *BusinessWeek* as one of the world's top 50 design schools, is, however, still the only school in the world which has social entrepreneurship at its core. Specialising in business design and social innovation and entrepreneurship, it addresses outer as well as inner globalization issues by operating with, among other things, 'outpost periods', where the whole team of students is relocated to another part of the world for three months.

The explosion of interest in business school programmes with sustainability and responsible capitalism on the agenda is often driven by students, who are founding their own organizations to support a social outlook on business. As Rakesh Khurana, a Harvard Business School professor, explains: 'Students are saying they want business education to operate in a different way and that they want higher expectations from faculty. Just telling them to maximize shareholder value does not satisfy them any more. They want to get away from the cartoon image of business that they are taught in the classroom, to get useful practical advice on how to lead a firm in the 21st century.'[23]

Stanford's Graduate School of Business, for example, has redesigned its curriculum largely based on student input from members of the US-based organization Net Impact, founded in 1993 for networking purposes by a group of business school students who wanted to use the power of business to address social and environmental challenges. Today, the network encompasses more than 10 000 young business leaders in 120 local chapters scattered across the whole continent, and 72% of the *Financial Times*'s top 50 global business schools now have active Net Impact chapters.[25]

Likewise, The Global Social Venture Competition – a competition which encourages business school students to develop the best business plan for creating financial benefits as well as measurable advantages for society – was initiated by students at the Haas School of Business under the University of California. And within the past five to seven years, socially responsible investment funds like the Haas Socially Responsible Investment Fund and the Microlumbia Fund have also been launched by students and alumnis in order to invest in a variety of areas right from non-profit projects to micro-entrepreneurial businesses.

Nevertheless, corporate responsibility and sustainability have not yet become fully embedded in the mainstream of business-related education, which is why the United Nations has developed its Principles for Responsible Management Education (UN PRME) for business schools and universities worldwide. The aim is to support the development of 'a new generation of business leaders capable of managing the complex challenges faced by business and society in the 21st century'.

The Principles for Responsible Management Education (UN PRME)

Principle 1

Purpose: We will develop the capabilities of students to be future generators of sustainable value for business and society at large and to work for an inclusive and sustainable global economy.

Principle 2

Values: We will incorporate into our academic activities and curricula the values of global social responsibility as portrayed in international initiatives such as the United Nations Global Compact.

Principle 3

Method: We will create educational frameworks, materials, processes and environments that enable effective learning experiences for responsible leadership.

Principle 4

Research: We will engage in conceptual and empirical research that advances our understanding about the role, dynamics and impact of corporations in the creation of sustainable social, environmental and economic value.

Principle 5

Partnership: We will interact with managers of business corporations to extend our knowledge of their challenges in meeting social and environmental responsibilities and to explore jointly effective approaches to meeting these challenges.

Principle 6

Dialogue: We will facilitate and support dialogue and debate among educators, business, government, consumers, media, civil society organizations and other interested groups and stakeholders on critical issues related to global social responsibility and sustainability.

We understand that our own organizational practices should serve as examples of the values and attitudes we convey to our students.

Source: www.unprme.org

Beyond doubt, the global consciousness movement is fostering a new breed of employees and business leaders, who want to use their competences in a social as well as a financial context. They do not want to risk compromising their inner values because of demands for profit maximization that may force them to put the company's interests above society's.

However, as long as the design and purpose of businesses evolves around profit making as the ultimate goal, conflicts of interest may arise. So although many MBA students say that they want jobs that allow them to make meaningful societal contributions, many of them feel that recruiters do not place a high value on personal integrity or the students' understanding of social issues. In fact, many of them predict that their values will conflict with what they are asked to do in business.[26]

At the same time, most still do not believe that corporate social responsibility makes a significant impact on a company's bottom line mainly because business schools and businesses are not good at providing solid business cases that show that corporate responsibility pays. A recent study (2003) showed that entering MBA students had idealistic ambitions, but by the time they graduated, these ambitions had been replaced by ambitions tied to financial performance.[27]

So although the ambitions of making a meaningful difference are present, there are still tensions between the notion of doing well in business and doing good for society as well as how to put this into practice.

So what are the business implications of all this? In short, the MeWe employees are pressuring companies to find an ideal blend of financial reward and personal fulfilment, because an engaged and committed workforce is a central route to increased productivity, performance – and innovation. Ethics, reputation and sustainability must take centre stage for companies wishing to attract employees in pursuit of the good (work) life. A shared purpose that goes beyond making a profit and a strong set of shared values is the key.

Adjusting to a global labour market also means that internationalization and diversity are becoming important human resource management words. This means looking for people from different social and educational backgrounds and with different social networks and personal interests to ensure the breadth of thinking required to respond in innovative and responsible ways.[8]

When the world becomes your home market, it is also critical to develop globally minded leaders and employees. Sustainable development requires what has been dubbed 'globally responsible leadership'. It requires CEOs, boards and executive teams who care as much about sustainability as their employees do.

The Global Brain
– hybrid markets

> 'A new mode of production is emerging and it's not the hierarchical form that we've known since the Industrial Revolution, and not quite the capitalist marketplace where people contract for services. It's a fluid way of producing value.'[28]
>
> Anthony D. Williams

> '[This is] a story about community and collaboration on a scale never seen before. ... It's about the many wresting power from the few and helping one another for nothing and how that will not only change the world, but also change the way the world changes.'

This is how the international news magazine *TIME* described its 2006 award of Person of The Year: YOU! The tool that makes the story about this unprecedented year of community and collaboration come true is Web 2.0: the new version of inventor Tim Berners-Lee's World Wide Web – or the Internet as we all have come to know it – which has led to a wide array of interactive tools like blogs, wikis and other community-enhancing websites like Facebook, Twitter, YouTube, Second Life and MySpace.

This powerful tool is opening up new democratic and collaborative ways of solving problems and creating positive change. Today, more than 1.5 billion people already have access to the Internet,[29] and within the next five to ten years an estimated more than five billion people[30] will be able to tap into this *Global Brain* where 'billions of messages continually shuttle back and forth in an ever-growing web of communication, linking the billions of minds and humanity together into a single system.'[2]

The implications are revolutionary. This new means of communicating is not only accelerating our inner globalization by making us more aware of the outer imbalances in the world, it is also empowering us to actually *do* something about it in each our own way. Billions of people can make their individual voices heard and put their minds to work on challenges of all kinds – no matter where they are or who they are. The old world of passivity defined by media is transforming into a new world with activity defined by media.

With 50 million blogs by 2006, and 7200 new blogs created every hour, 100 million clips viewed daily on YouTube and about 65 000 additional videos uploaded every day, over 47 million Facebook customers in two years, more than 200 million MySpace users in four years, more than 300 million users of China's social network QZone, with 25% of Western Europe's Internet users already posting comments and reviews about consumer products and user-generated media sites that are growing in numbers of visitors and participants by 100% per year, this is a massive technology-based social movement that cannot be stopped.[30,31,32,33]

The great power of social media became particularly clear with the US presidential election in 2008. It was dubbed an 'Internet election' after Barack Obama's 'YesWeCan' video generated more than a million hits a day and became one of the most popular videos ever uploaded on YouTube. The Obama campaign management was also successful in a strategy for political fundraising based on, among other things, online campaigning which secured a few dollars from millions of people rather than millions of dollars from a few people.

With the emergence of Web 2.0 we have, in other words, opened the doors to a 'massive social experiment', an 'explosion of productivity and innovation' with an 'opportunity to build a new kind of international understanding, not politician to politician, great man to great man, but citizen to citizen, person to person.'[34]

The power of YOU and the ability for us to exercise our individuality is really just as much the power of WE – in a 21st century MeWe kind of way – we are learning that the power of one can lead to the power of many.

It has taken decades for us to change from an industrial society to a knowledge and service society. But thanks to new technology, we are rapidly moving into the era of innovation, where all conventional rules and logics are being challenged, and where the effects of both inner and outer globalization are being accelerated and becoming more visible. It is a new world where creativity, responsibility, self-organization, participation and decentralization are key principles.

Today we live in an 'open source' society that enables us to share knowledge and establish virtual communities across geographical borders within a matter of moments. As a result, what we are witnessing or already actively participating in are:

- new expressions of collective action that extend and strengthen the power of civil society;
- new methods of idea generation and co-creation that draw on a collective pool of knowledge and wisdom;
- new kinds of self expression and participative involvement through sharing of experiences and personalising of products, services, content and designs.

Building open source software like Linux and Mozilla Firefox, sharing knowledge through collaborative encyclopedias like Wikipedia, reviewing books at Amazon, posting comments on news at aggregated blog and news website Huffington Post, videoconferencing via Skype, voting on which news stories of the day deserve attention at Digg.com, sharing your favourite websites with social bookmarking services like Digg or Del.icio.us, uploading personal videos on YouTube, sharing your photos at Flickr or setting up your personal pledge at Pledgebank.com in order to kick-off collective real-life actions are just some of the numerous examples of how technological development is putting millions of minds into play in new ways – and of how conventional border lines are being blurred.

Online chat forums and blogs, for example, have blurred the lines between writing and speaking, virtual reality technologies like Second Life have blurred the lines between the virtual and real worlds, home computing has blurred the borders between work and private life and online shops have made it possible for companies to do business and for us to shop regardless of traditional opening and working hours.

And with millions of people interacting, sharing and producing online every day, and even more to follow, the distinction between collaboration in a personal and business context is also blurring. As the late C.K. Prahalad, who has been among the top ten management thinkers in every major survey for over ten years, has pointed out, platforms like Google and Facebook are now becoming as critical to advertising and brand building as they are to creating individual networks of personal friends, just like large firms are using wikis and blogs inside their organizations to democratize access to information and knowledge and improve cycle time.[30]

In short, powered by new technology, our needs for social interaction and sharing are creating an explosion of technology-based social innovations and hybrid markets that are transforming how we think, learn, live, work and conduct business in ways we would never have dreamt of a century ago.

The new hybrids

The new online social arrangements, ranging from content sharing to organized collaboration, form what has been coined *The New Socialism* by Kevin Kelley, expert in digital culture and founder of *Wired* magazine. He argues that its ultimate goal is to maximize both individual autonomy and the power of people working together, and that it is an emerging design space in which decentralized public coordination can solve problems and create things that neither pure communism nor pure capitalism can.[35]

This is why we in the blended field of social and technological innovations also find hybrid systems of 'social economies', which blend market and non-market mechanisms and which blend capitalism with social purpose. The New Socialism is not only leading to innovations *in* business. It is also leading to innovations *of* business.

Who would have thought that the interaction of enthusiastic self-organized online volunteers would result in products which would become such a huge success that even corporate giants would start using them? Nevertheless, this has been the case with the open source Linux operating system – a model of production which was initiated by Finnish software engineer, Linus Torvalds, who has proved that an online community of like-minded IT nerds is able to create a product of such high quality that it is today used by major commercial companies such as IBM, Sun Microsystems, Hewlett-Packard and Novell.

But Linux's open source production model has not only changed the principles and practices of corporate giants. It has also had a replicative spin-off effect in areas other than the IT industry.

NASA in the USA, for example, uses the same principles to identify millions of craters on Mars with the help of amateurs. In Denmark, a community of IT students has, in collaboration with brewery experts and the artist company Superflex, created an open source beer – Vores Øl (Our Beer) – from a recipe published under the unrestrictive intellectual property licence Creative Commons licence, which means that anyone can use the recipe for pleasure or profit.[36] And in Australia the open innovation biotech institute Cambia has recently launched the Global Initiative for Open Innovation, which combines open-access software and sophisticated search features to make drugs patents for malaria, tuberculosis and other neglected diseases accessible to researchers worldwide.

That community-driven ventures can become big business is another implication of the activities on hybrid markets. T-shirt design company Threadless.com is a business that started by accident but now generates annual double-digit million dollar revenues. Just like iStockphoto started out as a community of amateur photographers sharing images and designs, initiated by web designer and entrepreneur Bruce Livingstone, who developed it into the pioneer of the 'microstock photography industry' as well as a solid business which was later sold to Getty Images for $50 million.

Threadless.com

The founders of Threadless, Jake Nickell and Jacob DeHart, really just wanted to create a website where people could submit designs for a cool t-shirt, vote for their favourite design and maybe win a free t-shirt. The design with the most votes would then be printed and sold.

Threadless has no budget for advertising or marketing, because the Threadless online community performs those functions primarily

continued on next page...

through peer-to-peer communication. Designers spread the word as they try to persuade friends to vote for their designs, and Threadless rewards the community with store credit every time someone submits a photo of themselves wearing a Threadless shirt or refers a friend who buys a shirt from the company.

This simple concept has turned into a whole new way of doing business, and in 2006 Threadless generated $17 million in revenues. Currently, the company sells an average of 90 000 t-shirts a month.

Source: Howe, Jeff: *Crowdsourcing*, Random House Business Books, 2009.

The advantage of mixing the speed of online technology with the expertise and engagement of human beings is, in other words, breaking the business-as-usual cycle.

Google is a textbook example of this. 'Democracy on the web' and 'You can make money without doing evil' are two of the ten things that Google has found to be true about conducting business in the digital age. Its status as the world's most popular search engine has been built almost entirely on word of mouth from satisfied customers. Business is based on revenue from online advertising, social networking and other online sharing services. It has donated one billion dollars to its charitable arm, Google.org, to fund social investment projects. It encourages its engineers to spend 20% of their work time on projects of own interest – 50% of its new product launches like Gmail, Google News and Adsense originate from this 20% time. By 2009 it had more than 19 000 employees and an annual turnover of more than six billion dollars. It has even become a verb in the Oxford English Dictionary.[37,38]

The mix of online technology and human engagement is also opening up new ways of meeting social needs. Refugee United, for example, is an Internet-based platform developed by Danish social entrepreneurs, who, free of charge, provide refugees with an anonymous forum to reconnect with missing family. By registering nicknames, scars, former locations and other markers only identifiable to family and close friends, everyone can remain 'invisible' to all but relatives at www.refunite.org and no official papers need to be filled in.

Social-capitalistic hybrid concepts like peer-to-peer lending, investment portals and crowdfunding have also grown out of cross-fertilising consciousness and digitalization. We find them in the shape of both non-profit and for-profit online start-ups like Kiva, MyC4, Rang De, Wokai, Prosper and Zopa, which build on the microcredit concept but use the Internet to connect several hundred thousand people to invest in each other in a way that is socially and/or financially rewarding.

Another variant is the non-profit project One Laptop Per Child (OLPC), created by employees of the American research laboratory MIT Media Lab, who, with support from the United Nations, produce computers with low power consumption, a crank handle and wireless broadband, so children in developing countries can access the Internet and thereby learn. The computer went into mass production in 2007 and the ultimate pricing goal is $100.

One Laptop Per Child (OLPC). *Photo courtesy of Design Continuum*

Implications for future business

With 250 000 people – almost the size of General Motors' workforce – working for free on 275 000 open source projects and other new low-cost, instantaneous, collaborative possibilities that follow in the wake of digitalization, these hybrid examples of making money and creating change in new ways show us alternatives to classic capitalism and corporatism.[35]

Labour, for example, can be organized more efficiently in the context of community than in the context of a corporation, and the online technologies operate like immense talent-finding search engines that match talent and knowledge with those in need of it.[39] They are expressions of how old business logics of ownership, innovation and profit making are being challenged and are 'opening up the economy', as co-author of *Wikinomics*, Anthony D. Williams, puts it, by changing 'the way we invent, produce, design and distribute products on a global basis.'[28] It is a rising economic force with a fluid way of producing both social and economic value.

In fact, the transformation of the Internet through the emergence of social media networks, user-generated content and open source approaches is the same transformation that corporate social responsibility (CSR) is undergoing right now. Like Web 1.0 was dominated by standardized hardware and software, but in its new version now encourages co-creation and diversity, CSR in its 21st century version is similarly opening up new possibilities for social interaction, involvement and participation in finding innovative ways of tackling some of the world's global challenges.

Web 1.0 and 2.0 – CSR 1.0 and 2.0

Web 1.0	CSR 1.0
A flat world just beginning to connect itself and finding a new medium to push out information and plug advertising.	A vehicle for companies to establish relationships with communities, channel philanthropic contributions and manage their image.
Saw the rise to prominence of innovators like Netscape, but these were quickly out-muscled by giants like Microsoft with its Internet Explorer.	Included many start-up pioneers, but has ultimately turned into a product for large multinationals like Walmart.
Focused largely on the standardized hardware and software of the PC as its delivery platform, rather than multi-level applications.	Travelled down the road of 'one size fits all' standardization, through codes, standards and guidelines to shape its offering.

continued on next page...

Web 1.0 and 2.0 – CSR 1.0 and 2.0

Web 2.0	CSR 2.0
Being defined by watchwords like 'collective intelligence', 'collaborative networks' and 'user participation'.	Being defined by 'global commons', 'innovative partnerships' and 'stakeholder involvement'.
Tools include social media, knowledge syndication and beta testing.	Mechanisms include diverse stakeholder panels, real-time transparent reporting and new-wave social entrepreneurship.
Is as much a state of being as a technical advance – it is a new philosophy or way of seeing the world differently.	Is recognising a shift in power from centralized to decentralized; a change in scale from few and big to many and small; and a change in application from single and exclusive to multiple and shared.

Source: Visser, W. (2008), *The New Era of Corporate Sustainability and Responsibility*, CSR Inspiration Series, No. 1, CSR International.

Within the next decade customer-driven innovation will therefore become mainstream, online communities will play a much greater role than today in gathering innovative ideas for products and services from customers and others, social networks will be common in the workplace, vast new stores of information will be generated by employees' and customers' use of digital collaboration tools, wider access to information will lead to less hierarchical organizations and greater autonomy for employees, and technology-based innovations may even be the breeding ground for completely new business models.[40]

Innovation will, in other words, no longer be in the hands of an elite group of specialists working in companies. Instead, it will result from an interactive process with professionals and amateurs, designers and consumers and from exchanging ideas with each other.[41] The future of responsible capitalism and sustainable development lies in knowledge sharing rather than protectionism, access to resources rather than owning them, in networks rather than organizations and in cooperation rather than competition.

Collaborative problem solvers
– collective intelligence markets

> 'A new era is dawning, characterized by participation rather than the command-and-control model so intrinsic to the institutions that dominated the 20th century: the military, corporations, centralized states. "Participation" is now the magic word. It's not about more stuff or more choice, but more say, more opportunities to contribute.'[41]
>
> *Marco Visscher*

Innovation has always been at the heart of modern capitalism and a key driver of competitiveness and economic growth. Just like innovation is a crucial driver for society to find solutions to some of the current global challenges. But the innovation formula is changing.

Global companies, governments, NGOs and citizens are – in the words of *Crowdsourcing* author Jeff Howe – discovering that 'the sum of our differences constitutes an immensely powerful source that can be applied to solving problems or developing new products or simply make the world, online and off, a more interesting place to live.'[39]

According to Jeff Howe, collective intelligence is an essential ingredient in one of the primary categories of what he calls 'crowdsourcing': the attempt to harness many people's knowledge in order to solve problems or predict future outcomes or help direct corporate strategy. A point that has also been made by James Surowiecki, who, with numerous case studies and anecdotes in his book *The Wisdom of Crowds*, argues that the aggregation of information in groups often results in decisions that are better than decisions made by any single member of the group.

This is why companies like General Electric use prediction markets to generate new business ideas, Hewlett Packard uses them for sales forecasting and Starwood Hotels & Resorts Worldwide uses them for developing and selecting marketing campaigns.[42] The markets simply outperform the experts because collectively they have access to far more data.

And this is also why the renowned research university Massachusetts Institute of Technology (MIT) has founded a Center for Collective Intelligence, which is attempting to use prediction markets to ultimately help us 'understand new and better ways to organize businesses, to conduct science, to run governments, and – perhaps most importantly – to help solve the problems we face as society and as a planet'.[43]

Millions of people already spend their free time contributing knowledge, feedback, ideas and innovations to numerous causes – in many cases without getting paid. The GlobalIdeasBank.org, for example, annually receives more than 250 000 unique visitors, who submit or vote on over 5000 creative ideas on how to meet the needs of societies and individuals, covering topics ranging from child education, relationships, crime, health and art to taxes, unemployment, welfare services, community politics, the environment and business models. Several of these social innovations have been developed into concrete projects, e.g. musical therapy for victims of stress, cars designed exclusively for women and People's Pubs where all profits go to charitable organizations.

Just like the MeWe employees, these people are driven by their intrinsic satisfaction of the top tiers of Maslow's hierarchy of needs. They have a need for involvement and participation, and are motivated by acknowledgement from the community, the pleasure of cultivating their talents and by passing on what they have learned to others. The work itself is meaningful.[39] And so, the Global Brain is generating a powerful global network of co-creative micro-innovators and online communities of empowered citizens that are contributing to economic and social development in decentralized and collaborative ways. It is creating a collective intelligence market for exchange of knowledge and wisdom to solve problems and generate ideas and solutions.

Online innovators

In the old world order a national crisis would lead to an extraordinary session of parliament, and a global crisis to a G20 summit. In the new world order, citizens are also directly involved in developing new solutions.

Glimpses of the new world are already here: in January 2009 Irish businesswoman Aileen O'Toole attended a TV programme to discuss how the Irish economy could recover and be renewed after the negative effects of the credit crunch. Two months later O'Toole launched IdeasCampaign.ie to encourage people to submit their positive ideas on how to preserve and increase employment, enrich local communities and stimulate the economy across 19 key areas including manufacturing, technology, retail, education, volunteering and community activity. 26 days later, 47 884 people had visited the website, 5284 ideas had been submitted and the Irish Prime Minister, Brian Cowen, guaranteed a 'fast track' arrangement to ensure that ideas were processed quickly by a governmental committee formed to address the economic crisis.

During the US presidential election in 2008 the Obama campaign management similarly launched the transition website www.change.gov to give ordinary people a voice in politics by encouraging them to submit their ideas for tackling issues ranging from the economy, education, energy and the environment to foreign policy, healthcare, homeland security and technology. More than 125 000 people accepted the invitation by submitting over 44 000 ideas, and cast over 1.4 million votes on the most popular ideas.

The need to involve social innovators from all sectors of society – NGOs, businesses, academia, development agencies, municipal agencies, etc. – in the development and implementation of problem-solving initiatives is giving rise to collaborative initiatives like the public services portal Participle.net; the large online community for youths sharing an interest in global development issues TakingItGlobal.org; and Social Innovation Exchange (SIX), which provides a set-up that connects a global community of over 400 individuals and organizations who want to learn, collaborate, replicate and develop innovative projects across the world.

For the same reasons, The World Bank, also known as The International Bank for Reconstruction and Development (IBRD), initiated a competitive grant programme, The Development Marketplace, in 2000, which is dedicated to a specific theme once a year. Winners receive grants of up to $200 000 to implement their projects over two years, and IBRD has so far awarded more than $57 million to over 170 early stage development projects in around 60 countries.

In 2009 alone 1700 ideas on how to save the planet were submitted to The Development Marketplace, with proposals ranging from 'Amazonian

Communities Teach Youth Traditional Knowledge to Meet Carbon Goals' in Colombia to 'Mobilizing Community Journalists for Participatory Disaster Risk Management' in Mongolia and 'Clay-Pot Microirrigation System for Food Security in a Dry Highland Village' in Ethiopia.

And the UK-based centre for social innovation, The Young Foundation, hosts Social Innovation camps in Scotland, New Zealand, Central and Eastern Europe to experiment in creating social innovations for the digital age by bringing together talented software developers and designers with teachers, students, carers – basically anyone with an idea that meets a social problem or need – to develop effective web-based solutions.

In short, the combined on- and offline world is creating a great social space with citizens that act as collaborative problem solvers to find solutions to some of society's greatest challenges instead of leaving it up to politicians and governmental institutions – simply because an increasing number of citizens both can and want to.

As US President Barack Obama concluded after his election: 'I think our campaign was an expression of people wanting to be engaged and involved in different ways. They didn't want to just be passive consumers of politicial television ads. They wanted to have their voices heard. They wanted to interact with their membership – or with their neighbor and their friends. They wanted to be part of something larger than themselves. And I think we tapped into it in technological terms. But it wasn't really the technology that was the story.'[44]

The end of the corporate expert

So what does all this mean for business? Traditional corporate innovation is part of a closed system where employees within the organization in great secrecy develop ideas that result in patent applications or new products and services. But with the open innovation systems that have emerged in the wake of technologization, sharing problems and solutions openly and involving external partners is becoming the new business norm.

Websites like NineSigma.com, InnoCentive.com, YourEncore.com and Ideastorm.com, where online communities of experts from all industries, geographies and technical disciplines or just ordinary citizens with extraordinary ideas are matched with the problems and needs of large commercial companies, are all examples of a new generation of open innovation and expert sourcing that is profoundly changing innovation models of companies like Procter & Gamble (P&G), Eli Lilly, General Mills and many other Fortune 500 companies.

Companies are simply recognising that the global pool of collective intelligence can be used as a source for product improvements and business innovations in supplement to their traditional R&D (research and development) or internal problem solving.

When the world's eighth largest company, P&G, for example, launched its pgconnectdevelop.com programme in the mid-2000s, inviting the outside world to contribute with ideas to some of its product and service development needs from packaging to design and marketing models, it gained access to 200 scientists or engineers for every one of P&G's in-house 7500 researchers – a total of up to 1.5 million external talents. It also led to some of P&G's most innovative products like the Swiffer cleaning products. Before the launch, P&G's ability to innovate had stagnated, and only 15% of its innovations originated outside the company.[39] Today, more than 35% of P&G's products have elements that originate outside the company, and overall R&D productivity has increased by nearly 60%.[36]

For the same reasons as P&G, InnoCentive was initially started as an R&D outsourcing programme by pharmaceutical company Eli Lilly. But in time InnoCentive has developed into a complete business of its own, and is now used by companies, academic institutions, public sector and non-profit organizations, who pay a participation fee for posting their challenges, whilst solvers who deliver the most innovative ideas receive financial awards ranging from $10 000 to $1 000 000 per solution. More than 30% of the problems posted on the site have been solved, which is 30% more than would have been solved using a traditional, in-house approach.[39]

An electrical engineer from New Zealand, for example, has developed a dual-purpose solar light to serve as both a lamp and a flashlight to be used in African villages and other areas of the world without electricity, thereby enabling children to study and allowing family members to safely walk to outhouses at night.

The inclusion of both commercial solutions and solutions to some of the developing world's challenges is the reason why Innocentive is today regarded as a pioneer with focus on 'sustainable breakthrough innovation'.[45] Similarly, other offline pioneers are challenging and inspiring the development of a sustainable future. Like the world's largest biannual international design and innovation award, INDEX: which brings together creative designers and innovators from all over the world to discuss and demonstrate how socially innovative design can improve human life. Since 2005, the award has brought life to several hundred new ideas, products, strategies and processes that redesign how we work and learn, how we care for our personal health, how we live and play together and how we live at home and in our cities. The 2005 winner was Vestergaard Frandsen's Lifestraw (mentioned in Chapter 1), a commercial product in support of social needs.

Innovative business ideas are also being democratized with the help of Web 2.0. At Quirky, for example, anyone can submit their business idea for $99. Ideas of the week are selected by Quirky's 'influencers', who also vote and advise on their further development. The best ideas are put into production and sent to market, at which point the person with the initial idea gets 12% of the top-line revenue, 70% goes to Quirky, which also funds the production, and the remaining 18% goes to the influencers who helped make the product a success. PowerCurl, a clip-on cord wrap for the price of $9.99 is just one of the results of a 24-hour design process with the Quirky community.

These different expressions of collective intelligence markets are, in other words, catalysts for business as well as social innovation.

The prosumers

A second factor on the collective intelligence market that is putting business-as-usual under pressure is the so-called 'prosumer' – an expression coined by futurist Alvin Toffler in his book *The Third Wave* back in 1980 when he predicted a trend of involving consumers in both product design and production.

At websites like RedesignMe.com communities of consumers and professionals help companies innovate through online collaboration, and consumers frustrated by their mobile phones, domestic appliances or other products can send their complaints so other site users can suggest ways to redesign these products. It is a shift towards mass participation and democratization in commerce rather than mass consumption.

Online sharing of experiences and opinions about corporate values, practices, products and services is also a part of this trend. Gone are the times when one customer would tell ten friends about their bad experience with a company or product brand. Today, public scrutiny is at a level where no companies can hide. All it takes is one dissatisfied customer, a laptop and an Internet connection – and soon the whole world will know all about a company's unethical behaviour or bad services. With one click of the mouse, one individual can force powerful companies to reverse unpopular policies.

In 1999, for example, Coca-Cola in Norway decided to take its 1.5 litre bottles of the popular citrus soft drink *Urge* off the Norwegian market due to unsatisfactory sales. But after a massive Facebook campaign, conducted by the 17-year-old Magnus Nyborg, who managed to mobilize 33 000 people to sign up, the 1.5 litre bottle was relaunched in 2008.

Together with Nyborg and his like-minded fellows of 'crowd surfers', 'consumer activists', 'customer evangelists' and 'citizen marketers' – just to mention a few of the terms that are being used to describe this participative consumer movement – this influential consumer army is using its power to shape and influence corporate reputation and practices.

In fact, a Google search by Forester Research on the world's 20 largest brands revealed that brand information is no longer in the hands of the owners. Fewer than 20% of the search results were linked to the companies themselves. Instead, voices of experts, media and consumers from blogs, forums and other websites dominated the search list.[36]

Consumer revenge sites like paypalsucks.com, saynotoo870.com, grumbletext.co.uk, consumeractiongroup.co.uk and gethuman.com are adding to the pressure on businesses. But sites like these do more than activate dissatisfied customers. They also offer companies an opportunity to learn how their customers view them, so they can change their practices accordingly. In some cases, as with gethuman.com – which now works together with software companies Nuance and Microsoft – what starts as consumer criticism may even end up as a business partnership.

The commercial companies, on the other hand, are not only institution-alising consumer feedback by engaging them in research or asking for their opinions and ideas, which they can post, view and vote on. They are also starting to actively join the debate with consumers – a trend that has been coined *feedback 3.0* – by posting their apologies and solutions alongside reviews from unhappy customers on sites like Bazaarvoice.com.

Others are going even further than that by quantifying their company's reputation through scores of insights, comments and opinions on how it treats its customers, employees, communities, the environment and society in general.

The corporate reputation tracking service, Vanno.com, for example, offers companies a Company Reputation Index and Company Reputation Trends based on tracks of online news sites, blogs and forums for stories and commentary about companies. And the online marketplace, Ethicaleconomy.com, makes it possible for companies, organizations and individuals to invite friends, colleagues, suppliers or customers to give their endorsements or suggestions as to how they can improve their ethical performance.

'CSR 2.0 – i.e. CSR in a Web 2.0 reality – means that corporations need to constantly be in many simultaneous stakeholder dialogues. In turn, Web 2.0 makes it possible for companies to communicate their specific ethical stances – and to ongoing develop the company and its products based on the stakeholder feedback they have access to online. Progressive companies no longer want to be measured by generic CSR codes and standards,' explains Nicolai Peitersen, the Danish founder of the UK-based company and site Ethicaleconomy.

So to sum up, the needs for involvement and participation which are fulfilled in the marketplace for collective intelligence are not only blurring the once clear borders between business and society. They have also led to a new culture of self-organization and involvement, which has formed a new breed of consumers who are involved in creating content and products. And dialogue, which used to be a controlled process, is now constant and out of corporate hands. All this is catalytic for new business innovation opportunities, problem-solving capacities which can make the world a better place and disruptive changes in the way that companies act and interact socially and ethically. It calls for socially innovative as well as responsible business conduct.

Civil power brokers
– *activism markets*

'If you want to make peace with your enemy, you have to work with your enemy. Then he becomes your partner.'

Nelson Mandela

It may be that business is one of the most dominant institutions of this century. But another powerful force has entered the globalization scene, putting pressure on governments as well as the corporate world: the activists.

Who doesn't remember when energy and petrochemical company Shell was struck by boycotts and activist campaigns conducted by hardcore NGOs like Greenpeace to prevent the company from sinking the oil platform Brent Spar? The actions of Greenpeace got worldwide media attention and damaged Shell's turnover by 30% in Germany alone.[46] In the end, Shell admitted defeat and sailed Brent Spar ashore in accordance with Greenpeace's demands instead of sinking the platform.

And who can forget *The Battle in Seattle* – the largest protest in America since 1968 – where more than 50 000 trade unionists, environmentalists and other activists from all over the world stood together in protest against the World Trade Organization's annual summit in 1999? The summit culminated in violent confrontations between protesters and police, negotiations broke down and the world leaders had no choice but to return home empty-handed.

Worldwide, the number of NGOs is growing year by year. In 2005 the number of NGOs was estimated at 50 000 compared to less than 20 000 only a decade earlier.[47] But with the development of online technologies the figures today are significantly higher. The WiserEarth Directory, for example, the world's largest free, open-source online index of NGOs and environmentally and socially responsible organizations, reveals a number of over 110 000 in 243 countries, territories and sovereign islands.

The civil numbers of this rising citizen force are staggering. For example, during the three so-called *White Band Days* in 2005, eight million people in the UK alone wore a white band, a common symbol of the global fight to end poverty that was agreed on by the Global Call to Action Against Poverty, historically the world's largest anti-poverty movement. Three years later, 116 million people in 131 countries – almost 2% of the world's population – came together at events across the world from Africa, Asia and the Arab states to Europe and North America as part of a *Stand Up and Take Action* campaign to remind world leaders that the first priority for them is to act decisively to end poverty and inequality.[48]

And when the world's leaders meet at the annual World Economic Forum meetings in Davos, Switzerland, its social counterpart, the World Social Forum, is around the same time able to gather up to 155 000 people from all over the world to meet, discuss and engage in concrete actions towards 'a more solidary, democratic and fair world'.[49]

The opportunity for global communication and coordination which the Internet has opened up has only strengthened NGO activities all over the world, making it almost impossible for governments, multinationals and other large organizations to operate under the public radar. In many cases NGOs have even replaced nation states as observers and upholders of international social and environmental standards, because national legislation falls short in regulating the actions of multinational corporations.

NGOs like Greenpeace, Friends of the Earth (FOE) and Via Campesina, for instance, have joined forces around a campaign website against agrichemical company Monsanto – www.combat-monsanto.co.uk – which includes sections with protests, whistleblower testimonials and articles about the negative effects of the company's products like GMO (genetically modified organisms) and herbicide Roundup as well as its usage of chemicals like P.C.B. and dioxin. The website also includes a world protest map with a country-by-country location guide to the GMO invasion and the resistance to Monsanto. So far, the victories of the anti-Monsanto activist community include Germany's and France's ban on the cultivation and sale of maize with GMOs. But the battle continues until their mission of 'building a world free of Monsanto' has been completed.

In short, 21st century companies have become more exposed than ever, making corporate responsibility a key issue that is keeping change-makers of all breeds active in the name of transparency and fairness.

The 'activism markets'

The word 'activism' often triggers associations with anarchism, demonstrations, campaigning, strikes, boycotts and protest marches along with grassroots groups, human rights and environmental organizations and movements. And although the classic manifestations of collective action still have the power to bring about change, new expressions of activism both inside and outside organizations are strengthening the power of society's civil watchdogs even further.

Today, the Internet as well as social networking forums like MySpace, Facebook and blogs are facilitating campaigns for both NGOs and individuals, 'providing campaigns with access to mounds of fresh ammunition, untapped legions of donors and armies of previously unmobilized activists', as *Times Online* put it in an article some years ago.[50]

The largest global online citizens' movement in history, Avaaz.org, for example, is taking the new model of Internet-driven, people-powered politics to international decision making by connecting people from all nations, backgrounds and ages to ensure that the views and values of the world's people shape global decisions. The core of Avaaz's model is a small team of global campaigners working in many countries plus their email list which is operated in 13 languages. By signing up, members are regularly alerted to urgent global issues and given opportunities to generate change by giving just a click vote or a donation via the web bank.

Since its launch in January 2007, Avaaz – which means 'voice' in many Asian, Middle Eastern and Eastern European languages – has grown to over 3.5 million members from every corner of the world, who are sending hundreds of thousands of messages to political leaders or donating hundreds of thousands of dollars to over 200 campaigns in support of democracy movements, humanitarian relief and non-violent protests. And for those who want to get further involved, volunteers can sign up for research, proof-reading and other tasks that match their talents and skills.

Avaaz's online approach to activism has also succeeded in attracting a new category of activists – those who may previously have been appalled or horrified by world events as they watched them on the evening news, but never found the time or the desire to participate in street demonstrations or other classic activist activities: the so-called *slacktivists.* These are slackers who care about causes just enough to sign online petitions, wear awareness bracelets or join Facebook protest pages but lack the time, money or drive to do much else. At other websites like Change.org they are provided with information about social and environmental problems ranging from healthcare and educa-tion to global warming and economic inequality, so they can translate their interest into effective action by signing or starting their own petition, which is then sent to more than 400 000 Change.org members.

The Point.com has made this kind of collective action even more sophis-ticated by putting the notion of the tipping point into practice and giving planners a way to organize fundraisers, rallies, boycotts and other events, by ensuring that no one acts until enough people have promised to join in.

Armed with powerful mobile devices, digital cameras, tiny recording devices, online connections and web publishing tools, ordinary citizens are now also becoming *citizen journalists* and active participants in the creation and dissemination of information for both activist movements and news media.

When citizen groups in Xiamen, China, for example, forced local govern-ment and business to suspend the development of a petrochemical plant, the demonstration looked spontaneous. But behind the scenes, activists were using mobile phones and text messages to coordinate it.[51]

Voices not usually heard in the international mainstream media have now also been leveraged by citizen-powered media like open source crisis and conflict reporting website Ushahhidi and participatory news networks like NowPublic.com and GlobalVoicesOnline.org.

Indeed, the only reason why it was possible for the whole world to follow the confrontations between demonstrators and Basiji militiamen in connec-tion with Iran's presidential election in 2009 was because of amateur videos, photo shots from cell phones and interaction with Iranian Internet users, who managed to post the latest news from Iran on Facebook, YouTube and Twitter, despite the website blocking filters that were set up by Iranian government officials to keep the civil protests against alleged electoral fraud away from public attention.

In fact, users of Twitter – the second most popular social network in the USA after Facebook – shamed the international news broadcaster CNN for not covering the Iran events that the 'twitterers' were following, which led to front page CNN presentations of videos and developing stories on the civil unrest in Tehran. The voices of people on Twitter had been heard.[52]

Media-related activism was also what hit McDonald's when the global fast food chain involuntarily became the main character in American journalist and film instructor Morgan Spurlock's documentary *Supersize Me* in 2004. The film documented the director's physical and mental reaction to just one month of exclusively eating food from McDonald's. Only half-way through the experiment, Spurlock's own doctor could no longer vouch for his safety and warned that he was in serious danger of physical collapse.

After Morgan Spurlock's film McDonald's changed the size of its menus and introduced healthier alternatives to the classic burgers and fries, such as salads and carrots, along with more readily available information about nutritional value and tools for health professionals on the fast food chain's corporate website. Under media fire for contributing heavily to the issue of widespread American obesity, McDonald's even launched a new *Go Active! Happy Meal* for adults in 2006, including a series of 15-minute *YourSelf!* Fitness DVDs as well as a *Get Up and Go with Ronald* exercise DVD for children.

The activism market has, however, expanded to include new actors – the pressure on corporations is also coming from the inside.

Activists in suits

In 2002 three American whistleblowers, Cynthia Cooper from telecommunications company Worldcom, Sherron Watkins from energy corporation Enron and Coleen Rowley from the FBI, were nominated *Persons of the Year* in *TIME* magazine. Cooper and Watkins publicized misconduct and giant financial scandals about their respective places of employment, and Rowley publicly criticized the FBI's slow reaction to the attacks on the World Trade Center in New York in 2001.

In the wake of these scandals the US Sarbanes–Oxley Act, also known as the 'Corporate and Auditing Accountability and Responsibility Act', was enacted in 2002. It requires publicly held US-based companies and their EU-based affiliates as well as non-US companies listed on US stock markets to

establish procedures that, among other things, ensure 'confidential, anonymous submission by employees of the issue of concerns regarding question-
able accounting or auditing matters'.

In the UK The Public Interest Disclosure Act (PIDA) already came into
force in July 1999 with the specific aim of protecting whistleblowers. In
France, the Commission nationale de l'informatique et des libertés (CNIL)
regulates the approval of whistleblowing schemes for organizations and companies either based or operating in France. And many other countries have
followed suit.[53]

As a result, systems of self-regulation have emerged inside companies
that have their own internal whistleblower schemes. More than 2200
organizations around the world are already using EthicsPoint's telephone
hotline and web-based reporting services to allow employees to report
incidents that are against company policy like theft, corruption, bribery,
discrimination, financial fraud and insider dealing. At the Danfoss Group,
for example, a global leader in development and production of mechanical
and electronic products that employs 22 000 people worldwide, its internal
tell-tale hotline has already led to the dismissal of 60 employees due to
'unethical conduct'.[54]

Even so, there are still autonomous insiders like Procter & Gamble's razor
brand Gillette's anonymous tell-tale who revealed to the media that its Fusion
Power razor heads were sold with a mark-up of more than 4750%.[55] And Peter
Rost, the former vice president at the pharmaceutical company Pfizer, became
famous all over the USA for his media crusade to legalize the re-importation
of drugs and for his disclosure of illegal practices in the company through
interviews, blogs and books.

Geraint Anderson, a financial analyst from the City of London, broke the
City's strict code of silence by writing columns in *thelondonpaper* under the
cover name *City Boy*, revealing the City's greedy bonus culture and short-term
gambling which he believed were the direct cause of the recent financial crisis.

Meanwhile, other activists are invoking the power of shareholder resolutions. Socially responsible investing (SRI) is – as we explored in the business
world of disorder section in Chapter 1 – already increasing the attention on
corporate social and environmental practices through either *positive screens*,
i.e. identifying companies that in some way benefit society, or through

negative screens which weed out poor SRI performers, including those who pollute or maintain poor working conditions.

But rather than passively following their investments in corporate activities, activist shareholders also exercise their right as part-owners of the company to influence corporate behaviour by using their proxy vote, attending annual meetings, corresponding with management or submitting resolutions and campaigns to promote their financial or non-financial priorities, ranging from increases in shareholder value and cost cutting to disinvestment from particular countries or adoption of environmentally friendly policies.

According to the Social Investment Forum the average level of shareholder support for resolutions on social and environmental issues rose by 57% from 2005 to 2007, from 9.8% to a record high of 15.4%. All it takes to file a shareholder resolution is to own at least $2000 worth of the company's stock and to have held it for more than a year. In 2007 institutional investors that filed or co-filed resolutions on social or environmental issues controlled $739 billion in assets. But resolutions are not the first step in shareholder activism. A dialogue or negotiation between management and shareholders can often produce the changes desired by investors.[56]

During the 1990s, for example, investors in athletic shoe and apparel company Nike became aware of the poor conditions that the workers in Third World supply companies were labouring under. So they began pressuring Nike to make changes. Some investors sold their stock, the share price dipped and the company was dropped from the stock index, the Domini 400 Social Index. Others maintained discussions with management. The company responded and instituted new policies to benefit its supply chain workers, and has improved its transparency so investors can find the names of countries in which it operates and even the names of contract factories with which it does business on the corporate website. Today Nike is back in the Domini 400 and viewed more favourably by socially conscious investors.[57]

Likewise, the US network of investors, environmental groups and other stakeholders, CERES, was involved in the decision by Dell Computer in 2008 to support national legislation for electronic product recycling, and in Bank of America's $20 billion initiative in 2007 to support the growth of environmentally sustainable business activity.[58]

Even socially conscious businesses like Whole Foods Market, the world's largest organic supermarket chain, regarded as exemplary by many, are not let off the hook. In 2005 the independent investment firm Trillium Asset Management introduced a resolution calling on the retail company to disclose any genetically engineered ingredients in its private label brands. After the vote, Whole Foods Market agreed voluntarily to comply with the measure.[14]

So the exchange of information and actions on the activism market may not necessarily lead to unresolvable conflicts. As in the cases of Nike and Whole Foods Market, it has rather led to a leap into setting new standards for their respective industries. And so, traditional archenemies are starting to partner around issues of mutual interest and benefit – the civil power brokers are becoming business allies involved in some of the social and environmental challenges that companies are facing.

As early as the 1990s, McDonald's and the Environmental Defense Fund (EDF) joined forces to target waste reduction opportunities in the fast food business. The most notable result of this alliance was McDonald's shift from polystyrene clamshell containers to paper wraps.[59] Even Greenpeace and Coca-Cola have acknowledged a mutual interest in combating climate change and have recently developed climate-friendly refrigeration equipment, on the one hand to reduce carbon footprints and on the other to increase business sustainability.

So what may start as a way for companies to manage their reputations can, in fact, give them access to the specialized knowledge and networks required to avoid pitfalls and to pursue new business opportunities. For NGOs, partnering with business gives them a means of persuading companies to change their ways, and – as we will explore later – is now also becoming a means for them to develop the competences and confidence to go into business themselves.[60]

In summary, the pressure on companies to act transparently and responsibly not only comes from watchdog organizations and on-the-street demonstrations. It also comes from global online NGOs, social networking forums, media-powered citizens, activist shareholders and insider whistleblowers who do not want to compromise their personal values in the name of profit maximization. But confrontations between civil power brokers and corporations may not necessarily always evolve around conflict – they may also lay the foundations for new business practices, indeed even new business models which meet social, environmental and economic needs in new ways. So, instead of fighting them or shutting them out, companies should invite the civil power brokers inside and use them as consultants and 'brand editors'. If not, they may threaten one of the most valuable assets a company in the new economy has: reputation.

Conscious buycotters
– ethical consumption markets

> 'Every time you spend money, you're casting a vote for the kind of world you want.'[61]
>
> *Anna Lappe*

In March 1989 three recent graduates and experienced campaigners launched the *Ethical Consumer* magazine from a council flat in Manchester. At that time no one had yet coined the expression 'ethical consumer', but even so it was clear to the trio that campaigns around ethical product issues were growing fast.

Soon the magazine grew into the Ethical Consumer Research Association (ECRA), a not-for-profit co-operative with more than 5000 dedicated subscribers who invested capital in the business when they were asked for it, and a dedicated team of more than 50 researchers and 70 volunteers, who were willing to work sometimes for free and almost always at below market rates for their skills, because it was a project they believed in.

Today, ECRA has become the UK's leading alternative consumer organization to 'provide information on the companies behind the brand names and to promote the ethical use of consumer power'. ECRA also hosts a Corporate Critic Research Database with corporate social responsibility records of over 50 000 companies as well as an online A–Z ethical score, Ethiscore, to help consumers identify the best products to support and the worst companies to avoid.

What we value rather than what we consume is a key issue today. And with around 60% on average of the world's GDP being accounted for by consumer spending on goods and services,[62] the shopping basket has indeed become an effective action platform for consumers in the 21st century. Or, as Vice Chairman of the Swiss National Bank Philipp Hildebrand puts it: 'Even with all the legal organizations in the world we would never be able to create a better means of control and punishment than the market itself provides.'[63]

But for companies this trend not only implies avoidance, boycotts and punishment. In the wake of the global consciousness movement, a whole new market for conscious consumption and *buy*cotting of values-based products and services has emerged.

While ethical boycotters in the 'hothouse of ethical consumption' – the UK – alone cost companies 2.6 billion British pounds a year according to the Ethical Purchasing Index (EPI) in 2004,[64] consumer boycotts in the UK declined by 21% in 2006 to £817 million.[65]

One feasible explanation could be the online activities that social media open up to enable consumers to make positive choices rather than to deselect. Another could be that other positive and innovative ways of motivating companies to change their unpractical and/or unethical practices are seeing the light of day.

'Boycotting, protesting, lawsuits – it's about going into attack mode,' explains Brent Schulkin, the 28-year-old San Francisco-based activist, now turned social innovator, with his new concept based on positive cooperation as the rewarding carrot for businesses to be socially responsible in a profitable way. Enter the *Carrotmobs* – a concept which is particularly appealing during tough economic times: participants do not have to donate anything. All they have to do is simply shop for products they are planning to buy anyway, adjusting the time and place of purchase.

So, in the spring of 2008, hundreds of carrotmobsters spent more than $9200 on energy-efficient lighting in the local San Francisco K&D Market, thereby helping the store fulfil its pledge to convert part of the revenues into greener lighting. The concept of rewarding businesses with mass purchases if they promise to use some of the money to become greener has since then branched out to ten other US cities with offshoots in Finland and France.[66]

The buycotting trend appears to be growing stronger. The fact is that an increasing number of consumers all over the world are turning to ethical consumerism to make companies more accountable. This was at least the conclusion of a global Synovate survey conducted in 2007 and again in 2008. Although the USA had the largest rise of all, from 57% in 2007 to 80% in 2008, Chinese consumers also showed an increased willingness to act on their concerns about climate change.[62]

This same tendency was also reflected in the 2008 National Geographic Society and Globescan survey, which reported that consumers from 14 countries including Canada, China, France, Germany, India, Mexico, Russia, the UK and the USA were taking action in their daily lives to reduce consumption and waste.[62] And one year later, 73% of 9000 consumers worldwide agreed that companies must have good environmental records, they should be clear about product risks and safety, provide information on environmental impact, have high ethical standards and treat their employees fairly. In fact, many of them were even willing to pay a higher price – despite the economic downturn – for green products if they were considered to be of higher quality.[67]

Similarly, the emergence of indexes on ethical and sustainable consumption like Co-operative Bank's Ethical Purchasing Index, Good Businesses' Concerned Consumer Index and Globescan and National Geographic's Greendex indicate that the ethical consumer trend is indeed here to stay.

Instead of demographic factors like age, income and profession, the common denominator for these conscious consumers is their values. Issues like environmentalism, feminism, globalization challenges and spiritual searching are reflected in their lifestyle interests and product choices, ranging from green building supplies, socially responsible investing, alternative healthcare, organic foods and clothing to eco-tourism, personal development media, yoga and other body-mind-spirit products.[68]

And so, with the mere use of supply and demand of sustainable products, conscious consumers are not only changing the rules of business, they are also opening up new, lucrative business opportunities.

Just a luxury market?

When the upmarket New York-based shop ABC Home Furnishings allowed two Harvard University researchers to conduct an experiment on two sets of towels – one set with a label with the logo 'Fair and Square' and a message that the towels had been made under fair labour conditions, the other set without any label, the results were striking. Not only did the sales of towels increase when they carried the Fair and Square label but they carried on increasing each time the price was raised.[69]

Luxury consumption is already being redefined as responsible and sustainable. *Green Living* or *Style & Design* magazine supplements include features about everything from ecotourism and green restaurants to furniture and beauty products, hybrid taxi companies and advice on eco-parties and recipes. Jewellery brands like Tiffany and Cartier are championing ethics alongside aesthetics by supporting their responsible use of non-renewable resources like gold. And one-off products like British bag guru Anya Hindmarch's anti-plastic effort, the $15 'I'm not a plastic bag' limited-edition canvas bag, has made fashion addicts camp outside supermarkets and even caused a stampede in Taipei.

This could lead sceptics to think that ethical consumerism is just a luxury that only the rich can afford. And in many cases this is true. But the figures also tell a story about how awareness of the purchasing power of conscious consumers is entering the mainstream and gaining commercial significance.

In the UK, for example, which has some of the world's most aware and critical consumers,[70] the market for ethical consumption has grown almost 40% in just five years (1999–2004). In 2004 it reached a turnover of £25 billion.[64] All in all, there has been an increased predisposition to ethical behaviour, which has led to an increase of household expenditure on ethical goods and services ranging from ethical banking and investments to organic foods and Fairtrade products, ethical clothing and energy-efficient light bulbs.[65]

And in the USA, one in four adult Americans – nearly 41 million people – are so-called LOHAS (Lifestyles of Health and Sustainability) consumers,[71] a segment which is formed by the so-called Cultural Creatives described in the Introduction.

The purchase decisions of these values-driven consumers have contributed to the commercial successes of, for example, the Toyota Prius, the world's first mass-produced hybrid car, and Whole Foods Market, today the world's largest organic supermarket chain. In the USA alone their values and lifestyle choices have developed a market of $209 billion.[71] And the market for sustainable products and services appears to be growing stronger year by year.

In 2002, for example, natural products, from food to personal care items, were a $36 billion market – up from $15 billion five years earlier.[14] Likewise, the American market for organic foods has grown 20% since 1990, and it is now growing five times faster than the market for conventional foods.[46]

A closer look at the many surveys on ethical consumerism, however, reveals consumer sub-segments of hardcore advocates that back up their statements with conscious buying behaviour, aspirational followers that are regular consumers of ethical products and services, although they don't always practice what they preach, and non-believers who at best are passive ethical consumers.[14,65,72,73] Three segments which *TIME* magazine dubbed 'the Responsibles', 'the Toe Dippers' and 'the Skeptics' in connection with a US poll in 2009.[74] So there is still a gap to fill in terms of addressing the needs of the last two categories.

Interestingly, the rise of ethically conscious consumers is creating a 'rub-off' effect on other consumer segments and non-ethically based companies. 'Conventional' consumer segments have come to appreciate the value and attributes of green, Fairtrade, eco-friendly or organic products – but instead of converting to the existing ethical companies and brands, these consumers are looking to their favourite brands to incorporate sustainable, green practices.[75] And so, mainstream brands are now jumping on the ethical bandwagon.

Big business

Although consumers from all parts of the world are willing to act on their concerns about, for example, climate change, it is not always easy to convert the good intentions into action. The barriers: lack of knowledge about the environmental effect of products, the bad image of the quality of green products, distrust of the credibility of product information, lack of clarity about financial benefits from buying green, accessibility to green products and a lack of useful guidance on which products and services are more sustainable.[76]

These barriers constitute new business opportunities that can be grouped into three broad business approaches:[62]

1. Sustainable innovation – the development of sustainable products, services, processes and business models by integrating eco-efficiency and sustainability into life cycle processes and product designs in ways that do not compromise on quality, price or performance.
2. Choice influencing – the use of marketing communications, awareness-raising campaigns and other means to enable and encourage consumers to choose and use products more efficiently by working in partnership with consumers, NGOs, governments, media, opinion-makers and other key stakeholders around sustainable production and design of products through to their selection, use and disposal.
3. Choice editing – the removal of unsustainable products, product components and services from the marketplace in joint initiatives with other actors in society like retailers, suppliers, authorities and policy-makers by eliminating hazardous products from the shelves, demanding certain standards of supply chains or educating consumers on how to lead sustainable lifestyles.

There is, in other words, a huge market potential for companies if they attach values and sustainability principles to their products and services.

The Danish food supplier Aarstiderne, which delivers ecological food and food recipes in wooden boxes directly to the customer's front door, is one example of the socially innovative business concepts that are evolving around these needs. By combining existing social and technological innovations, it has created an ethical and sustainable business that generates both social and economic value: the traditional grocery-shopping concept (the supermarket) in combination with a new technology (the Internet) together with delivery of exclusive ecological groceries that are delivered in wooden boxes. These are later recycled and used to heat and power Aarstiderne's organic farm, which not only supplies 60% of Aarstiderne's power needs, it has also changed the shopping patterns and improved the eating habits of more than 40 000 Danes and thousands of Swedes and Germans. The co-founder of Aarstiderne,

Thomas Harttung, was named one of *TIME* magazine's Heroes of the Environment in 2009.

The development in a market otherwise dominated by special offers and discounts is so noticeable that traditional brands like the world's largest supermarket chain Walmart and British supermarkets Tesco and M&S are also addressing sustainability and climate change as part of their business strategies. Just like strong sportswear brands like Puma, Adidas and Nike have begun to produce eco-friendly lines that appeal to conscious consumers and *Greenagers*.

This is also the reason why one of Britain's largest coffee producers – and most boycotted company – Nestlé, launched its own ethical brand *Partners Blend* in 2005 in the hope of riding the Fairtrade wave. The move attracted criticism, since Partners Blend is the only Fairtrade offering that Nestlé has in a portfolio of 8500 products which include the baby foods and powdered baby milk that campaigners have accused the company of marketing aggressively and unethically in the developing world by undermining the benefits of breast-feeding.[77]

Nevertheless, Nestlé was ranked no. 1 in Spain on the 2007 list of the most ethically perceived brands in five of the world's leading economies. And along with ethically born brands like Body Shop, Green and Black's, innocent, Bio Produkte, Ben and Jerry's, Lush and Alter Eco, classic brands like Coca-Cola, Danone, Adidas, Nike, Procter & Gamble, Philips, L'Oreal and Kellogg's were also represented.[70]

This is no coincidence. Mainstream commercial companies are realising that practices built on ethics, responsibility and sustainability are simply business opportunities that cannot be missed, and hope to get a piece of the growing, lucrative market for conscious consumerism. Some – like Nestlé – by developing their own ethical brands or by branding some of their socially responsible practices; others by adopting green or socially responsible brands that give them both respectability and profitability.

British confectionery and beverage company Cadbury Schweppes is just one of the increasing number of companies that have been quick to respond to this aspirational and lucrative market by buying one of its competitors, the largest organic chocolate company, Green and Black's, but the company has continued to operate it as a separate brand.

The same goes for multinational beverage giant Coca-Cola, which, in 2009, bought a minority stake for £30 million in innocent, the UK-based fruit smoothies company, which, in 2007, already had a 69% share of the £169m UK smoothie market.[78] innocent has pioneered the use of better socially and environmentally aware ingredients, packaging and production techniques, while donating 10% of its profits to charity as well as retaining its sense of fun.

Add to them companies like the international consumer product giant Unilever, French food products company Danone and the world's largest cosmetics and beauty company L'Oreal, who respectively have bought shares in or acquired ethically based brands like ice cream producer Ben & Jerry's, organic yoghurt maker Stonyfield Farm and the legendary cosmetics company The Body Shop.

It is, in other words, largely due to the paths that have been paved by idealists and visionaries with entrepreneurial genes that commercial companies are adapting new responsible approaches to their existing businesses.

As was concluded at the annual LOHAS Forum in 2008, '... it takes a core group of pioneers and truly organically grown green businesses to set the standard for all to learn from, take ideas from and hopefully follow'.[75]

The founders of retail companies like The Body Shop, Ben & Jerry's, Stonyfield Farm, Whole Foods Market and Patagonia have not only shown that building a company around their personal values and ideals of ethics, responsibility and sustainability is an effective way of changing the rules of business – they have also been rewarded financially for their ethical stance by conscious consumers.

In the case of Whole Foods Market, the story started in 1980 when John Mackey opened a small natural foods store in Texas. Twenty years later the business with the holistic slogan *Whole Foods, Whole People, Whole Planet* had turned into the world's largest organic retailer with more than 50 000 employees and more than 270 large, luxurious stores in the UK and the USA.[79] Its sales have tripled again and again since 1994, and today even the world's largest mainstream supermarket chain, Walmart, is falling behind Whole Foods Market's annual sales increase of more than 20% in a business otherwise close to stagnation.[80]

The recipe for their commercial success: '... we're not retailers who have a mission – we're missionaries who retail ... we put our customers and team members before our shareholders. We deliver results by being a mission-driven business,' as their US CEO, Walter Robb, puts it.[81]

Yvon Chouinard, passionate environmentalist and founder of the Patagonia sportswear business, which was the first major retail company to switch all of its cotton clothing to organic and the first to make fleece from recycled soft drink bottles, is of the same species: 'I'm not in the business to make clothes. I'm not in the business to make more money for myself.' Instead, Chouinard has created the business to promote ethical product sourcing and environmental campaigning. 'That's the reason why I'm in business – to try to clean up our own act, and try to influence other companies to do the right thing.'[36]

All of these companies belong to the category of business that is driven by the founders' personal passion and values-based convictions – pragmatic idealists who, over the past two to three decades, have built their companies on eco-friendly and/or socially conscious missions, while at the same time building economically sustainable businesses.

They operate like 'corporate Trojan horses' where idealists and activists smuggle in humanistic values disguised as capitalist business, and are part of the visible top tier of socially rooted companies of all sizes that are successfully bridging the gap between economics and humanism – not only in the USA and the UK but all over the world. They are a part of the force for good that is creating a new face of capitalism.

Part II

New Needs – New Solutions

Chapter 3

The new social contract between business, government and civil society is blurring lines between sectors. It is giving rise to dynamic alliances and new business logics cultivated by social entrepreneurs who are creating growth and value in innovative ways – and by strategic businesspeople who are tapping into the unique business opportunities emerging in the seemingly paradoxical field between economics and humanism. Together they are reshaping the face of capitalism with blended value creation as the foundation for sustainable development.

The new faces of capitalism
– blurring sector borders and the fourth sector

> 'What's needed is the next iteration of capitalism – a new model that stems from an understanding that our common goal should be to maximize our value potential ... it should be a blend of economic, environmental and social factors.'[1]
>
> *Jed Emerson and Sheila Bonini*

Sustainable development as the future foundation for growth, innovation and value creation has already become an overall vision for many institutions, companies, organizations and citizens that, in each their own ways, are committing themselves to contribute to a better world. They start from different places but are heading toward the same destination. The travellers on the sustainability journey are, in other words, diverse and their routes to long-term social and economic value creation manifold. But together their journeys represent the new global mindset that is transforming business and society at large, and with their respective pioneering efforts they are laying the initial trails for a new roadmap to a sustainable market economy.

Whereas the purpose of Part I of this book was to take a closer look at *what* the new business paradigm looks like and *why* it has emerged, the purpose of this second part of the book is to look at *who* the different travellers are, and at *how* they are paving the way for responsible and sustainable business by:

1. Coupling capitalism with social purpose – and vice versa.
2. Incorporating externalities into their business models through solutions to environmental or social problems or needs.
3. Applying principles of industrial ecology, inclusive growth and/or immaterial growth.
4. Integrating environmental, social and economic value creation as a part of their bottom line thinking.

We will explore how they, in their efforts to bridge economics and humanism, have discovered new partnerships, new resources, new organizational forms, new systems, processes and work methods, new products and services and indeed new business models that address some of the world's most pressing social and environmental challenges. They have developed new expressions of capitalism that create value for individuals and for society as a whole.

But let us start by looking at who some of these travellers are.

Wealth and welfare in new ways

In the 20th century the 'tri-sector model' of the classic welfare state roles and tasks was crystal clear: the private sector made money, the civil sector ensured social cohesion and solidarity and the public sector provided order, legal rights and welfare. But this is all changing.

In the civil sector (also referred to as the third or social sector), NGOs and social organizations are being put under pressure to change their ways because of cutbacks in public funding and corporate philanthropy, increasing competition from private (online) fundraising initiatives and demands for transparency, efficiency and measurable results from private donors and sponsors.

More than ever, social organizations must look for alternative sources of revenue as well as original branding strategies to make them visible, attract volunteers and to ensure funding. Oxfam's hugely successful Christmas gift catalogue, which offers gifts like sponsoring a goat in an African village for £25 or five bags of seed for a local farmer for £10, is just one example of how charitable organizations develop market-based fundraising alternatives that, at the same time, meet the popular demand for transparency and direct involvement in the distribution of donated money.

Reducing dependence on grants and donations by setting up a social enterprise is another strategy that social organizations are applying. Some of their routes to financial independence are, for example, through fee-generating services, working for the government as professional welfare providers or engaging in commercial activities to finance the social mission. Some organizations in fact believe that applying business methods helps them achieve their social goals more effectively, and some engage the corporate sector through formalized social partnerships.

Meanwhile governments, mainly in the OECD countries but also in some developed and transitional economies,[2] aim at improving procurement. They commission services and find innovative approaches to effective and efficient welfare solutions through privatization, deregulation and liberalization by, among other things, collaborating with or outsourcing to actors from the civil sector.

In the UK, for example, the government has launched a Partnership for Public Services (PPS) programme that aims to involve charities, social enterprises and voluntary groups in delivering innovative and improved services. And its Right to Request programme helps National Health Service staff start their own social enterprises to give them freedom to use their talents in finding innovative ways to improve quality of care for patients.

Governments are also starting to advocate CSR through promotional initiatives to address fundamental welfare state dilemmas such as (un)employment but also global challenges like poverty, human rights and climate change. In Denmark, for example, the government has, since the early 1990s, been a key driver of formalized approaches to CSR. The most extensive government-driven CSR effort of its kind both in Denmark and internationally has, so far, been the People & Profit 2005–2007 campaign which offered free CSR conferences, training programmes and materials to more than 12 000 managers and employees in small- to medium-sized companies.[3]

The 'philanthrocapitalists' – also known as *venture philanthropists, new donors, high-engagement philanthropists* or *social venture capitalists* – are also proponents of the business-oriented view to addressing social objectives. In their search for efficiency and visible concrete social returns, this new breed of philanthropists are adopting a high-impact, entrepreneurial approach to their giving.

They do not talk about 'funding applications' or about 'giving back to society' but about 'business plans' and 'social investments' because that is how they view their contribution. Sometimes they even start their own foundation or an organization to make sure that social issues and development challenges are resolved in what they believe is the best possible way. Like eBay founder Pierre Omidyar, who shook the traditional philanthropic world by converting a foundation established by his wife and himself in 1998 into The Omidyar Network – a hybrid of philanthropy and venture capitalism, where the money is not merely invested in traditional, non-commercial organizations but also in commercial businesses. Or former eBay director, Jeff Skoll, who established the Skoll Foundation in 1999 with the mission to 'drive large-scale change by investing in, connecting and celebrating social entrepreneurs and other innovators dedicated to solving the world's most pressing problems'.[4]

Microsoft billionaire Bill Gates – who has called for 'creative capitalism' by using the power of the marketplace to help the poor – is another example. Together with his wife he co-chairs the Bill & Melinda Gates Foundation, which manages the world's largest fortune earmarked for charity, around $34 billion, an amount that was practically doubled in 2006, when American billionaire Warren Buffett donated approximately $30 billion. The foundation has ruffled many NGO feathers by imposing the same standards of accountability and transparency used by business on the projects it funds – and cutting off those who don't comply.[5]

Companies, on the other hand, are entering formalized partnerships with social actors like NGOs, UN agencies and bilateral agencies. For instance, over half of the Global Compact's corporate members are already engaged in partnerships with NGOs and the UN around areas such as microfinance, employment opportunities, food, healthcare, women's rights, education volunteering/secondment, environmental protection, logistics, agriculture and fisheries.[6]

When a tsunami devastated parts of Asia in December 2004, for instance, the United Nations' Development Programme (UNDP) enabled private companies to 'adopt' an island and manage the reconstruction of ruined homes in the Maldives. And the global transport service provider TNT has, since 2002, been engaged in a *Moving the World* partnership with the United Nations' World Food Programme (WFP) to fight hunger. TNT provides hands-on support in emergencies, engages in knowledge transfer projects and initiates advocacy and fundraising activities to help WFP be more efficient and effective. So far this has resulted in €32.5 million in-kind donations to WFP operations, €5.5 million donated in cash and €9.0 million raised by TNT employees.[7]

The main reasons for these various corporate acts of kindness are still to ensure successful implementation of CSR programmes, to build trust with stakeholders, engage in corporate citizenship, improve employee morale and enhance the company's reputation.[6] But some companies are starting to realize that they can create more value from their philanthropic contributions if they relate them to their core business.

One of these companies is the multinational technology and services conglomerate General Electric (GE), which donates more than $200 million through contributions from the GE Foundation, GE businesses and GE volunteer hours. GE has had huge success in applying its special knowledge and other internal resources to building hospitals in Ghana in partnership with local stakeholders. Its 'citizenship strategy' is, in fact, integral to its business strategy, which means that it now invests $6 billion each year in research and development, of which $4 billion is allocated to solving the problems of clean energy and affordable healthcare.[8]

General Electric's healthcare initiative in Africa

The devastating poverty and disease that prevail over much of the African continent were of deep personal concern to the 4000 employees in GE's African-American Forum. But instead of a large cheque, GE decided to dedicate some of the company's extensive experience with water, energy and sanitation.

First, GE applied its highly disciplined six sigma problem-solving approach to develop an effective plan and conducted over 100 interviews with experts from the EU, UNICEF, Africare, the US Agency for International Development and the US Department of State to select a suitable area.

A team of senior executives from GE's water, energy and health businesses then travelled to Ghana in December 2003. The district they chose had a population of 100 000, but no reliable power, clean water or access to healthcare other than a single midwife.

In collaboration with Ghana's ministry of health, local members of parliament, the mayor, tribal leaders and residing non-profit organizations, GE started working on the construction of a hospital. By October 2004 – nine months later – the hospital was complete, fully staffed and functioning – a pace that few non-profits could have matched, and an experience that has profoundly changed GE's thinking about corporate philanthropy.

The company now has eight other similar projects in Ghana, and is considering extending its work to South Africa, Malawi, Tanzania and Uganda.

Source: Stanford Social Innovation Review [9]

In sum, the mindsets and models of society's three main sectors are in sharp contrast to those of the 20th century. Today, social and economic obligations go hand in hand, and the hybrid blend of market and non-market mechanisms is finding expression in all sectors of society: public organizations must be economically efficient while providing effective welfare solutions; NGOs and charities must be effective and economically sustainable while doing good; and companies must be socially responsible while making a profit. As a result, reinvention, innovation and new alliances are new and important key words in 21st century wealth and welfare creation.

Societal problems and needs do not fall neatly into designated sector boxes. Addressing social issues and development challenges efficiently and effectively is therefore no longer a question of who does the work, but rather of who can deliver the best solutions. And sustainable solutions require a collaborative cross-sector effort. In fact, cross-sector fertilization supports three crucial mechanisms of social innovation: exchanges of ideas and values, shifts in roles and relationships and the integration of private capital with public and philanthropic support.[10]

But referring to the 'blurring' of sector borders encourages people to continue looking at the world through the old tri-sector lens rather than rising above the present framework to understand the deeper shift in the nature of how all organizations operate and need to operate.[1]

Maybe this is the reason why the concept of social entrepreneurship has been off the radar for many years. For it is in this cross-section between the public, private and civil sectors that social entrepreneurs are often found. They encompass all three sectors: like the public sector they provide welfare solutions, like the private sector they run their ventures as businesses and like the third sector they are values-based and work with a clear social mission.

Their 'mixing of genes' is drawing the contours of a metaphorical *fourth sector* with companies and organizations of all shapes and sizes that work for the wellbeing of society in new ways. You could go as far as to call social entrepreneurship an expression of a mindset with the same overall objective that many other institutions, companies, organizations and citizens of the global consciousness movement are increasingly committing themselves to: the contribution to sustainable development.[11]

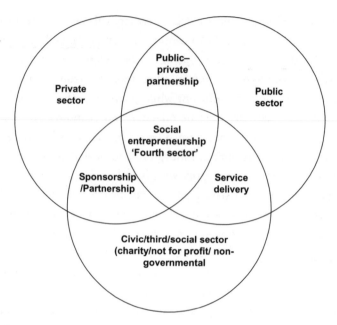

The 'fourth sector'. Figure by Tania Ellis with inspiration from Clark, Martin, *The Social Entrepreneur Revolution*, 2009.

It's a jungle out there

Social entrepreneurs come from all walks of life and span all educational levels. Though social ventures are more likely to be started by men, the gender gap is not as high as in business entrepreneurship.[12] Social entrepreneurs may be idealists or activists motivated by social indignation or love for their fellow men. They may be wealthy individuals interested in giving back to society, or they may be businesspeople looking for a sustainable business model to help them 'do good by doing well'. Some social entrepreneurs have spent most of their careers in one sector. Others have moved between positions in the business community, non-profit organizations and the public sector.[13] What they do have in common, however, is their ethical fibre and engagement in social issues.

Because the travellers on the sustainability journey come along different routes, entering the field of social entrepreneurship is entering a jungle of definitions and concepts that criss-cross industries, sectors and legal units, ranging from non-profit to for-profit forms and hybrids of the two.

Sustainable companies, fourth sector companies, high purpose companies, for benefit businesses, double bottom line businesses, affirmative businesses, values-driven enterprises, social intrapreneurship, civic entrepreneurship, social purpose ventures and *social enterprises* are just some of the terms that are used in attempts to cover the field. Even within a single term the definition may vary, depending on the source. One study of 'social enterprises' from 2001 showed as many as 16 different variants.[14] In short, neither practitioners nor academics have found common ground on a definition.

Mirjam Schöning, director of the Geneva-based Schwab Foundation for Social Entrepreneurship, recognizes the terminological confusion: 'I attended the first academic conference in 2004 in search of a more concrete definition of social entrepreneurship, only to discover that the spectrum was even broader than I had previously thought. The only common denominator the participants could agree on in their definitions was the element of social change.'

However, some researchers refer to a *European* and an *American* approach to social entrepreneurship. The European approach emphasizes the collective, associative or cooperative *social enterprise* with commercial activities and earned income supporting traditional social services in the third sector; the American approach centres on *social entrepreneurship* with bold individuals launching new activities in the blurry zone between traditional sectors, dedicated to a social mission while maintaining a market focus.[15]

Nevertheless, leading researchers in the field warn against prematurely defining the field because fuzzy boundaries allow for a continual and fluid conception not only of social entrepreneurship but also of social and institutional change, of social and economic wealth creation and of social and economic development.[16] In other words, the field of social entrepreneurship is constantly developing and its terminology must develop with it.

This book builds on a purposely broad definition of social entrepreneurship, which includes individuals, privately and collectively owned organizations as well as businesses engaged in innovative or entrepreneurial activities with a social purpose. Because social and environmental aspects of sustainable development are inextricably linked, the term *sustainable entrepreneurship* would also be applicable, but I have chosen to keep the most commonly used term 'social' here in its broadest sense, i.e. including the environment.

An exploding phenomenon

Socially entrepreneurial opportunities arise particularly when the prevailing systems are weakening or even failing. The concept of building a business around a social purpose in new ways has therefore been promoted and shaped in different ways around the world, depending on different social, political and economic traditions.

It can be traced as far back as to the 19th century with the co-operative movement. And in the late 1980s new co-operative initiatives started to emerge in Europe to compensate for governmental shortcomings concerning issues like long-term unemployment, social problems, immigration and work integration of disadvantaged people.

Poverty-related issues, illiteracy, natural disasters, population pressures, growing environmental problems, health problems like HIV/AIDS and governments that have been historically weak, corrupt or ineffective are also some of the drivers behind socially entrepreneurial activities that have been recorded in all regions of the world like Asia (especially India, Pakistan and Bangladesh), Latin America, Africa, Australia, North America and Europe.[7]

In fact, social entrepreneurs in developing countries tend to focus on fundamental needs like basic healthcare provision, access to water and sanitation and agricultural activities in rural areas. While social entrepreneurs in the so-called 'innovation-driven economies' like France, Italy, Denmark, Hong Kong, Japan, the UK and the USA are particularly active in launching culture-related organizations, providing services for disabled people, focusing on waste recycling and nature protection and offering open-source activities such as online social networking.[12] As a result, their contributions to sustainable development can be found in 'clusters' of, for example, recycling and waste, economic development, transport, education, employment, health or ethical consumer products.

Although the field is difficult to quantify accurately because of the unclear definitions, there is universal agreement that it has grown significantly over the past two decades. One of the indicators of the growth of the field is the increasing public attention over the past five to ten years. In addition to the educational institutions mentioned in Chapter 2, dedicated organizations and foundations, online networks and innovation intermediaries, physical hubs and awards, competitions and TV series are today promoting, supporting or paying tribute to social entrepreneurs from all corners of the world.

For example, international research, community-building and awareness-raising organizations like The European Research Network (EMES), the Geneva-based Schwab Foundation for Social Entrepreneurship, the US-based Ashoka and Skoll Foundation and the UK-based Skoll Centre for Social Entrepreneurship are some of the more established actors. But also online networks like Young Social Enterprise Initiative (YSEI.org), SocialEdge.org and i-Genius.org and physical working spaces that serve as social innovation incubators like the London-based The Hub, which is rapidly spreading to other parts of the world, offer and share resources for practitioners and others with an interest in social innovation and entrepreneurship.

In the media world as well the scope of social entrepreneurship is made visible. To name just a few initiatives, there is *The World Challenge* brought by BBC World News and *Newsweek*, Fast Company's annual *Social Capitalist Awards*, CNBC's *The Good Entrepreneur*, Deutsche Welle's portraits of 25 social entrepreneurs as part of its *Global 3000* programme and PBS's critically acclaimed *e²series* with stories about innovators and pioneers who envision a better quality of life, socially, culturally, economically and environmentally.

It was, however, not until 2003/4 that the first pilot Global Entrepreneurship Monitor (GEM) survey was conducted in the UK of 'businesses with social objectives whose surpluses are principally re-invested for that purpose in the business or in the community, rather than being driven by the need to max-imize profit for shareholders and owners' — the now most widely used defini-tion of social enterprises and social entrepreneurship in the UK.

Among other things, the GEM survey showed that 6.6% of the British population was involved in some form of social entrepreneurship activity, that companies with mixed sources of revenue created more jobs and higher turnover per employee than their mainstream counterparts and were more likely to be started up by women, members of ethnic minorities and people with low incomes.[18] A 2005 survey showed that 775 000 people in the UK were employed by social enterprises that generated a total annual turnover of more than £18 billion.[19]

In 2009 GEM took the first significant step to a global examination of the prevalence and nature of both business entrepreneurship and social entrepreneurship in 49 countries.[12] The survey was built on a broad definition which included the start-up, ownership or management of 'any kind of activity, organization or initiative' with a 'particularly social, environmental or community objective' which was then qualified into four typologies in order of prevalence:

1. *Innovative not-for-profit social enterprises* with high levels of social/environmental goals.
2. *Hybrid social enterprises* with high levels of social/environmental goals with an earned income strategy integrated or complementary to the social mission.
3. *For-profit social enterprises* with high but not exclusively social/environmental goals and an earned income strategy.
4. *Traditional not-for-profit NGOs* with high levels of social/environmental goals.

The GEM survey shows that social entrepreneurial activity rates to this point are, in general, much lower than the total entrepreneurial activity rates (the average social entrepreneurship rate ranges from 1% to 4.3%). But interestingly, a significant minority of social entrepreneurs, particularly in developing countries, wants to have a profitable business that at the same time addresses social issues, demonstrating a need for more holistic definitions of entrepreneurship – rather than dividing it into a respectively social or business category.

So, although the growth rate within the field of social entrepreneurship has already led experts to call the development of social entrepreneurship a 'worldwide explosion of dot-orgs' that exceeds the explosion of commercial companies that emerged during the dot-com wave in the 1990s, there is still some way to go before we capture the full value of the economic, social and innovative potential that lies in this cross-section between business and social change.

The focus of the next section is to try to capture the true extent of this phenomenon by looking into the three *dimensions* of social entrepreneurship that are commonly referred to:

1. Social change is the main purpose.
2. Innovative problem solving is the solution.
3. Business methods are the means.

We will look into these three dimensions to gain insight into how social entrepreneurs in the cross-pollinated 'fourth sector' are responding to needs, developing solutions and creating value in ways that mainstream companies, social organizations and governments have either failed to do or have never thought of.

The value of social entrepreneurship
– three dimensions of the new business paradigm

1. **Social change is the main purpose.**
2. Innovative problem solving is the solution.
3. Business methods are the means.

When young Ibrahim Abouleish returned to Egypt in the mid-1970s after studying medicine in Austria, he was met with an Egypt he could no longer recognize: dirty streets, diseases, poor people and social problems he would never have imagined.

After three years of analysis Abouleish came to the conclusion that part of the explanation was an imbalance between economic growth and declining environmental quality caused by years of extensive use of pesticides in Egyptian agriculture. Another part was the imbalance in the pharmaceutical industry, which would hear nothing of natural healing methods.

In 1979 Abouleish founded the SEKEM company on 70 hectares of desert 60 kilometres outside Cairo. Today the once barren desert has been turned into an area of flourishing biodynamic agriculture with 150 biodynamic farms and 2000 hectares of land which produce fruit, vegetables, herbal medicine and clothes sold in more than 8000 shops across Egypt, Europe and the USA. SEKEM deployed a new system for protecting cotton crops, which led to a ban on crop dusting throughout Egypt, and by 2000, pesticide use in Egyptian cotton fields had fallen by over 90%.[20, 21]

More than 2000 people are employed in the various SEKEM business units. The Co-operative of SEKEM Employees ensures that the human and democratic rights and values of the company are adequately implemented, and addresses issues regarding civil rights in the workplace to guarantee a healthy and productive work environment. Every morning the employees meet to report briefly on the accomplishments of the previous day and their plans for the current day to give them a sense of equality as members of the SEKEM community. Every business unit also has a human resources officer to take care of employee training, career development and medical care.

The profit from the business is reinvested in, among other things, schools run according to Rudolf Steiner's anthroposophical principles (a spiritual philosophy), an adult education centre and a holistic medical centre.

In 2003 Ibrahim Abouleish received the Alternative Nobel Prize (an award which honours those 'working on practical and exemplary solutions to the most urgent challenges facing the world today') as an acknowledgement of what the jury called 'the healthy business model of the 21st century'. The model combines profit and success on the global market with a human and spiritual approach to people and with respect for the environment. The same year Abouleish was awarded the accolade Outstanding Social Entrepreneur by the Schwab Foundation for Social Entrepreneurship and invited to partici- pate in the following World Economic Forum meeting in Davos. At the same time 'The Society of SEKEM's Friends' was founded in Switzerland, and similar companies were established in Tanzania, Kenya and South Africa.

SEKEM is an example of how social entrepreneurs drive change under the premise that it is not at the expense of society, the environment or human wellbeing. And because sustainable social change is the main purpose of their activities, social entrepreneurs typically work for the long term rather than for the quick gain – in SEKEM's case with a 200-year strategy built on anthropo- sophical principles, an holistic approach to people management and a busi- ness model which creates economic, social and cultural value.

Value creation in multiple ways

Working with social change as the main purpose implies the creation of social value such as a cleaner environment, better education and childcare, improved health, reduction of poverty, more justice and fairness and housing of homeless people. Social value is, in other words, created by addressing societal needs or problems in ways that go beyond private gains.

Balancing social, environmental and financial value creation is, however, the key to sustainable development. As the originator of the concept of 'blended value', Jed Emerson, argues: '... if you want to maximize economic value by generating financial returns for investors, you should no longer be able to do it without taking into account how your execution of a business strategy is affected by social and environmental factors. And if you want to achieve greater social and environmental justice in the world, you shouldn't be able to unless you understand the economics of modern business.'

The Base of the Pyramid concept, for example, creates value but does not automatically make a company's activities sustainable. BOP-customized products like single-serve plastic packaging, for instance, are criticized for causing environmental problems because they are not biodegradable. And weaving and clothing manufacture in emerging markets have proven unsustainable because they have ignored the long-term needs of the communities in preserving their social fabric and natural environment.[22]

Social entrepreneurship offers new models of sustainable change by blending, generating or even renewing the use of four kinds of capital to create social value.

Financial capital – use of (new forms of) money

In Brazil, sustainable community transactions in the slum districts of the town Curitiba have, since 1971, been reinforced by the use of complementary money systems, as the residents of Curitiba have been rewarded for gathering garbage with a coin that can be used as a free bus ticket or as payment for food. In a three-year period over 100 schools gathered 200 tons of garbage, and as payment received 1.9 million writing slates. In two decades, from 1975 to 1995, the local economy of Curitiba grew by 50% above the Brazilian average, and in 1992 the UN declared Curitiba 'the world's most ecological town'.[23]

US-based RecycleBank's value proposition is to make it financially attractive to recycle, and it has, since 2004, rewarded households for recycling by letting them earn RecycleBank Points on a dedicated Visa Card that can be used to shop at over 1500 local and national businesses. In 2009, it already served over one million people in 20 states across the USA, which has enabled RecycleBank to save cities tens of millions of dollars annually in landfill disposal fees, saved over 1.5 million trees and saved millions of gallons of oil. In 2004 it was designated Champion of the Earth by the United Nations' Environment Programme (UNEP), and is now expanding its services to Europe.

And in more than 400 towns in the UK a Local Exchange Trading System (LETS) works as a supplement to the traditional government-issued monetary system. The purpose is to stimulate the local economy in deprived communities, where electronic points can be earned and spent on exchanges of different kinds of social services. Thereby, tangible value is put on relationships, networks, cooperation and community work even when there is no official financial market for these transactions. In the final instance, this creates social cohesion as well as employment instead of reliance on state welfare benefits, and governments in New Zealand, Australia, Scotland and over 30 American states have therefore supported the start up of these types of local monetary systems.[24] In 2005, more than 5000 different trade systems of this kind existed worldwide in local communities of 500 to 5000 people.[23]

Environmental capital – use of natural resources

Green Works, a UK-based award-winning registered charity and social enterprise, uses environmental capital to achieve the twin goals of zero waste and support of people from marginalized communities by applying the four Rs – Reduce, Re-use, Remanufacture or Recycle – to collect and process unwanted office furniture, which is then sold at a discount to schools, colleges, housing associations and businesses, and by employing physically and socially disadvantaged people.

Since 2000, Green Works has taken more than 60 000 tons of furniture that would have ended up in landfill. Meanwhile, schools, charities and small businesses have saved around £2.5 million from Green Works, which achieved a turnover of £2.1 million in 2007.[25]

Peepoople is a Swedish company that addresses one of the United Nations Millennium Development Goals: to halve the proportion of people without sustainable access to drinking water and sanitation by 2015. Its contribution is the single-use, biodegradable and self-sanitising Peepoo plastic bag which serves as a personal, portable and low-cost latrine for the 2.6 million people – 40% of the world's population – who lack regular access to a toilet. The bag is lined with a coating that disinfects the waste, it is odour-free for at least 24 hours and within two to four weeks after use the bag content constitutes high-quality fertilizer – a usually expensive and scarce commodity in developing countries. The fertilized Peepoo bags turn contaminants into a local resource which improves the soil's structure and water-holding capacity and which, in the long term, will improve the potential harvest from the fields and enable simple economic systems to develop.

The Peepoo toilet. *Photo courtesy of Camilla Wirseen/Peepoople*

UK-based Worn Again, voted 'number one eco brand' by *The Independent* in 2008, uses the combination of aesthetic and environmental capital by 'upcycling' corporate waste materials into new, design-led products.

Worn Again has, for example, turned the raincoats, jackets and train seat antimacassars of high-speed train service company Eurostar into bespoke train managers' bags for Eurostar staff, taking decommissioned textiles and returning them to the company as new products. A percentage of Worn Again's income goes to Anti-Apathy, a registered charity which promotes and supports people who take creative and innovative approaches to social and environmental issues.

Aesthetic capital – use of design, art, music, architecture, etc.

The Danish art company Superflex has designed a commercial brand – Guaraná Power – for local farming co-operatives in the Brazilian Amazon to create a counter economic position that empowers farmers of guaraná (small dark red berries containing caffeine) from corporate monopoly on guaraná soft drinks from multinational soft drink companies. The farmers are now paid five times the former market price, and all earnings from Guaraná Power benefit the local guaraná farmers, who use the surplus to improve their local community. Superflex is currently relaunching the product in an organic version.

Guarana Power. *Photo courtesy of The Power Foundation*

Participant Media uses quality film entertainment that shows creative and commercial potential as well as raising awareness of the environment, health, human rights, institutional responsibility, peace and tolerance or social and economic equity. With award-winning films like Al Gore's *An Inconvenient Truth*, the documentary *Darfur Now*, the geopolitical thriller *Syriana* and the drama *The Kite Runner*, Participant Media has been a catalyst for a wide range of social action campaigns as well as being instrumental to progressive social development through active, working relationships with 83 non-profits reaching over 20 million people. In connection with *The Kite Runner*, for example, Participant Media teamed up with NGOs to support literacy by rebuilding libraries, training teachers and providing computers and other educational materials for war-torn Afghanistan.

In the same country, the Mobile Mini Circus for Children (MMCC) uses educational entertainment to bring hope and joy to war-ridden Afghan children. Since its foundation in 2002 the NGO has presented workshops and travelling circuses for more than 460 000 children. It also runs a Children's Cultural House in Kabul with creative activities for up to 350 children each season, and financial capital comes from creative teaching workshops for schools and other educational institutions which generate an income for the artists.

Social capital – building human relationships, trust, networks and cooperation

The business model behind the largest North European culture and music festival – The Roskilde Festival, which houses an annual audience of more than 75 000 people – is based on using a combination of social capital, which enables the festival to attract about 25 000 volunteers every year; environmental capital in terms of its Green Footsteps campaign, which promotes and engages festival guests in sustainable activities; and aesthetic capital in terms of music in support of humanitarian and cultural purposes by reinvesting all its profit via the association behind the festival, The Roskilde Festival Charity. Since the early 1970s the charity has distributed more than $25 million to various NGOs with humanitarian and cultural purposes. The Roskilde Festival has also created economic growth by generating trade in the local community around the festival which in 2008 amounted to around $8 million in only eight days.[26]

With corporate sponsors like Nike and MTV, Copenhagen-based GAM3 uses street basketball, breakdance contests and other urban sports tournaments to create social capital by bringing together marginalised youth from ethnic minorities with Danish youth so they can find common ground. The vision is to empower youth and prevent conflict and marginalization on a local and global level. GAM3 is already well on its way, with 55 coaches, more than 70 volunteers and two Country Directors that run activities in Egypt and Lebanon. There they use sports to promote equal opportunities for all, tolerance, trust and mutual respect to more than 6000 young displaced children, refugees, orphans and street kids, of which 34% are girls.[27]

One of the key success factors of Grameen Bank (described in Chapter 1) comes from putting social capital first by building on principles of trust rather than paperwork, and by building on networks rather than legal systems. Credit officers visit the villages, enabling them to get to know and explain the purpose of the bank to the borrowers, and local solidarity groups with five prospective borrowers are formed. If the first two borrowers repay their loans plus interest, the other members become eligible for a loan, and so the collective responsibility of the group serves as the collateral on the loan. Which leads us to the second dimension of social entrepreneurship:

> 1. Social change is the main purpose.
> 2. **Innovative problem solving is the solution.**
> 3. Business methods are the means.

'I started a bank with $27 and wanted to do it in a different way than the banks do. I wanted to lend money to the poorest people. And when people ask me, "How did you design it? How did you figure it out?" I said it was very simple. I knew nothing about banking. That helped me a lot.'

This is how the textbook example of a social entrepreneur, Bangladeshi economist, Nobel Peace Prize-winner and microcredit pioneer, Muhammad Yunus, introduced his Grameen Bank concept in a speech for more than

50 000 people at the Roskilde Festival in Denmark on a hot summer's day in 2009.

Like Yunus, many of the world's social innovators have, throughout time, created many of the institutions, principles and concepts that we today take for granted. Their common denominator? They have an almost unshakable optimism and strong belief that the impossible is possible, and they do not wait for others to pave the way for them. They develop innovative solutions that solve society's problems and meet people's current needs rather than creating new ones. They are the ones who see opportunities where others see insoluble problems, empty buildings, people unfit for work or undervalued resources. They are not limited by scarcity of resources, but are rather masters at attracting or combining them in new ways. So on their way to accomplishing their social goals they challenge the status quo and often break with established structures, logics and mindsets.

In the case of Yunus he just looked at how the conventional banks work – and did the opposite. As he explained at the Roskilde Festival event: 'They go to the rich, I go to the poor. They go to men, I go to women. They go to the urban centre, I go to the rural village. They ask their customers to come to their office, I said, "forget it!" I said, "People should not come to the bank, banks should go to the people." Conventional banks wanted collateral. I said, "forget about collateral. Poor people don't have any collateral." So our bank is without collateral. We don't need any collateral. Our bank is without lawyers. We don't need any lawyers. And it works beautifully!'

So although many social entrepreneurs, like Yunus, are initially met by scepticism, disapproval and rejection from naysayers, industry insiders and experts who do not believe in their ideas, they have both the persistence and skills to communicate and market their innovations to the outside world so that what once was a marginal idea becomes the new standard.

With his Grameen Bank concept Yunus has introduced a business innovation that recognizes the multidimensional nature of human beings – a social business that is designed to make money. Not for personal gain, but to pursue broad social goals. And 33 years after Yunus presented the idea of microloans to conventional banks, many of these same banks have collapsed, whereas microbanks are flourishing and have even spawned commercial followers. Today there are more than 3000 microbanks in over 50 countries, even in welfare states like Canada, France, the Netherlands, Norway and the USA which, it has turned out, also constitute markets for social and economic value creation.

It is not without reason that social entrepreneurs are often described as 'pioneers of innovations that benefit humanity', and that they have a 'mission to change society – if not the entire world'. Or, as Bill Drayton, founder of the global social entrepreneurship association Ashoka, puts it: 'They are not content just to hand out fish or teach others how to fish. They will not stop until they have revolutionized the entire fishing industry.'

Interview with Muhammad Yunus at The Roskilde Festival. *Private photo*

Society's problem solvers

Bill Drayton knows what he is talking about. With the mission of building a world where everyone is a change-maker, Drayton's global organization has, since 1980, spent its $30 million annual budget (2006) to invest in more than 2000 social entrepreneurs – Ashoka Fellows – in 60 countries all over the world, supporting innovative projects in the fields of education, environment, human rights, citizen involvement and economic development.

Key selection criteria for Ashoka Fellows are social impact and innovative problem solving. So it is not just another orphanage or daycare centre they look for. It is *new* rather than traditional social solutions that are called for. And to ensure maximum effect, the solution should have the potential to create systemic social change.

One of Ashoka's Fellows is Bart Weetjens, a Belgian product development engineer with a long-time fascination for rodents, who wanted to use his skills to benefit communities in Africa. When he analysed the landmine problem in Africa in 1995 he was surprised by the complexity and high technological levels of expensive mine-clearing solutions that were largely proposed by research institutions outside the continent.

By relying on locally available resources his model has turned out to be cheaper, quicker and more scalable, yet efficient: his organization, Apopo, trains the widely present African Giant Pouched Rat to detect landmines (they have now also been trained to detect tuberculosis) at landmine detection testing facilities (in partnership with the Tanzania People's Defense Forces) which, at the same time, provides local jobs for the economically disadvantaged.

In short, his innovation not only creates jobs and saves lives as well as costs – it also represents a significant shift in the field from landmine-affected countries depending on foreign expertise to having the power to control the demining process, and is now replicable across Africa and other continents affected by landmines.

Apopo's hero rats. *Photo courtesy of Christophe Cox*

The Apopo case is illustrative of how social entrepreneurs create value: they develop social innovations that meet needs that are either overserved because the existing solutions are more complex than required – or not served at all because of market or government failure. They often do this more efficiently, effectively and, if not profitably, at least sustainably by combining resources and tools from different worlds, blending market and non-market approaches, building alliances across sectors and professions and by having lower cost structures and more efficient delivery channels.[10]

This is why The Organisation for Economic Co-operation and Development (OECD) has worked with social enterprise since the late 1990s. And this is why the UK Government has launched a *Social Enterprise Action Plan* and established a £73 million Social Enterprise Investment Fund (SEIF). It believes that successful social entrepreneurs can play an important role in delivering many of its key policy objectives, including showing new ways to deliver public services, helping to increase productivity and competitiveness and contributing to socially inclusive wealth creation by tackling some of society's most entrenched social and environmental challenges.[15]

For similar reasons, the US White House Office of Social Innovation and Civic Participation has founded its recent $50 million fund. 'Instead of creating new top-down programs, we want to partner and build upon the innovative ways people are already solving problems across the country,' Office director Sonal Shah explains.[28]

Partnering or involving users, citizens, local governments or other stakeholders is, in fact, the key to creating better and more viable solutions than the social entrepreneurs would be able to achieve on their own. Not only because of the intersectorial nature of their activities, but also because it gains access to, for example, more competences, increased capacity and infrastructure. A huge amount of value can, in other words, be realized from social capital as a bridging capacity in terms of strong social networks and a wide range of strategic alliances.

This is the reason why visibility, credibility and networking are, next to financing, crucial for the success of social entrepreneurship. The Schwab Foundation for Social Entrepreneurship, for example, does not provide financial support to its more than 150 social entrepreneurs, but runs a

Social Entrepreneur of the Year selection process with partner companies in 15 countries and on five continents to identify the world's leading social entrepreneurs. It provides media exposure and networking opportunities at the World Economic Forum meetings, including the Annual Meeting in Davos and the numerous regional meetings. 'Most social entrepreneurs concentrate on delivering impact on the ground. At Davos and through other platforms, we draw the attention of business and public leaders to the social innovations pioneered by social entrepreneurs. We offer the platforms for representatives of all sectors of society to bring their strengths to the table and partner with social entrepreneurs,' explains director Mirjam Schöning.

Collaborative innovation is also the principle behind the first American non-profit pharmaceutical company, Institute for OneWorld Health, which was established by American scientist Victoria Hale in 2000 as a response to one of the great problems in the world: the combating of epidemic diseases in developing countries.

Victoria Hale has challenged the prevailing logic of the pharmaceutical industry that research and development of medicines for developing countries is too expensive because of economic and logistic barriers by redesigning the entire value chain with the use of different types of partnerships:

- The company is financed by large foundations (among others, the Bill & Melinda Gates Foundation and the Skoll Foundation), government institutions and private donations.
- OneWorld Health's own scientists work closely together with research centres, institutions, universities and individual scientists who offer voluntary work hours, knowledge and resources as a contribution to the research work itself or to the operation of the company.
- Alliances have been formed with drug companies like Roche and Novartis who give the institute access to their proprietary research or donate patent-free licences from which the companies are unable to achieve any commercial gain.
- The research and production capacity of the developing countries is used for clinical testing and production, and for getting the medicine distributed to those areas where it is most needed.

Results: the philanthropists are happy to support the cause, the scientists are highly motivated, the biotech companies have gained an attractive marketing channel for their unused intellectual property and jobs have been created in the developing countries. But most important of all, the Institute of OneWorld Health has succeeded in delivering cheap, effective and relevant new medicines to those places where the need for them is greatest.

The efforts of OneWorld Health have, among other things, resulted in the introduction of a $46 million dollar programme for the development of a new, cheap malaria medicine, and the non-profit pharmaceutical is currently waiting for regulatory approval of a new medicine to combat the fatal visceral leishmaniasis disease which causes over 200 000 annual deaths.

So what started out as an oxymoron that people laughed at, saying 'oh, that'll never work' has proven that global health no longer needs to be an insurmountable problem, and potential investors are now asking the institute to consider a *not* non-profit model. So would OneWorld Health be willing to open up to other possibilities? Victoria Hale's answer is clear: 'Absolutely.'[29] Which leads us to the third dimension of social entrepreneurship:

---

1. Social change is the main purpose.
2. Innovative problem solving is the solution.
3. **Business methods are the means.**

Before his youngest son was diagnosed with Autistic Spectrum Disorder (ASD) Technical Director Thorkil Sonne had never thought of starting his own business. But watching the boy's ongoing hardship and looking at the poor work opportunities for people with ASD, Sonne realized that his son's future did not look too bright. It was not, however, that his son lacked skills. In fact, the boy had a highly unusual ability to concentrate on details and submit to an exact standard. It was just that the labour market was not geared for harvesting these special skills. And so, in 2004, Thorkil Sonne started his own IT company Specialisterne (The Specialists) with a business concept centred on utilising the special skills of people with ASD.

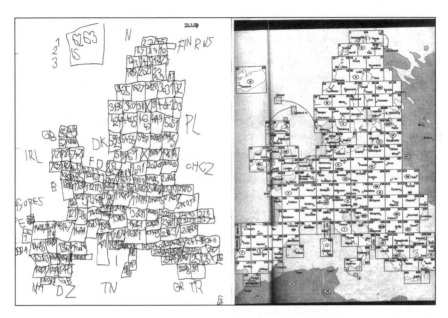

Unusual aptitude for detail: Thorkil Sonne's seven-year-old son reproduced a numbered European roadmap from memory. *Photo courtesy of Thorkil Sonne.*

When Sonne started his business, which tests software and conducts quality controls for companies like Siemens, Microsoft, Cisco and CSC, he had no idea that his social business model would receive numerous prizes and international media attention. Nor would he have believed that Specialisterne – only four years after its foundation – would become a Harvard Business School Case Study.

Nevertheless, all this has already come true, and today Sonne is upscaling with a licence concept in Glasgow, Scotland, and he has a short-term goal to start licences in three major European cities by the end of 2010 and a long-term goal to create one million jobs worldwide for people with ASD and similar challenges like ADHD (Attention Deficit Hyperactivity Disorder).

The business potential of Specialisterne is huge, but for Thorkil Sonne it is about more than that: 'In the traditional market the goal is to make products attractive enough so you can sell them with a profit. In my case the goal is to create a better future for my son and all the others with ASD and other invisible disabilities. We want to change society's view of the large group of people with ASD.'

Sonne's business model may be unique, but his motivation for starting a commercial company is not. He is a textbook example of the growing number of social entrepreneurs who engage in commercial activities to create sustained social value – the social business entrepreneurs who turn the failures of government or market into social business opportunities by grounding the 'let's-go-change-the-world movement' into value-adding actions. For them, generating their own revenue streams is becoming a high priority because it can lead to economic sustainability, independence and the opportunity to accomplish more of their social mission.

The value-adding business strategies

The socially innovative business model of Specialisterne is a new segment of the so-called *affirmative businesses* or *social firms* that build on hiring individuals with mental, physical, economic or educational disadvantages by offering them real jobs, competitive wages and opportunities to build careers and to gain their sense of self-worth and self-sufficiency.

Within just this particular type of social business there are opportunities for creating both social and economic value: in the UK alone, nearly one in five people of working age is disabled. Almost half of these 6.9 million people are unemployed, which means dependence on welfare benefits and personal low self-esteem. From 1997 to 2007, the number of social firms grew from just 5 to 127, creating a total of 1625 jobs for disabled people.[15] These figures are admittedly small, yet the results reveal a huge potential for economic and social value creation: cost reductions on welfare benefits, new manpower, increased revenues and tax incomes on the one hand – and improved life quality, raised self-esteem and a meaningful life on the other.

The social entrepreneur and mainstream business entrepreneur share many of the same characteristics like passion, goal-orientation, a willingness to take chances, the ability to mobilize resources and the ability to see opportunities and turn vision into concrete actions. However, there are three fundamental differences which are often highlighted in distinguishing the social entrepreneur from the business entrepreneur: opportunity, motive and purpose.

The prototypes of social and business entrepreneurship

The Social Entrepreneur	The Business Entrepreneur
Social mission ('help others').	Economic mission ('make a profit').
Meets social/society's needs.	Meets financial/commercial needs.
Creates social value.	'Creates financial value.
Socially driven, charitable dimension, sense of justice.	Profit-driven, commercial dimension, business sense.
Profit as means to succeed with social goals – to secure financial independence.	Profit as goal in itself – to secure owner's financial welfare.
Value is measured through social effect 'Social return on investment'.	Value is measured through financial income 'Financial return on investment'.
Whole/parts of surplus is reinvested in organization or in new social projects.	Surplus goes to owners/shareholders.
Sustainable growth.	Growth.

Table by Tania Ellis

The business entrepreneur recognizes gaps in the economic system (*business opportunities*) whereas the social entrepreneur recognizes the gaps in the social system (*social opportunities*).

The intention or *motivation* in terms of empathy and moral judgement as opposed to rational business actions is another distinction that is used to differentiate the two.[30] The degree of exposure to social issues and moral background of the social entrepreneur is a contributing factor to recognising the social opportunities in the first place. The social entrepreneur's ability to link his or her knowledge of a social need with a means of satisfying the need is another.[31]

And this is where the *purpose* of exploiting the opportunities comes into the picture. For the business entrepreneur the purpose is to create financial value whereas the social entrepreneur is in business with the purpose of creating social value.

So, contrary to the commercial business that uses market methods – or social responsibility – as a means to make a profit for its owners, the social entrepreneur uses market methods and makes money as a means to meet social goals for the benefit of society. Social entrepreneurs are promoters of heartcore rather than hardcore business.

The motto of Greyston Bakery, a New York-based social business which hires people who are long-term unemployed, former addicts or criminals, makes the distinction between means and ends clear: 'We don't hire people to bake brownies. We bake brownies to hire people'. A Zen Buddhist meditation group founded the company in 1982 with the mission of using business as a force for personal transformation and economic community renewal. The bakery is the supplier to, among others, the popular ice cream company Ben & Jerry's, and has an annual revenue of around $5 million.[32] All profits are reinvested in daycare centres, health clinics and minority counselling via its Greyston Foundation.

Whether a profit should be reinvested or not has, however, led to a heated debate among experts and practitioners in the field. For some it is crucial that all or a part of the profit is reinvested – they do not believe in personal gain from activities with a social purpose. Others are more pragmatic and argue that it is *the way* they make their money which is central, not how they spend their surplus – they believe that it is OK to cash in on the profit and focus on the social *outcome* of their business efforts. Others, like Grameen Bank, leave the profits in the hands of those who need it by giving the borrowers (or employees) ownership of the business so the profit goes back to them as dividend.

The social value created can, in other words, be divided into two categories: products, services or operating systems of the business that create social benefits like housing, healthcare and education or business ownership which belongs to, for example, the poor or disadvantaged.[33]

Putting social value creation at the centre of its business is precisely why the Indian Aravind Eye Care Hospital – a bottom-of-the-pyramid institute which treats more than 2.5 million patients a year to eliminate needless blindness through comprehensive eye care services that restore sight – measures value by its ability to restore sight rather than by dollar-denominated value. But because it is a financially self-supported company, operating with an annual budget of $13 million (2008–9), it can do 60% of its work for free or significantly subsidized for low-income families.[34, 35]

Some social entrepreneurs are – as the earlier mentioned 2009 Global Entrepreneurship Monitor also showed – driven by a profit motive as well as a desire to address social issues. A definitional overlap which may in time make it more difficult to cling to the either/or differentiation of the two entre-preneurship categories and which may arguably be reinforced by the entry of an increasing number of socially oriented business school students who want to combine market and meaning.

As the Schwab Foundation's director, Mirjam Schöning explains: 'Many business school students have been exposed to the subject, and so we see a new generation of social entrepreneurs taking a business approach to social value creation. Witnessing the recent collapse of capitalism in its current form has only accelerated the need for a new aspirational model.'

One example of a socially conscious business student who has started his own social business is Sam Goldman – founder of d.Light which sells $10–25 solar-powered lamps in more than a dozen countries where people lack electricity.

Goldman spent four years in the Peace Corps in Benin before earning his master's degree in business at Stanford Graduate School of Business. During his stay in the West African republic Goldman learned firsthand of the prob-lems of using kerosene lamps: it is expensive, it provides poor light and it is extremely dangerous. And when his neighbour's son nearly died after suffer-ing severe burns from spilled kerosene, Goldman realized that he wanted to create a venture to solve both the social and economic problems caused by these lamps.

Like Goldman, many social business entrepreneurs are pragmatic ideal-ists who want to make money – they just don't want to make it at any price. This is also the reasoning behind Sam Goldman's pursuit of finding ways of lowering the costs of d.Light's lamps: 'I'm not satisfied with $10,' he says. 'The real customers that we started this business for can't afford that.'[28]

The choice of business model depends on the social venture's value-add-ing proposition as well as growth ambitions in the short and long term. And because social entrepreneurs are in business to create social value and change, they put effectiveness before scale.

Some, for example, focus on scaling the social solution rather than scaling the actual business. Others operate with concepts that are not even suitable for upscaling or replication because they may depend on rare conditions, scarce skills or business models that are neither transferable nor cost-effective if repeated elsewhere.[36]

Consequently social entrepreneurs apply different growth strategies depending on their company's development stage and whether they have quantitative or qualitative value-adding ambitions. It is about finding the optimal organizational size and the right way to grow in terms of development, rather than pursuing growth for the sake of growth. In other words, size does not always matter, and small can be beautiful too.

In the field of social entrepreneurship, one of the following *seven growth strategies* are, therefore, typically applied:

1. Remain small in organizational size and focus on other growth parameters, e.g. employee happiness, environmental improvements or building local economies.
2. Grow quantitatively in size, e.g. turnover and number of employees by attracting investors, expanding into new markets and/or increasing the customer base.
3. Replicate the business concept to other national or global regions, e.g. through systematic franchising or 'amoebic' multiplication of small independent units.
4. Build a movement, e.g. by spreading the core idea and principles so that governments, mainstream businesses, local communities or other entrepreneurs decide to work in support of the same purpose.
5. Collaborate or merge with other social ventures in the same cluster to develop processes, products and services or engage in 'network production', e.g. so micro-entrepreneurs can join forces to supply large companies.
6. Enter into partnerships with actors in the private, public or civil sectors, e.g. to gain access to knowledge, skills, infrastructure and/or capital.
7. Sell parts of or the entire social venture to a mainstream, commercial business, e.g. to increase the knowledge and impact of the concept or so it goes mainstream.

The choice of growth strategy is also closely linked to the financing of the social venture: models range from what the Schwab Foundation for Social Entrepreneurship categorizes as *leverage non-profit ventures*, i.e. 100% external financing through, for example, donations, sponsorship and public funding but where upscaling is generated through private or public sector partnerships; *hybrid non-profit ventures*, i.e. a mix of external financing like grants or subsidized loans and revenue income from own products or services; or *social business ventures*, for-profit entities with 100% revenue income from own products or services, also referred to as for-profit social enterprises, 'FOPSEs'.

Therefore, you find social businesses with legal entities ranging from associations, self-governing institutions, member service organizations, charities with trading arms, development trusts and mutual benefit and cooperatives to business foundations, companies limited by guarantee or limited by shares and listed companies.

So far, legal labels for companies that provide social good and yet make a profit are limited to the British legal form, Community Interest Companies (CIC), which has been developed for social businesses whose surpluses are principally reinvested in the business or the community; the American low-profit limited liability company status I3c; and the B Corp certification for purpose-driven companies that have social/environmental standards built into their foundation, and where directors are not legally required to exclusively maximize shareholder value (so far, however, with no legal ramifications other than in Philadelphia[37]).

To overcome the limitations that either purely charitable or commercial companies entail, the hybrid not-for-profit model is, according to the Schwab Foundation for Social Entrepreneurship, increasing in popularity. It enables social entrepreneurs to use the profits from their main business to cross-subsidize their charitable work. It also enables them to take up other forms of capital, such as debt and venture capital through the for-profit entity, while the non-profit entity can receive tax-exempted grants and provide non-profit-making services to a community – a blended value space that is also seen in the private sector where some companies place their altruistic or CSR-related activities in a company foundation.

Nevertheless, the largest increase in organizations going through the Schwab Foundation selection process is in the social business venture category. One explanation offered by director Mirjam Schöning is that most recent social enterprises are started by business school graduates who choose to design their ventures as financially self-sustaining. Another is that this particular business model offers the greatest opportunities for rapid scaling.

With an ambition of driving down the price of d.Light's lamps, economies of scale make sense in Sam Goldman's case, because the bigger you get, the cheaper your product can be. So it was clear to Goldman that a project of this kind would only become large enough to reach the great number of people who use these lamps as their primary source of light if it were organized as a profit-making business. 'We could have done it as a nonprofit over a hundred years, but if we wanted to do it in five or 10 years, then we believed it needed to be fueled by profit. That's the way to grow.' In May 2007 d.Light raised $6.5 million from a combination of investors.[38]

Not all social entrepreneurs are able to raise commercial funding though. Many end up falling between two stools when operating in the cross-section of commercial and non-commercial enterprise: social foundations are reluctant to give grants to profit-making companies, and commercial investors hold back because it takes too long for them to create a financial return on investment.

As Jonathan Bland, former director of the Social Enterprise Coalition (SEC), explains: 'Social enterprises will normally not be able to access conventional sources of equity, as they can't offer the usual rates of return or exit and protect the social mission of the business. For this reason, new forms of patient capital are starting to be used, such as community share issues and bonds and quasi equity products such as participating loans from social investment funds.'

This is one of the reasons why Specialisterne, for example, has recently converted its limited liability company status to a not-for-profit foundation: it gives access to grants and capital with investors who invest their assets over a longer period to ensure that society benefits from the investment.

If Specialisterne had been operating in the Third World, a potential investor could have been one of *TIME*'s Responsibility Pioneers in 2009, the Acumen Fund. Founded by social entrepreneur Jacqueline Novogratz as a non-profit organization but which operates like a venture capital firm, the Acumen Fund takes donations from philanthropists and invests its portfolio of $38 million in a businesslike way by lending to or taking stakes in social ventures that offer services within water, health, housing or energy at affordable prices to people earning less than four dollars a day.

There are, however, also other options. 'What we see at the moment is a new wave of funds that operate with a hybrid of investments where capital is prepared to take a risk and longer return because they are motivated by social returns on the investments (SROI),' explains Sarah McGeehan, Head of Social Finance at one of the UK's leading expert organizations on innovation, the National Endowment for Science, Technology and the Arts (NESTA).

Here they work with social investments from a three-legged perspective that addresses some of the key growth levers that social entrepreneurs call for: (1) the *supply of money* by mapping social investment and funding initiatives; (2) the *demands for money* by seed granting a bespoke investment service that supports other business resource issues required to attract investments and growth like a board, technical support or marketing needs; and (3) the *enabling infrastructure* of how to make the money work, e.g. effective tax code policies, European state aid competitive rules, social charters for banks and other social financing strategies.

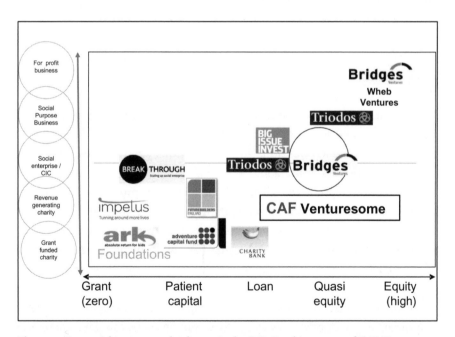

The emerging social investment landscape in the UK. *Graphic courtesy of CAF Venturesome*

There are, however, still paradoxical gaps that need to be closed: social entrepreneurs are often able to raise start-up capital from $100 000–250 000, but it is more difficult for them to raise money from $250 000 to $2 million in growth capital for their venture.[39] Many of the new social venture funds are finding it hard to find social business opportunities to invest in that satisfy their expectations. As Mirjam Schöning from the Schwab Foundation explains, 'At the same meetings, social entrepreneurs complain that they can't find any investors and the social venture fund representatives say there are too few social businesses to invest in. The conundrum is based on the discrepancy between the financial return most social entrepreneurs can offer and the financial return expected by most investors.'

Measures of social value and impact are therefore imperative. And although qualitative social metrics in the triple bottom line methodology, social audits and balanced scorecards already exist, other quantitative models like The Measuring Impacts Toolkit,[40] the social return on investment methodology (SROI),[41] the RBS SE100 Index[42] and Social Impact Bonds[43] are charting and uniting growth with social impact and long-term savings to society.

Ethical bourses or matchmaking exchanges that connect investors of all kinds with social businesses that generate social value as well as financial return are also emerging – for example the Global Exchange for Social Investment (GEXSI), the South African Social Investment Exchange (SASIX), Brazil's Social and Environmental Stock Exchange and the UK-based Social Stock Exchange, which was initiated in 2008 with a £250 000 research grant from The Rockefeller Foundation.

Not all social problems respond well to the for-profit social business venture. One reason is that profit-making companies may find it difficult to build communities based on volunteering, trust or goodwill. It all really boils down to one central question: as you grow, will the economics of your business work in favour of your mission or will they work against it?[38]

In other words, the pursuit of profit can become damaging because it may entail less trust or take away the focus on the social mission. Therefore, the choice of business model is based on how the social mission is achieved best.

Key learnings from social entrepreneurship

There are many lessons we can learn from exploring the three dimensions of social entrepreneurship.

First, social entrepreneurship is a process of creating value by combining resources in new ways (= social innovation). Second, these resource combinations are intended primarily to explore and exploit opportunities to create social value by stimulating social change or meeting social needs (= social value). And third, when viewed as a process, it involves the offering of services and products but can also refer to the creation of new organizations (= social business opportunities).[44]

A closer look at the three dimensions shows us that social entrepreneurs integrate different kinds of capital and 'blended value' thinking into the core of their activities and thereby provide new breeding grounds for innovative approaches to social cohesion and economic growth. Even the concept of money as a transaction method is being renewed.

Furthermore, they generate both direct and indirect value, or what economists call *positive externalities*, through positive side-effects or 'external benefits' that go beyond the benefit of an individual's or organization's activities.

Roskilde Festival, for example, has indirectly generated trade in the local community, SEKEM has influenced a dramatic fall in the use of pesticide spraying of cotton crops and RecycleBank and Green Works have saved the environment from tons of waste from households, commerce and industry.

So, by extending the concept of capital to include other aspects than the purely financial – and by using it as a means to ultimately enhance the well-being of people and society at large – they advance the principles of sustainable wealth and value creation. They define the new economy.

Social entrepreneurs challenge prevailing logics by asking 'why not?' instead of 'why?' They acknowledge problems but do not dwell on them.

Instead, they prefer to focus on positivity and the power of the collective intellect and will to tackle apparently insoluble problems. They overcome the fear of failure and show us that what nay-sayers label 'impossible' is indeed possible, because they have the perseverance to keep on going until what once was a marginal idea can be replicated by others or even become mainstream.

The combination of local knowledge, specialized skills and motivation to find solutions to social problems enables them to see and construct opportunities that governments, corporations and profit-seeking business entrepreneurs miss.[36] They show how growth and value can be created in new and sustainable ways by demonstrating what the world looks like through what Muhammad Yunus calls 'social business glasses' as opposed to 'profit-maximising glasses'.

Giving importance to growth goals that appeal to a larger part of the human spirit than purely financial growth goals also enables them to attract business partners, volunteers and employees. Thereby they offer organizational prototypes that demonstrate how cross-sector collaborative partnerships can be used to address social needs or societal problems in new ways.

By addressing market and government failures and coupling capitalism with social purpose, social entrepreneurs also develop new business models ranging from non-profit to for-profit that shape cost-effective, sustainable and scalable innovations with proven impact. For example, they – like Specialisterne – work with people that governments have been unable to reach effectively with basic public welfare services. Or they – like the Institute of OneWorld Health – provide access to products and services to markets where business does not operate because the risks are too great and financial rewards too few.[45]

With their frontrunning ways of creating value, social entrepreneurs show us how to tackle economic, social and environmental challenges in new ways. And because they are uninhibited by the biases, standard operating procedures, bureaucracy, cultures, strategic commitments and other rigidities common in established organizations, they constitute an important test and learning centre. Every social (business) venture – whether it succeeds or fails – is an important experiment for developing and trying out new models and solutions.[36]

Apple's homage to the Crazy Ones

Here's to the crazy ones. The misfits. The rebels. The trouble-makers. The round pegs in the square holes. The ones who see things differently. They're not fond of rules, and they have no respect for the status quo. You can quote them, disagree with them, glorify or vilify them. But the only thing you cannot do is ignore them. Because they change things. They push the human race forward. And while some may see them as the crazy ones, we see genius. Because the people who are crazy enough to think they can change the world, are the ones who do.

Think Different. Apple commercial, created by TBWA Chiat/Day, Los Angeles (1998)

The field of social entrepreneurship, in other words, constitutes 'society's department for research and development' which businesses and governments can use as a source of inspiration and market intelligence for prototyping new products, services or even entirely new industries. It holds a corps of ground-breaking pioneers that play a catalytic role by kickstarting systemic changes, preparing the ground for tomorrow's markets and promoting new logics in business and society. They push society forward by providing aspirational trails on the map of future sustainability-oriented companies.

In a nutshell, social entrepreneurs hold what the founder of the World Economic Forum, Klaus Schwab, believes is the key to sustainable capitalism: reasonable profits as opposed to maximising profits. Or what Muhammad Yunus calls 'the missing piece of the capitalist system' – the second half of the currently incomplete structure of capitalism that fosters cooperation and community, reconciles markets and meaning and bridges profit and purpose. They are the counterparts of classic capitalism, and are paving the way for a sustainable market economy. Social entrepreneurship *is* the new (business) paradigm.

Responsible business 2.0
– from CSR to CSI and the four enabling Cs

'We operate on the core theory, on the belief that doing well and doing good are not separate ideas: they are inseparable ideas. That, in fact, they are inextricably linked and that everything we do, every business decision we make, every strategy we promulgate, every speech we make, or every pair of boots or shoes that we ship, have to be the embodiment of commerce and justice, and that's a different model.'[46]

Jeff Swartz

'We believe that the leading global companies of 2020 will be those that provide goods and services and reach new customers in ways that address the world's major challenges – including poverty, climate change, resource depletion, globalization, and demographic shifts.'[47]

This is the manifesto for tomorrow's global business by the World Business Council for Sustainable Development (WBCSD), a CEO-led global association of some 200 companies from more than 30 countries and 20 major industrial sectors, dealing exclusively with objectives for bridging business and sustainable development. Amongst its members are companies like Novo Nordisk, Grundfos, Unilever, General Electric and CEMEX – all described in Chapter 1 as cases in point of how companies can differentiate themselves by putting innovation and sustainability at the core of their business thinking. Just like many social (business) entrepreneurs they have realized the potential in turning unaddressed development challenges into innovative solutions and value-creating enterprises.

The concept of companies voluntarily integrating social and environmental concerns into their business operations and in interaction with their stakeholders – commonly referred to as CSR – is, however, still under development.

Many corporate acts of responsibility have been and still are nice-to-have 'add-ons' to the core business with initiatives ranging from cause promotions and cause-related marketing to community volunteering and corporate philanthropy, managed by the departments for public relations, human resources or marketing. As a result, there are still those who perceive CSR as an altruistic liability to the bottom line or a risk factor that needs to be managed.

In 2005 the concept of CSR was challenged when international news magazine *The Economist* published a critical editorial, questioning initiatives meant to further CSR in private companies. The growing support for CSR, *The Economist* argued, was 'based on a faulty – and dangerously faulty – analysis of the capitalist system' which serves public interest by driving high living standards in the West. So why not let corporate leaders focus on what their stakeholders pay them for – and leave social and economic policy to governments?[48]

But as the world grows smaller and stakeholder demands grow bigger – and as the MeWe generation of new leaders become vice presidents and CEOs – CSR is moving from a philanthropic conception of responsible capitalism into a new version of CSR, which is placed at the very core of business strategy. Indeed in some cases at the very core purpose of the business.

Only three years later, *The Economist* published a special report which marked a clear new stance on the responsible business agenda. This time the report featured numerous examples of large companies like Marks & Spencer, Walmart, Coca-Cola and PepsiCo changing the way they work by embracing purpose as well as performance with products that 'contribute positively and responsibly to human civilization', as PepsiCo's CEO Indra Nooyi put it.[49]

Like an increasing number of other companies, these featured companies believe that CSR offers clear business benefits. To them, the 21st century business of business is still business. But the rules of *how* to stay in business have changed, and they are responding with attempts to reconfigure their DNA as pure profit seekers through responsible business actions.

Traditional business models are consequently being stretched. And with the reinforcing impact of the economic crisis, some of them are being stretched to a breaking point where business as usual is no longer an option. Many business executives believe that growth – perhaps even survival – will depend on fundamental changes. Not in terms of developing new products or services, but in terms of *how* business is done. Consequently many of them are already focusing their efforts on business model innovations. In fact, they experience significantly better operating margin growth than their competitors because of this.[50] Business model innovation is the new route to competitive advantage.

The many examples in Chapters 1 and 2 show that pressures and expectations of business engagement in global development and responsibility issues are already high – and that the business opportunities are consequently many and diverse. In the new business paradigm sustainable value creation constitutes a competitive advantage, a valuable source of innovation and driver of future business – it is something that lies at the very heart of the social entrepreneurship mindset. In short, *The Great Trade-off Illusion* coined by Stuart Hart (and referred to in Chapter 1) is therefore being replaced by *The Great Business Opportunity*.

The evolution of CSR

That economy and humanism can – or rather must – go hand in hand is something that challenges world views in both the social and capitalistic camps. Is CSR shrewd marketing to give unscrupulous companies a halo effect, or is it just a sophisticated way of giving – pure philanthropy just in a new wrapping?

As former IBM executive and expert in sustainable business strategies, Bob Willard, observes, there are 'groups that believe that all this talk about corporate sustainability and CSR is some type of socialist conspiracy, so to speak. They believe it's all about giving additional power to the NGOs of the world.'[51]

Adapters to the responsible business ethos, however, come along different routes. Some companies have a reactive, risk management approach and arrive by way of regulatory threat or compliance, scandal or crisis. They view CSR as a necessary licence to operate and believe that complying with regulatory requirements will sufficiently benefit society – so-called *compliance CSR*.

Other companies are shaped by their founder or CEO's personal passion and ethical values, and may engage in philanthropic activities as well as business-related altruism in the name of enlightened self-interest. They view CSR not only as good business but as the right way to do business – so-called *conviction CSR*.

And yet others have a proactive, business development approach and arrive by a logical process of reasoning and analysis by linking solutions to society's problems or needs to their business. They view CSR as a good business opportunity – so-called *strategic CSR.*

The international carpet manufacturer Interface is a prime example of the evolution of CSR. In search of inspiration for a speech on the company's environmental vision, which was non-existent at the time, founder and chairman, Ray Anderson, felt a 'spear in the chest' when, in 1994, he read environmentalist Paul Hawken's book *The Ecology of Commerce.* Anderson's moment of truth kickstarted the company's *Mission Zero* journey, which has moved Interface from no CSR or compliance CSR to conviction CSR and strategic CSR. Over time, this has fundamentally changed the way Interface does business, putting the company at the forefront of the new business revolution.

Interface's European CEO, Lindsey Parnell, who worked in the carpet industry when Interface entered the European market, recalls: 'My experience of sustainability back in the 1990s was in the shape of a couple of A4 pages that were kept for forward-thinking customers who might ask about our policies. It didn't go deeper than that. In 1998 the company I worked in was bought by Interface, and the first thing that struck me was how actively engaged and enthusiastic people inside the company were, while others in the industry still saw environmental issues as a soft issue without relevance to the business, a cost pressure and something they had to comply with.'

For those who have started with a predominantly defensive corporate stance, the learning costs have, in many cases, been high.

Coca-Cola and Pepsi, for example, were, in 2003, targeted by a study from an NGO, the Center for Science and Environment (CSE), which alleged that samples of the companies' drinks in India tested high for pesticide residue. The reputations of both companies were hit hard, and in a rare moment of solidarity the two soft drink giants teamed up to attack the NGO at a joint press conference. But this defensive move proved insufficient and annual sales continued to plummet. Finally, the two giants publicly outlined social and environmental initiatives like conserving water resources. Among other things, Coca-Cola now has a water preservation scheme in place with the Worldwide Fund for Nature (WWF).[52]

The value of a company's reputation is, in other words, high – and a bad reputation is more likely than ever to negatively affect the company's bottom line. Concerns about ethics, economy, reputation and innovation are therefore now the most common drivers for CSR as opposed to risk reduction or improving relationships with governmental authorities.[53]

American investor and billionaire Warren Buffett once stated that it takes 20 years to build a reputation and five minutes to ruin it and, knowing this, you will do things differently. Sportswear company Nike experienced this first hand after being accused of child labour, low wages and unreasonable work hours in sweatshops run by the company's suppliers. This blow to Nike's reputation fundamentally changed its business strategy.

Initially, CSR was integrated into Nike's business system with Sustainability Directors as well as a Nike Compliance Team of more than 80 employees who ensure that the working conditions in its more than 700 factories are in line with standards and regulations. Nike even became the first major brand to publicly disclose the names and addresses of the factories in its global supply chain.

Over the past three years Nike has, however, started to move beyond corporate responsibility and into what it calls 'Sustainable Business and Innovation', integrating sustainability principles and practices into every aspect of its business – design, developing sustainable materials, rethinking processes and advocating systemic change in the footwear, apparel and equipment industries. And to measure its progress, Nike has set ambitious long-term targets and reports on its performance. As Nike states on its website, 'success relies on our ability to transition into the sustainable economy'.[54]

In sum, in the new world economy compliance CSR is no longer sufficient. Reactive methods like lobbyism, PR, marketing or other cosmetic measures can no longer stand alone. Investing time, money and involving people in sustainability practices is essential, whatever the motivation of business may be. Which is why CSR in its new version has been labelled Corporate Sustainability and Responsibility, with intertwined strands of economic sustainability and financial responsibility, human sustainability and labour responsibility, social sustainability and community responsibility and environmental sustainability and moral responsibility.[55]

These perspectives on sustainability and innovation will change the way companies view the purpose of their business and how they map their future strategies.

New world CSR

Classic corporate philanthropy such as donations, sponsorship and volunteering creates social value. But if unrelated to the company's business, this will be the first aspect to suffer cutbacks in times of crisis because it is not viewed as a source of revenue.

By shifting from 'philanthropic CSR' as a distinct add-on activity to 'strategic CSR' with activities that complement – or maybe even become – the core of business, more value is added to both society and the company: externalities are internalized and corporate benefits range from improvement of the corporate brand, differentiation from competitors and increased operational efficiency to attraction and retention of employees, development of new (premium price) products and services and access to new markets and customer segments. In short, the in-built weaknesses of old world CSR are overcome.

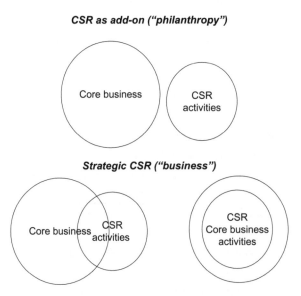

CSR approaches. *Figure by Tania Ellis*

For this very reason, British retail giant Marks & Spencer budgeted $215 million in 2007 for Plan A, an in-house five-year environmental programme which includes cutting the company's fuel and electricity use, charging customers for plastic bags, sourcing merchandise from green factories and farms and a dedicated 'Plan A champion' at every store.

The company has already saved 55 000 tons of CO_2 in a year, it has recycled 48 million clothes hangers, tripled sales of organic food and aims to convert over 20 million garments to Fairtrade cotton. And according to the company's sustainable development manager, Plan A is so far paying for itself because it has lowered the company's energy expenses as well as other costs.[56, 57]

This is what director of the Doughty Centre for Corporate Responsibility at Cranfield School of Management, David Grayson, and his co-author, managing director of the International Business Leaders Forum, Adrian Hodges, have dubbed *corporate social opportunity* (CSO) – i.e. commercially attractive activities which also advance environmental and/or social sustainability – in their book with the same title.

When CSR is built into business purpose and strategy, they argue, CSR becomes an exciting source of creativity that can lead to innovation in products and services, access to new or under-served markets as well as new business models in terms of how products are conceived, developed, marketed, distributed, financed, staffed, etc.

Thereby corporate social responsibility can be transformed into *corporate social innovation* (CSI) – a term that was first introduced in 1999 by Rosabeth Moss Kanter, who argued that companies should use social issues as a learning laboratory for identifying unmet needs and for developing solutions that create new markets, while also addressing societal concerns.[58]

The right strategic move based on <u>*value innovation*</u> – rather than racing to beat competitors by building a defensible position within the existing industry order – is what INSEAD business school professors Chan Kim and Renée Mauborgne call *the* key factor that helps companies create profitable growth in the future, a conclusion they base on a study of 150 strategic moves spanning more than a hundred years, 30 industries and companies of all sizes.

Kim and Mauborgne call it a *blue ocean strategy*, a metaphor for companies that create new, uncontested markets by creating true value based on customer needs, rather than focusing on battling over market shares in existing overcrowded markets that are 'bloody red oceans' with rivals fighting over a shrinking profit pool. In the case of CSO/CSI, *sustainable value creation* is the focal point for developing new blue ocean business opportunities.

Existing CSR activities – add-on or strategic – can be a good starting point: a survey amongst 60 small- to medium-sized European companies (in Europe, 99% of companies fall into this category) shows that those companies which tend to implement CSR are also the most innovative.[59]

Take employee-engaging CSR programmes like corporate volunteering, which are usually associated with a philanthropic add-on approach: the benefits are many and diverse, and studies already show that volunteering can be used by companies to develop business skills including decision making, problem solving, negotiating and leadership skills.[60] If linked to business strategy, corporate volunteering can be leveraged to use as field research to develop potential CSI-based products, services or business models, because it puts the company in closer touch with potential customer needs or new potential marketplaces.

Benefits of *Corporate Volunteering*		
For company	**For employees**	**For NGO/society**
Increases and improves public image and reputation.	Contributes to employee's professional and personal development by expanding their foundation of experience.	Improves life quality in (local) community by supporting solutions to social problems.
Corporate branding	*Personal development*	*Social value*
Improves employee team work, work morale, productivity, engagement, retention, performance, loyalty.	Increases interaction between employees in different departments and levels of the company.	Increases number of volunteers and supply of talents/competences in (local) community
Knowledge and competences	*Cross-organizational cooperation*	*More hands*
Increases corporate competitiveness in connection with, among other things, talent recruitment.	Improves employee initiatives, teamwork, social competences and cooperative skills.	Enables exchange of competences and knowledge between private companies and organizations.
Employer branding	*Empowerment, pride*	*More competent heads*
Increases innovation of e.g. new products,services		Increases innovation of e.g. new products, services
(Corporate) Social Innovation		*(Corporate) Social Innovation*

The benefits of corporate volunteering. *Modelled after the United Nations Development Programme's table on benefits of corporate volunteerism and further developed by Tania Ellis.*

Adding to the jungle of definitions, a new term has recently surfaced: *corporate social entrepreneurship* (CSE), i.e. the process of extending the company's domain of competence and corresponding opportunity set through innovative leveraging of resources, both within and outside its direct control, aimed at the simultaneous creation of economic and social value so these returns are complementary and synergetic rather than competing.[46]

Cases of corporate social entrepreneurship usually tend to fall into different stages of development, ranging from remote arms-length development to full integration with core business, and with focus, ranging from today's risks to tomorrow's opportunities.[61]

For example, Hindustan Unilever's Shakti initiative is run out of its core business; Coca-Cola's Water Stewardship Initiative is blurring the boundaries but firmly connected to core strategy; what began as the Patrimonio Hoy bottom-of-the pyramid project has led to a new business segment at CEMEX; and what was originally created as a pilot funded jointly by Vodafone and the UK Department for International Development led to the M-PESA mobile money transfer service which is opening up potential new markets, as we saw in Chapter 1.

So existing companies can, on the one hand, gain an advantage by creating sustainable value innovations which build on their strengths. But, on the other hand, most companies are designed to support and ensure the success of their existing business models which equals in-built limitations as to how radical the innovations can be. It is a challenge for them to disrupt themselves.

For companies to accelerate their CSR journeys and move into CSO/CSI/CSE they must therefore adopt an entrepreneurial mindset and cultivate an entrepreneurial environment that enables fundamental organizational transformation.[46]

Reinventive businesses

The blue ocean strategy of Danish insulin producer Novo Nordisk emerged in the 1980s when the company shifted its historical attention from doctors as key influencers to the users themselves. This shift transformed Novo Nordisk from insulin producer to diabetes treatment provider and led to the invention of the user-friendly NovoPen that gave the company a long-standing market lead. To counter the hassle and social stigmatism that diabetes patients felt from using the traditional insulin needles and syringes, the NovoPen, which resembles a fountain pen with an in-built injection needle, insulin and dosage mechanism, has improved the life quality of millions of diabetics worldwide. Since then, as mentioned in Chapter 1, the multinational has taken yet another major strategic shift by moving away from 'sick care' and taking a more progressive view of 'healthcare'.

The former textile company Vestergaard Frandsen, which used to produce work clothes and uniforms for the Scandinavian market, is another company that has successfully reinvented its business by building core activities around corporate social innovation.

While the pressure from low-priced textile manufacturers in China, Pakistan and India was building at the beginning of the 1990s, Vestergaard Frandsen partnered with former US president Jimmy Carter's Global 2000 guinea worm eradication programme to develop the Pipe Filter, a plastic pipe with a stainless steel mesh that filters out guinea worm larvae from contaminated water. The result: with a very simple water filter as the cornerstone in the programme, guinea worm-related diseases are now on the brink of eradication. In fact, guinea worm disease is poised to become only the second disease in history to be eradicated and the first without the use of a vaccine. This was the turning point for Vestergaard Frandsen.

'We found out that, one: we could use our textile skills in developing health products, two: this is where the highest margins were, three: we were unique – we had no competition. So we decided to split our portfolio into generic and non-generic products,' explains the founder's grandson, an entrepreneur by heart and mind and today the CEO of the Group, Mikkel Vestergaard Frandsen.

Today Vestergaard Frandsen's entire business is built on developing textiles and inventing technological breakthroughs in the field of disease control (for example the earlier-described LifeStraw) for the world's most vulnerable people. They have found that this niche holds huge market potential and is indeed good business. And although the company originally had no explicit social mission, the positive effects of doing business to promote a humanitarian purpose have, over time, transformed the mindset of the company as well.

'When you realize that you are saving the lives of hundreds of thousands, that's when you start to understand the responsibility that your product innovations carry with them – that the purpose of what we are doing reaches far beyond making a profit, which is actually the very reason why we are able to attract the best people,' argues Mikkel Vestergaard Frandsen, who firmly believes that serving a humanitarian purpose and making a profit are not mutually exclusive: 'Doing good is linked to our brand equity, to our R&D, to basically everything in the company. So when times get tough, we can never cut away the humanitarian purpose as other companies with CSR-programmes may have to do. If we chip away at our 'profit for a purpose' approach, we chip away at our future.'

Greenwash or clean conscience?

When old world logics meet new world practices paradoxes also emerge. The concept of 'green munitions', with biodegradable plastics for missiles, 'reduced smoke grenades' and 'quieter warheads' from the weapons industry is a case in point.

'Weapons are going to be used and when they are, we try to make them as safe for the user as possible, to limit the collateral damage and to impact as little as possible on the environment,' is the argument of director of corporate social responsibility at munitions and defence systems manufacturer British Aerospace (BAE).[62]

At the same time new actors are continuing to jump on the sustainability bandwagon. Take the recent pledge to green energy and organic foods by the bête noire of the American retail family, Walmart, which is still struggling with public attacks and accusations of discriminatory and unfair labour practices, including its minimum wages, resistance to union representation and dominant effect on small local businesses.

With its business-related sustainability initiatives like the construction of new stores that are 25% to 30% more energy efficient, boosting the sales of energy-efficient lightbulbs by giving them more shelf space, announcing plans for a sustainability index that will rate its 100 000 suppliers on issues like energy use and labour and selling more organically grown food, Walmart has – not surprisingly – been accused of *greenwashing* (a portmanteau of *green* and *whitewash* used to describe deceptive use of green PR or green marketing).

Walmart's CSR efforts are, however, more than mere window dressing if you ask CEO, Lee Scott, and the company's motivation is simple: 'We are not being altruistic. This is a business philosophy, not a social philosophy,' he explained to *TIME* magazine some years ago, while acknowledging that the new business strategy had also been launched partly to shield Walmart from bad press.[63]

But any motivation is good motivation if you focus solely on the end-results: when the world's largest retail chain with more than two million employees in over 7000 department stores worldwide and over 100 million customers every week, for example, asks its truckers to shut off their engines when stopping for a break as a part of its pro-environmental policy changes, this not only yields estimated savings of $25 million a year – it also has a positive impact on the environment. Just like the retail giant's other efforts have improved energy efficiency not only in its stores, but in its supply chain, convincing its suppliers to reduce the amount of packaging they use, enabling them to put more on delivery trucks, which has meant fewer deliveries and less gas consumed. So who cares if they are doing it to improve their image or bottom line?

Nevertheless, it is examples like Walmart and British Aerospace that mark a dividing line: companies that one investor would dismiss as unethical are models of change to others. Insiders from the investment world estimate a 50–50 split around, for example, Walmart, with those who do not want to own a company which they are uncomfortable with because of the way it treats its people, and those who believe that the company is profitable, well run and is doing things that they want to reward by investing.[64]

So, on the one hand, critics like environmentalist Paul Hawken deride the regulation of the so-called 'sustainable funds', pointing out that 90%

of Fortune 500 companies are included in such funds as leaders of a sustainable economy, including American weapons manufacturer Halliburton and pesticide and biotech producer Monsanto. 'The term "socially responsible investing" (SRI) is so broad, it is meaningless,' Hawken argues.[65]

Whereas, on the other hand, pragmatists like long-time sustainable business advocate and economist Hazel Henderson argue that SRI is an incremental approach and needs the time and space to experiment. The first step is, in other words, not perfection but to put social or environmental issues on the business agenda in the first place as opposed to not addressing them at all. As Henderson determines: this is a *movement* for social change.[65]

Nevertheless, the pressure for truly and fully sustainable practices continues – and sustainability pioneers are not spared either. For although greenwash is more likely to occur in companies without cultures based on honesty, transparency and trust or in companies that are in transition with some parts of the business still occupied with old world industries or practices there is also the risk of unintentional greenwashing because of lack of awareness, the temptation to jump the gun before the aspiration has been fully implemented or because all proof points are not yet in place.

This happened to Seventh Generation, a founding B Corporation member and pioneering US brand of household and personal care products like 100% recycled fibre paper towels, organic cotton hygiene products and natural cleaning and laundry products. Its worst nightmare came true when it was met with headlines like '"Organic" and "Natural" consumer products found contaminated with cancer-causing chemical'. A report had shown that the company's dish liquid contained detectable levels of the contaminate 1,4-dioxane, a by-product of a process used to improve the degreasing agent in detergents, although Seventh Generation had managed to strip the dioxane to minute levels that were fifty times lower than other so-called 'natural' brands.

Seventh Generation's mistake was excluding its consumers and key stakeholders from its hundreds of meetings and conversations about how to purge dioxane from its products. 'We ran many of our own tests and worked closely with suppliers and manufacturers. But we didn't take that one essential step:

to share our trials and tribulations with everyone who wanted to weigh in, express concerns, ask questions, and challenge our progress. ... The problem wasn't highlighted on our website or detailed in our earlier corporate responsibility report. And so, we failed,' Seventh Generation's CEO, Jeffrey Hollender admits in the company's 2007 *Corporate Consciousness Report*. After the dioxane story, Seventh Generation has consequently shared its work-in-progress challenges by, among other things, using the forum section of its website to engage consumers.

Interface CEO Lindsey Parnell offers another example of how to overcome the paradoxical pitfalls of sustainable business from the time when the company worked on producing carpets from polylatic acid, a product made from corn as an alternative to nylon. 'It looked really good, it would reduce our dependence on oil and at the end of its life it would compost. But then we found out that it was made from American genetically modified corn, which they don't mind in the USA but are much more sensitive about in Europe. So we took the debate to Forum For the Future and Greenpeace to ask what they thought. They appreciated what we were doing to reduce dependence on oil, but could not approve of the usage of GM. So now we are working with a European company that is trying to make it from sugar beet.'

These cases show that sustainability efforts can be not only rewarding but also risky business. With sustainability it is, however, not important to be perfect, but to be humble, open and honest about doubts and errors – and to proactively inform and involve the organization as well as the outside world in the long-term sustainability plan as well as of the shortcomings. Because no matter how well-run or heart-driven a company may be, this will never prevent it from making mistakes.

How to get started

There is no one formula for sustainable value creation, partly because it is a journey more than an end-state, but also because it depends on the company's culture, ambitions, market challenges, etc.

In addition to the already numerous guidelines for reporting, ESG frameworks, certifications and standards mentioned in Chapter 1, other guidelines and principles for sustainable business success in the new economic world order are emerging.

For example, The British think-tank Demos has defined the shift from CSR to CSI through 'Five Ideals',[66] David Grayson and Adrian Hodges have developed the 'Seven Step Model for CSO' for companies that want to leverage their CSR activities into new business opportunities,[67] the white paper 'A New Mindset for Corporate Sustainability' introduces ten steps that will turn companies into 'sustainability-driven innovators'[22] and the Danish Ministry of Economic and Business Affairs has developed the Ideas Compass (www.ideascompass.dk) to guide small- and medium-sized companies in developing CSI.

Other methodologies and tools now seeing the light of day include sustainability management systems like *Total Responsibility Management* (TRM), used by, among others, UK retailer Sainsbury's. It is an explicit parallel to Total Quality Management involving systematic approaches for setting and managing goals and key performance indicators of responsibility, which enable companies to respond more explicitly to all kinds of new external pressures and open up innovation opportunities.[22]

Taking a fresh look at the company's operations through sustainability glasses by using the Life Cycle Analysis (LCA) methodology to review the manufacturing process piece by piece – including product development, sourcing and assembly, distribution, use and end of life – for innovation opportunities is another tool that some companies choose to use. At Interface, for example, they use a sustainability scorecard rooted in LCA to score all their products and development initiatives that are gathered in their so-called 'Innovation Pipeline'.

And the Sustainable Balanced Scorecard, a broader version of the traditional Balanced Scorecard, helps companies to achieve strategic alignment by linking strategic sustainability objectives with measures and actions.

Reviewing these guidelines as well as the practices of current champions, there are some enabling factors that recur and which I have compiled into four essential cornerstones: *The Four Cs* of Clear Purpose, Corporate Engagement, Collaborative Co-creation and Clear Communication. They can be used as guidelines on the road to sustainable business success.

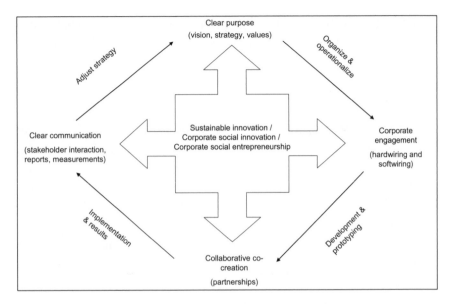

The Four Cs: the four cornerstones of sustainable innovation
Figure by Tania Ellis

Clear purpose

One important key is to select social and/or environmental activities to match the company's business competences and reflect its culture, values, challenges and business strategy. For example, by identifying some of the global forces for change (political, economic, social, technological, environmental), looking into changing stakeholder needs and expectations on societal, sector or organizational levels, and examining in more detail whether they represent risks or corporate social opportunities.

This may imply a new vision of business outcomes, a more proactive role towards sustainability and asking fundamental questions like 'Where can we add value?' rather than 'Where can we make money?' Also, 'What does sustainability mean to our business?' and 'How genuinely committed are we to creating sustainable value?' Is it to improve public relations, win over competitors, develop new product lines or to ultimately transform the whole business in the long term? And, because businesses must plan for the long term in a climate still dominated by quarter-to-quarter thinking, equally important is 'How much are we willing to invest before there is a return?'←

Consequently, this first enabling C can only happen if company gate-keepers – CEOs, CFOs and board members – give permission to and lead the change.

Corporate engagement

The vision and strategy must also be accompanied by changes in the company's 'hardwiring' as well as 'softwiring', i.e. with accompanying structures, processes, performance and measurement systems in support of the sustainability ambitions as well as communications, employee and leadership development programmes designed to encourage sustainable value creation thinking, skills and practices.

Ideally, it should permeate the DNA of the entire company, so it is not something companies are 'doing' but something they 'are'. Therefore, it is important to involve not just CSR-responsible employees but the entire company across all divisions of the organization, e.g. sales, marketing, finance, so they can recognize and understand their respective economic, social and environmental impacts and can become co-creators of sustainable value design and implementation in a systematic and integrated approach. This can be underpinned by sustainability ambassador programmes or cross-departmental/cross-hierarchical committees that enable voluntary change agents to spend time and develop ideas and initiatives together and to assist in, for example, sustainability training delivery, awareness campaigns or review and implementation follow-ups within departments and functions.

In addition to top management, catalysts include vice presidents responsible for, for example, sustainable development and/or corporate responsibility, human resource managers, external consultants – or dedicated social *intra*preneurs.

Collaborative co-creation

Sustainable value creation also implies that external stakeholders – online as well as offline – are turned into potential strategic partners by inviting them to join the innovation process. They could be actors on the hybrid, collective intelligence, activism or conscious consumption markets (described in Chapter 2) who are involved through open innovation processes or open dialogues. Not only because they hold unique knowledge that can renew and improve business activities, but also because they can infuse mainstream companies with new mindsets, values and energy.

Potential collaborators include citizens and local communities with grass-roots initiatives; social entrepreneurs that may have already developed the required solutions; cultural innovators, opinion-makers or special consultants within, for example, social science disciplines that can provide ideas and insights into the selected challenge; other companies – even competitors – with complementary core competencies; networks, organizations or bodies dedicated to sustainable business; NGOs, governmental organizations or academic institutions with specialist knowledge as well as other cross-sector alliances.

This third enabling C requires technologies as well as people inside the company with relevant specialist and networking skills that enable them to connect with others and build successful partnerships.

Clear communication

Working with sustainability is a learning journey, and we will never know what stumbling blocks we may need to cross along the way. What may appear sustainable today may turn out to be unsustainable tomorrow. Navigating the waters of social and economic value creation may also attract attention from critics and sceptics because compromises may need to be made in the short term to achieve long-term sustainability goals. Openness, transparency and clear communication of both successes and failures towards internal as well as external stakeholders in order to build trust and mutual understanding is therefore critical.

But communication is more than advertising to sell a product or traditional PR-driven communication with glossy or defensive messages. It also implies involving the outside world. If, in other words, traditional communication channels are combined with, or even turned into, interactive activities, it will be possible to react quickly to mistakes as well as to harvest potential ideas and feedback from stakeholders outside the company.

Communication channels include annual reports, non-financial accounts, corporate websites, PR and publications, social media like blogs and other online forums. But also books, speeches, articles and public engagements by key people in the company, including the CEO, are important for authenticity and credibility.

The stress test of sustainable business

In 2001 the British business thinker, John Elkington, who has been described as 'a dean of the corporate responsibility movement for three decades', foresaw in his book *The Chrysalis Economy* that in the 21st century the world would have to experience an economic meltdown in order to be able to rebuild a sustainable economy – and was heading into one. Today, Elkington believes that the recent economic crisis will drive new rules for the global economy as a range of economic, social, environmental and governance priorities into core corporate strategy and business models.

Before the credit crunch, companies which proactively designed environmental, social and governance practices to create sustained competitive advantage appeared to have a stronger financial performance than those which did not. For example, a 2007 Goldman Sachs study of corporate responsibility leaders in six industrial sectors showed that they had outperformed the overall stock market by 25% over a two-year period, and within their own sectors 72% of the companies had outperformed their peers.[22] The reason for this, according to a number of experts, is that corporate responsibility is a proxy for good management – and good management is *the* prime indicator of superior financial performance.[68]

But in 2008, almost a third of global companies surveyed by Business for Social Responsibility, a global network of firms with an interest in CSR, said that they expected to cut their spending on sustainability as a result of the crisis, which would, at first glance, confirm CSR critics' belief that this is a trend that only thrives during economic booms.

Nevertheless, the economic crisis – as it turns out – is an effective way of separating the sheep from the goats by shaking out unsustainable, unrooted or greenwashed·CSR efforts while showcasing the longevity of sustainable business models. In fact, a recent A.T. Kearney analysis of 99 companies on the Dow Jones Sustainability Index and Goldman Sachs's SUSTAIN focus list revealed that during the current economic slowdown, companies that show a 'true' commitment to sustainability appear to outperform their industry peers in the financial markets.[69]

Europe's biggest social bank, Triodos Bank, is a case in point. While large commercial banks were either nationalized, put into administration or were forced to ask their shareholders and governments for money to make up for their losses in the midst of the economic crisis in 2008–9, Triodos Bank experienced renewed growth and an unprecedented interest in its sustainable approach to banking which builds on financing companies, institutions and projects that add cultural value and benefit people and the environment with the support of depositors and investors who want a sustainable society. The bank has, in fact, generated continuous growth of 25% annually over the past two decades with assets under management of almost $5 billion; it has close to 200 000 customers and almost 10 000 sustainable businesses and projects in its loan book.[70] Our growth is faster than foreseen; we continue to thrive despite the financial crisis, and have no shortfall of capital. This year we have grown faster than ever before, with more than an 18% increase in our customer numbers since January 2009. If nothing else, the financial crisis has taught us that it pays to choose sustainable,' says Triodos Bank's CEO, Peter Blom.[71]

Feminine and masculine values

The combined values of economics and humanism constitute what are also classified as so-called 'masculine' and 'feminine' values – with, among other things competition, linear and rational thinking on the one side and cooperation, holistic and intuitive thinking on the other.[72, 73]

The late Anita Roddick, founder of The Body Shop and a global role model for social entrepreneurs, described her personal leadership style like this: 'I run my company according to feminine principles – principles of caring, making intuitive decisions, not getting hung up on hierarchy, having a sense of work as being part of your life not separate from it, putting your labour where your love is, being responsible to the world in how you use your profits, recognising the bottom line should stay at the bottom.'[74]

In Iceland, which suffered a major collapse during the economic crisis in 2008 and where the collective understanding is that it was 'young men in black suits' who caused the crisis,[75] there is much talk about a new culture and new values. In a way it is now operating as the world's 'credit crunch lab' with women at the forefront of the clean-up that are determined to reinvent business and society by injecting values of openness, fairness and social responsibility, including its new female prime minister, Johanna Sigurdardottir, a higher number of female cabinet members and women bankers in charge of some of the collapsed banks that used to be governed by men.[76]

One of the few firms in the Icelandic finance sector that is actually turning a profit is Audur Capital – an innovative CSR-driven business that was set up by former managing director of the Iceland Chamber of Commerce, Halla Tómasdóttir, and former senior banking executive, Kristin Petursdóttir, just before the credit crunch.

At Audur, there's a simple recipe for success: 'We've brought greater female values into the financial world,' says Tómasdóttir and explains the company's five core feminine values:

> 'First, risk awareness: we will not invest in things we don't understand. Second, profit with principles – we like a wider definition so it is not just economic profit, but a positive social and environmental impact. Third, emotional capital. When we invest, we do an emotional due diligence – or check on the company – we look at the people, at whether the corporate culture is an asset or a liability. Fourth, straight talking. We believe the language of finance should be accessible, and not part of the alienating nature of banking culture. Fifth, independence. We would like to see women increasingly financially independent, because with that comes the greatest freedom to be who you want to be, but also unbiased advice.'[76]

This, of course, has nothing to do with men or women per se. In the business world there are also men exhibiting softer, collaborative and intuitive behaviour. Howard Schultz, founder of CSR-oriented coffeehouse chain Starbucks, describes his own leadership style as 'sensitive, passionate and responsive', which is also reflected in one of his mantras: 'People aren't interested in how much you know. It's how much you care.'[74] Add to him the many New Pioneers that are bridging economics and humanism and you will find similar traits of how both feminine and masculine values go hand in hand. The 21st century is the time for 'women to reclaim their voices and men their hearts', as feminist Jane Fonda once put it. It is sustainability made manifest at all levels.

Long-term efforts and future levers

A sustainable business is not a guarantee against losses. But for first-movers it means a better chance of survival. 'We have reduced volume and decreased our sales and costs, but we are still quite profitable, and that is due in part to the efficiency in our factories and the power of our brand, thanks to our Zero Mission quest,' explains Interface CEO Lindsey Parnell, who also sees what effect the credit crunch is having on other mainstream companies. 'When I look around our industry some of our competitors are in really bad shape and not all can survive. Some of them had started working with sustainability but have had to integrate all these principles in a much shorter time frame than us, making the learning curve much steeper. And so, they are still very vulnerable. On the other hand, before the recession it was getting really embarrassing with all the companies jumping on the sustainability bandwagon with forward-looking claims and huge amounts of marketing. That has disappeared now.'

So for companies that have put stakes in the ground for their sustainability ambitions there is no way back. Turning back on sustainability will only damage their reputation and reduce their brand value. Now is the time for them to prove that their commitments are more than fair weather words motivated by short-termism. Meanwhile, the credit crunch is eating away at unprepared businesses. 'Innovate or die' appears to be the challenge faced by businesses today. The crisis is, in effect, driving a maturation of the entire CSR field and taking it to the next 2.0 level. It is opening up an opportunity to push the social entrepreneurship mindset and approach to profit making and problem solving into the mainstream.

Consequently, most of the reported cuts have so far been limited to activities peripheral to business interests, whereas activities involving the company's enlightened self-interest like Marks & Spencer's Plan A are on the rise. In May 2009, for example, General Electric introduced a $6 billion plan to increase profits in its healthcare division while broadening people's access to low-cost healthcare around the world. And confectionery makers Mars and Cadbury are both planning to increase the amount of cocoa they harvest from sustainable sources because it is good for the environment and will also relieve potential future shortages.[77]

So while charities and NGOs have been hit by cancelled or postponed corporate philanthropy commitments, the global imbalances are – just as Elkington foresaw – forcing their way into the core of business as market needs just waiting to be met.

Multinational household-products giant Unilever, for example, has felt the sting of global recession. Yet one part of Unilever's business is flourishing in the face of the crisis: the previously described Shakti programme operating at the bottom of the pyramid by hiring more than 40 000 Indian women to sell the company's products in their home villages. Initially designed to aid some of Unilever's poorest customers, the Shakti programme has turned out to be lucrative for the company, providing a reliable income even in a downturn. 'Because of the financial crisis this project has become even more important for us. If we want to continue to grow during difficult times, we will have to leverage this,' says Hemant Bakshi, Unilever executive director for customer development in Mumbai, India.[57]

Summing up, the fact that the current capitalist system is only half developed is reflected clearly in the emergence and subsequent development of CSR. CSR is therefore not a trend that will just fade away but rather an important first step and expression of a transition stage – a half-way house towards a renewed version of capitalism with business models that build on a purpose that goes beyond profit maximization and have sustainable development integrated into their core.

A business force for good
– the power of partnerships and converging fields

'Coming together is the beginning. Keeping together is progress. Working together is success.'

Henry Ford

Hardcore businesspeople have realized that they can increase their profits by incorporating social responsibility as a part of their business strategy, and heartcore idealists have recognized that the use of market methods gives them the opportunity to create even more social value. Both categories are moving in the same direction.

The blended value proposition of social, environmental and financial value all being parts of one essential value and therefore non-divisible is, in fact, the future way of thinking of value creation, as already promoted in CSR, social investing, venture philanthropy and indeed social entrepreneurship.[78]

Social entrepreneurs and big businesses each play their roles in the transformation of industries and markets toward sustainable development. Their seesaw interaction pushes transformation in different ways depending on the stage of development.

The small and relatively new social ventures with primary social/environmental objectives function as 'innovation labs' because they are able to identify unmet needs, develop solutions and utilize local resources in ways that can be transformed into new (business) opportunities or markets in unlikely places. The big, established companies with complementary social/environmental objectives function as 'accelerators' because they have volume, resources and complementary business skills that can refine or upscale the social business opportunities.

The new business revolution is, in other words, being driven both top-down from some of the world's largest companies and bottom-up from entrepreneurial activists and social change-makers. As a result, both are navigating in the crossfields between business and humanism, although they have different aims and motivation for doing so.

Although the respective motives for meeting both inner and outer globalization needs range from altruism to enlightened self-interest or pure profit-seeking, they are all contributing to an increasingly powerful 'force for good' that is not only changing the world – it is also changing the face of capitalism to a renewed version where profit is reconciled with our inner values.

Both are, however, mutually dependent on each other in order to become successful with their economic and social missions, because a top-down approach alone does not work, just like a bottom-up approach alone is not enough.

The needs

For mainstream companies it is no longer an automatic advantage to be big: in a highly connected world, small-scale actors – as we saw in Chapter 2 – have the capability to achieve large-scale impacts in ways that used to be reserved for companies that had the power to be globally dominant through scale, scope and closed system development.[35]

Instead, globally integrated enterprises must today develop 'glocal' solutions that are devised by global businesses *and* local entrepreneurs.[79] When global challenges on top of this are integrated into the strategic core of big business, with an emphasis on corporate social innovation, effective partnerships and co-creative innovation become key. Not only because of the need for local or specialized knowledge, but also because profit-driven companies often require a legitimising seal of approval that can hold up under public scrutiny.

In other words, progress in sustainable business requires authenticity, transparency and close interaction with concerned stakeholder groups like NGOs and investors, by involving users throughout the development process – and by collaborating with social entrepreneurs.

In fact, to maintain high performance and create renewed growth, smart mainstream companies bypass radical innovation by imitating and adapting rather than innovating to enter and dominate new markets – they apply what has been dubbed the *fast-second strategy*.[80] Pioneering entrepreneurs are, in other words, not necessarily those who are able to turn new markets into mass markets.

The field of social entrepreneurship, on the other hand, is, to some extent, still in its nascent stages, dominated by young, small and vulnerable businesses that suffer from resource constraints and need professional business tools and skills to ensure their quantitative and/or qualitative growth and longevity.

But in other ways the field of social entrepreneurship has also grown out of its baby shoes and reached a crossroads with proven concepts of social value creation and effectiveness that now need to be taken to the next level, as we have seen with cases like Stonyfield Farm and The Body Shop. Many innovative approaches and a wealth of new models that have emerged over the last ten years have not yet been fully explored, and therefore remain in their infancy awaiting a 'quantum push' to exhibit widespread benefit.[81]

There is, in short, a need to create a critical mass of better and stronger social business ventures. The fundamental questions for social entrepreneurs to consider are therefore how to acquire resources, how to build successful organizations and how to build support to gain maximum social impact.

So first, they need to build legitimacy for their ideas and approaches, next they must find ways of gaining access to people and organizations that will embrace and help leverage their innovative approaches and then they must attract the necessary resources to develop, test, refine and scale their initiatives.[17]

And this requires social support in terms of efficient networks of suppliers, customers, investors, etc. who can raise awareness and gain access to resources and skills.[30]

In fact, cooperation and partnerships will infuse all parties involved with new perspectives and new knowledge that may lead to better results than they would be able to create individually.

So, by joining forces big mainstream companies may gain access to new markets or new product and service innovations or even new business models that build on corporate social innovation more easily and at greater speed, because the smaller social ventures may have spent years or even decades designing, testing and implementing their social innovations as well as building a relationship of trust, local knowledge and credibility amongst their users or customers.

The social ventures, on the other hand, may leverage their innovations with less risk and may release extra capacity to either replicate or even start up more new social ventures because the big companies may not only provide management skills and resources but also identify potential spill-over effects and synergies between initiatives that the entrepreneurs themselves may not recognize because they are so focused on their existing innovations.

In other words, partnerships open up the opportunity for each party to concentrate on what they do the best, and on what is their primary purpose. The key is to have operationally separate structures that are devoted to maximising both economic and social benefits, and that cooperate to create a complete business model.[82]

The benefits of partnerships between mainstream business and social entrepreneurs

Contributions from Mainstream Business	Contributions from Social Entrepreneurs
Access to strategic, managerial, technical assets and skills, e.g. corporate volunteering	Specialist know-how, local knowledge, innovative ideas, motivation and immaterial fringe benefits (e.g. meaningful work)
Volume, upscaling, e.g. access to larger customer base, new markets, distribution channels	New products, services, customer groups, markets, business models
Increased awareness, PR, marketing	Positive image, storytelling
Redefine corporate philanthropy as 'social venture capital' to support early stage social ventures	Legitimacy, credibility, trust in (local) community
Outsource CSR tasks and social innovation (e.g. fulfilment of Millennium Goals)	Manage outsourced social tasks (e.g. Millennium Development Goals)
Nework contacts (e.g. policy-makers, executives, investors)	Network contacts (to grassroots, other social entrepreneurs, etc.)

Table by Tania Ellis

Three social business partnership categories

So how do we capture the full value of the economic, social and innovation potential that lies in this cross-section between mainstream business and social entrepreneurship?

Expert researchers Johanna Mair and Christian Seelos from IESE business school present three partnership models for global strategies that will serve corporate sustainable development needs while also serving society's need for innovation (1) integrated, (2) complementary, (3) symbiotic.

The first model is built on integrating resources to serve more people. Like the partnership between social business Aravind Eye Hospital and AuroLab, a commercial manufacturing company for affordable high quality lenses, who work together to treat as many cataract patients as possible at the lowest possible price. The result: delivery of annual eye examinations for two million patients and 220 000 sight-restoring operations. And although 47% of the patients are too poor to pay for anything, their health service partnership model earns a 60% profit which enables rapid capacity build up and replication in other countries.[83]

In the second model partnership is built around complementary services that provide mutual benefits. Like the Bangladeshi hybrid non-profit business, WasteConcern, which has succeeded in turning the problem of waste into a business opportunity through a composting scheme that provides organic fertilizer to poor farmers. To collect the waste – 4635 tons of waste is generated every day in the capital city Dhaka alone – it has created a door-to-door rickshaw van collection service for a small fee which covers both the drivers' and waste collectors' salaries. To ensure distribution of compost, WasteConcern has developed a partnership with local chemical fertilizer producer MAP Agro to whom WasteConcern sells the raw compost which is then enriched in MAP Agro's specially built compost nutrient enrichment plant before it is sold on to the farmers. Benefits: for the farmers the compost is an ideal substitute for chemical fertilizer because it is cheaper and reduces the need for it by 30%. It has reduced public agencies' need for land for landfill areas, increased public awareness of the hazards of crude waste dumping and has created employment. And the private companies gain access to a new stream of income by selling the compost. In 2006 WasteConcern ran 38 composting plants in 20 towns in Bangladesh, and the model is now being replicated in ten Asian and ten African cities.[84]

The third model is built on establishing a joint venture around a mutual area of interest. This is how, among others, Grameen Bank has succeeded in expanding its microfinance activities into, among other things, communications, healthcare, technology and nutritional foods with companies like Telenor, GE Healthcare, Intel and Danone to meet its overall vision of reducing poverty by providing business and employment opportunities.

The social business venture Grameenphone, for example, was established in 1997 in a partnership between Grameen Telecom Corporation (38%) – a non-profit sister concern of Grameen Bank – and Norwegian mobile phone company Telenor (62%), which recognized the huge business potential of only 2.5 million telephone lines (mobile and land combined) in Bangladesh, a country of 147 million people.

Today Grameenphone has over 23 million subscribers, more than 5000 full and temporary employees and another 100 000 people who earn a living from Grameenphone as dealers, retailers, scratch card outlets, suppliers, vendors, contractors and others. The revenue of $4.6 million already represents more than 15% of the company's total revenue.[22] Besides providing a livelihood Grameenphone has also provided crucial access to communications in remote areas with weak infrastructure and to rural people who cannot afford to own a telephone.

In the case of one of Grameen's other joint ventures, Grameen Danone Foods, a *Shakti Doi* yoghurt has been developed from pure full cream milk that contains protein, vitamins, iron, calcium, zinc and other micronutrients, sold at the equivalent of €0.05 (five cents) per cup. This innovation has also had a positive influence on Danone's use of containers in its mainstream business.

During his visit to Denmark's Roskilde Festival in 2009, Muhammad Yunus mentioned the Grameen effect on Danone's packaging policy: 'Danone was using plastic containers. We said "no, in the social business we want to use biodegradable containers", and they agreed to make them. There are lots of synergies like this that create value for both the social and commercial business.' Danone executive, Emmanuel Marchant agrees: 'This is not charity for us. This is about business and building our brand. The lessons we learnt when we had to get the price down, without compromising quality, and improve taste, are valuable across our business.'[85]

So if social entrepreneurs and mainstream businesses can overcome the potential barriers and difficulties that may follow because of, for example, differences in values between the partners, the amount of capital costs and resources needed to establish and manage the partnership and the patience, perseverance, time and effort that must be invested, such partnerships can result in a multitude of benefits for all involved.

Buy-in or sell-out?

Most successful large companies excel at business planning, allocation of capital and execution and improvement of existing products, but few are good at exploring significantly new ideas and radically different business approaches.[86] When pioneering social businesses, on the other hand, reach a certain size and volume they are often confronted with the choice between growing bigger or finding other ways in which to develop.

To the delight of hardcore capitalists – and contempt of many heartcore idealists – companies such as Ben & Jerry's, Stonyfield Farm and The Body Shop have explored one of the routes to growth by selling their businesses or parts of them to larger mainstream corporations.

The idealists have criticized the pioneers for selling out on their principles and for diluting the values behind their ethical brands. A critique that has been answered with the argument that with growth and profitability follows more strength and influence – that it enables them to continue their social mission and act like a kind of 'Trojan horse' in large corporate settings.

The 'Trojan horse' effect became particularly visible when ice cream idealists and founders of Ben & Jerry's, Ben Cohen and Jerry Greenfield, in 2000 conditioned their over $23 million deal with Unilever who were obliged to donate $5 million to anti-corporate campaign groups, one of which paradoxically staged a boycott of one of Unilever's largest customers, Walmart.[74] Nevertheless – although the sales contract ensured Ben & Jerry's its own board and management – the once-radical ice cream maker four years later admitted that it was 'beginning to look like the rest of corporate America'.[87]

For the incarnated environmentalist Gary Hirshberg, who, in 1983, founded Stonyfield Farm which was to become the USA's fastest growing and fourth biggest yoghurt producer with $330 million in annual sales, the 2001 takeover by French food giant Danone has been more uneventful. Danone owns 85% of Stonyfield Farm's stock, and the remaining 15% belong to the employees and Hirshberg himself, who is still CEO and chairman of the company. In 2009, *Business Week* awarded the company the accolade 'America's Most Promising Social Entrepreneur'.[88]

When The Body Shop went on the market, buyers did not exactly line up in spite of the company's more than 2000 shops and 77 million customers in 50 different markets. In the investment community, The Body Shop business was not considered lucrative enough. But L'Oreal, part-owned by Nestlé, decided to buy because it had seen the growth of both ethical and naturally based products in the cosmetics industry. (In 2006, the market for natural, organic and non-animal-tested cosmetics grew by 22%, reaching £386 million.[89])

And though The Body Shop came under fire for 'selling out' after the £652 million takeover in 2006, the company suffered no ethical losses by becoming part of a larger set-up, according to its director of global values, Jan Buckingham: 'I think what The Body Shop has done is to try and mainstream the whole idea of having social and environmental objectives as a part of your mission statement'.

Under the leadership of its late founder, Anita Roddick, The Body Shop succeeded in taking a high-profile political stance on environmental and human rights issues with in-store campaigns on causes like women's rights, climate change, homelessness and trade justice through Community Trade programmes with indigenous peoples and marginalized communities in developing countries.

According to Jan Buckingham, whose primary function is to ensure that the company does not compromise its values-based principles in the name of commerciality, The Body Shop's trading has remained healthy and the take-over has not had any limiting effect on its idealistic values and activist spirit. 'It's not in L'Oreal's interest to make The Body Shop look like everything else in their product portfolio,' Buckingham explains and mentions professional management training, branding skills, economies of scale in the supply chain and huge financial security (particularly in times of recession) as some of the positive impacts that the takeover has had on The Body Shop.

The Body Shop, on the other hand, has also had a positive influence on L'Oreal, although the two companies are by nature of business quite different. For example, their respective development teams are working closely on developing formulas and exchanging knowledge on recycling and packaging. The Body Shop mindset that what you do as an ingredient buyer has an impact on the agents you buy from has also led L'Oreal to initiate direct trading relationships with small suppliers. Retaining the social technology of The Body Shop is, in other words, a learning opportunity that can enrich the mainstream company's operations.

Losing intimate control of the company, a more formal set-up with suppliers and strains on customer relations are, however, some of the drawbacks of choosing this kind of growth rather than taking it more slowly and organically, warns Buckingham. 'We don't know whether the takeover has changed our customer profile noticeably, but we do know that there are people who just don't like big companies, and obviously you lose them if you choose to grow in the way that The Body Shop has,' she admits.

Clear communication is therefore just as essential as for mainstream businesses. For bought-out companies like The Body Shop, Ben & Jerry's and Stonyfield Farm the task is to prove that what they stand for, what they believe in and what they are trying to achieve is still at the top of their agenda. They have to prove that they are buying in, rather than selling out. They have to be much more transparent and back up their social and environmental claims. And they have to show that they are improving their parent companies, rather than being abused by them.[90]

Converging fields

With an accelerating convergence between what first-mover corporations are already doing, what mainstream companies are striving to do and what social entrepreneurs are showcasing in their field, there is a growing potential for fruitful 'cross-fertilization' through partnerships and upscaling of solutions.

The growth and impact of socially entrepreneurial and corporate social responsibility need not be mutually exclusive. And although effective social ventures are often described as small- to medium-sized, this does not prevent them from being large corporations, as we have seen in the cases of Stonyfield Farm and Ben & Jerry's. Just like large corporations can be socially innovative as we have seen in the cases of Vestergaard Frandsen, Unilever and Interface.

So while social entrepreneurs tug at heartstrings, large mainstream companies are also creating social value, although in each their own way. For instance, all the Grameen-related social businesses are already well on the way to fulfilling the vision of eradicating poverty by making a difference for millions of people. But when greenwash-labelled Walmart incorporates its environmental policies, this also has a significant impact with a rub-off effect on its millions of customers and thousands of suppliers as well as local communities.

This simple but hard logic of scale that stands together with the soft logic of values and innovative power is what is accelerating the current sustainable business revolution.

But the subtle – yet important – difference is still purpose and motive, which is closely linked to the innovative power of new solutions as well as perseverance. Because whilst commercial companies are, in many cases, still governed by quarter-to-quarter thinking, social entrepreneurs work with a more long-term goal and are willing to go much further with their endeavours before they pay off. The delicate balancing act is to stay focused on the long-term trends despite short-term pressures – to balance long-term sustainability strategies with short-term margin improvements. The current economic system and short-term financial demands of shareholders may, in many cases, still conflict with long-term sustainability goals. And this may be over-come by entering into alliances.

However, when commercial companies operating in the new business paradigm integrate social and environmental bottom lines parallel to their economic ones – or even incorporate social or environmental solutions as part of their core business (CSI), they may eventually resemble social business ventures.

As these two fields of practice continue to evolve, it will, in other words, become increasingly harder to distinguish the two from each other, because social entrepreneurship will become more of a mindset around blended value creation rather than a specific category of start-up companies.

As Mirjam Schöning from the Schwab Foundation for Social Entrepreneurship experienced at a World Economic Forum meeting: 'We had two representatives from large corporations together with two social entrepreneurs on the same panel, and they were all fighting over who's the *real* social entrepreneur.'

And when the MeWe generation of leaders and employees with the same values, characteristics and motives as the social entrepreneurs start building their actions on their inner values, they may become *corporate change-makers* or *social intrapreneurs* that apply the principles of social entrepreneurship by developing socially innovative solutions that have both an ethical fibre as well as business potential for mainstream companies. Maybe even with a stronger effect because they – contrary to the social entrepreneurs – have access to more resources to put their ideas into practice.

The social entrepreneur and the social intrapreneur

Characteristics	Social Entrepreneur	Social Intrapreneur
Shrug off constraints of ideology or discipline.	X	X
Identify and apply practical solutions to social or environmental problems.	X	X
Innovate by finding a new product, service or approach to a social challenge.	X	X
Focus – first and foremost – on societal value creation.	X	X
Successfully navigate corporate culture, strategy and process.		X
Communicate social entrepreneurship in compelling business terms.		X
Build and inspire teams across a multiplicity of corporate divisions.		X
Jump in before they are fully resourced.	X	X
Have a dogged determination that pushes them to take risks.	X	X
Combine their passion for change with measurement and monitoring of impact.	X	X
Have a healthy impatience – they don't like bureaucracy.	X	X
Run their organizations.	X	

Source: *The Social Intrapreneur: A Field Guide for Corporate Changemakers*, SustainAbility, 2008.

Creating a socially entrepreneurial organization within an existing structure is no doubt difficult, but mainstream companies can succeed if they offer resources and managerial support and more general reward and incentive systems designed to nurture new ideas and encourage experiment without fear of sanctions – or by reversing the bureaucratic effects of organizational ageing through incubators, acquisitions or spin-offs.[91]

Social intrapreneurs are, in fact, already promoting corporate social entrepreneurship in large corporate settings. At Nike, for example, Sam McCracken has launched the company's Native American Business which leverages the power of the Nike brand to drive athletic participation among Native American communities. At CEMEX, Luis Sota works with the company's executives to develop its low-income housing solutions for Mexican consumers. And at Unilever, Vijay Sharma heads up the Shakti programme which cultivates women entrepreneurs in Indian rural villages.[61]

In short, the point at which future conversions take place may well be when it is in business's self-interest to embed the values and principles of social entrepreneurship – and when individuals make a meaningful difference both for themselves and others in a social as well as a business context.

This may not be the ideal scenario for some social entrepreneurs, but maybe this is still an ambition worth striving for. To work towards better business overall rather than creating new categories that segregrate rather than integrate.

Some of the entrepreneurs I have met do not even use the words social business or social entrepreneur. They see themselves as entrepreneurs who want to make money in the way they believe it should be made. They want to prove that you can make a profitable business and play in the same markets as everybody else – although there are some things they will never do in the name of profit. Their vision is a complete transformation of the economy over the next 20 years to a new system that builds on principles of sustainable growth.

But as one of them, strategic director and co-owner of Worn Again, Jamie Burdett, points out: 'It is a big shift that will take quite a few years before it is at the heart of business because current mindsets have to be changed as well. And this requires an enormous amount of internal cultural change and recognition that you cannot squash margins as much as you may want to, and you have to educate shareholders on that.'

So it will not be until the term 'social entrepreneur' has metaphorically disappeared from the dictionary and has broken into the mainstream that we can celebrate its triumph. One thing is for certain though: the businesses of the future will have both flavours.

Chapter 4

The world is changing, and so is humanity. We are reaching a critical mass of people who are conscious about the consequences of humanity's unsustainable growth – and want to do something about it. Old and new paradigms co-exist, and this creates paradoxes. But paradoxes give us the opportunity to progress. Just like optimism and utopias do. The future is not something we predict. It is something we collaboratively design and co-create. A will to change is the first step. The next is to take action.

An evolutionary revolution
– in the midst of a paradigm shift

'Like the discovery of DNA did for the theory of evolution, the economic crisis could solidify social entrepreneurship as the most compelling model for lasting social change.'[1]

Jeff Skoll

'If you were to guess our development stage as a species, where would you place us? Are we toddlers, teenagers, adults or elders?' American social scientist Duane Elgin asked his audience when he visited Copenhagen in 2005.

The majority of the audience agreed that we were probably teenagers. This did not surprise Elgin, who is the author of numerous publications on voluntary simplicity and personal and collective dimensions of the human journey.

It was the same response that he had received from other audiences, no matter whether they were in Japan, New York, California or Brazil.

⌐Just like teenagers who are reckless and tend to think they will live forever and seek instant gratification, these characteristics also apply to humanity: we have acted recklessly in our rapid consumption of natural resources, behaving as if we would last forever. We tend to express our identity and status through material possessions. And we seek our own pleasures, largely ignoring the needs of future generations.[2]⌐

Today, however, metaphorically speaking, the human family appears to be moving into early adulthood. We are on an evolutionary journey that is being pushed forward by experience, greater knowledge and consciousness. The age of globalization has made the effects of our unsustainable actions more visible which has served to heighten our awareness of the consequences.

This evolutionary journey is the reason why values like ethics, responsibility, meaning and sustainability are starting to predominate. It is the reason why there is a need to re-evaluate, adjust and possibly fundamentally change our basic assumptions about how to work, live, learn, cooperate, conduct politics, manage economies, technologies, solve problems and do business. And it is the reason why social innovaton has become more important than ever.

The journey towards sustainability

Changes usually happen quietly and gradually over a longer period of time. In Nature evolutionary changes are often first noticed when they have reached a critical mass or *tipping point*, a concept that was popularized in 2000 when American author Malcolm Gladwell published his bestseller with the same title. In his book Gladwell illustrates how ideas, trends and social behaviour spread like viruses. Among other things, he shows how small adjustments in, for example, language, packaging, timing and location combined with involving few, but particular, people (he describes them as 'Sales Men', 'Mavens' and 'Connectors') can create change – or 'social epidemics' – with massive effect. In fact, studies suggest that it only takes 5% of 'informed individuals' to influence the direction of a crowd of up to 200 people.[3]

This is precisely what the global consciousness movement has contributed to: it has spread a positive virus of life quality, wellbeing and sustainable development. A virus that has already become an overall vision for many institutions, companies, organizations and citizens – for travellers like the philanthrocapitalists, the social enterprises, the social entrepreneurs, the responsible businesses, the social intrapreneurs – who, in each their own ways, are working in support of the new 21st century paradigm.

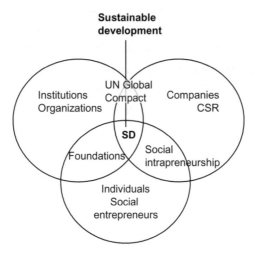

Sustainable development – the common vision. *Model developed by Johanna Mair and Christian Seelos, IESE Business School.*[4]

As a result, we can find traces of the positive virus of change in every corner of society. It is already making its mark on financial markets as well as on new standards, guidelines and legislation. It is manifested in the three new growth principles and in the five markets of change. It is reflected in people's needs for balanced lives and employee demands for meaningful work. And it is a driver of ethical consumerism and activism as well as social entrepreneurship – all factors that motivate, force or inspire corporations to operate in a responsible and sustainable way no matter whether their main purpose is to do good or do well – or both.

The journey towards sustainable business has – so far – been shaped by a series of societal pressure waves and entrepreneurial solutions:[5]

- Wave 1 (peaking 1969–72) focused on new policies, rules and regulations, largely in the environmental, safety and health areas. Counter-cultural entrepreneurship, particularly in the areas of whole foods and 'alternative' or 'intermediate' technology emerged.
- Wave 2 (peaking 1988–91) drove voluntary market initiatives like responsibility reporting and certification. Much of the entrepreneurship focused on environmental and sustainability-related services and socially responsible investment.
- Wave 3 (peaking 1999–2001) drove concerns about globalization, global and corporate governance. There was a dramatic increase in the number of networks linking social and environmental entrepreneurs.
- Wave 4 (now) involves a growing focus on innovation and entrepreneurial solutions to sustainability challenges. The promise is that mainstream players are getting involved. The prospect of alliances, partnerships, mergers and acquisitions will likely grow.

Throughout the book I have presented a wide range of pioneers in the business of social innovation who are developing and scaling market solutions to a broad range of global challenges. These pioneers are leading entrepreneurs, organizations and businesses like Apopo, Grameen Group, Aravind Eye Care System, Institute for One World Health, Ashoka, Participant Media, Better Place, General Electric's Ecomagination, Google.org, Innocentive, Novo Nordisk, the Oxford Health Alliance and the World Business Council for Sustainable Development just to mention a few. All of those have also been included in a recent report, *The Phoenix Economy*, on organizations of all sizes with innovative business models that are paving the way for the new paradigm in terms of scalable sustainable solutions that deliver blended value across the 'triple bottom line' agenda.[6]

With their groundbreaking actions they show us how business can be positioned to be a positive force in protecting the environment, reducing poverty, improving wellbeing and promoting ethical consumption. And they show us that in the interface between social entrepreneurship, the social missions of public and civil organizations and commercial companies, there is a wide range of opportunities with the potential to solve many of society's yet unsolved problems – but also new opportunities to create sustainable business innovations that embrace value creation for the common good as well as the bottom line.

Following their trails will, therefore, help secure stable and safe societies, preserve open and free markets, ensure access to critical resources, avoid abrupt social and environmental changes, provide new products and services and, for the fast first-movers, carve out competitive advantage.[7]

But there are still obstacles that need to be overcome before we succeed in creating a global economy that builds on sustainable growth and progress.

Forever blowing bubbles?

Many of the growth challenges that have been covered and discussed throughout this book are not new. We can go 20, 30, 40 years back in time to find warnings and revelations of the flaws in our current systems' design.

In 1968 Senator Robert Kennedy pointed out in a speech that the gross national product as it was designed then – and still is today – ignores all non-monetary aspects of the economy. That it 'measures neither our wit nor our courage, neither our wisdom nor our learning, neither our compassion, neither our devotion to our country'. In short, it measures 'everything except that which makes life worthwhile'.

Even the creator of GDP national accounts himself, Simon Kuznets, warned back in 1934 that such a limited, one-dimensional metric should not be used as an index of overall social progress.[8]

In 1992, the economists' practice of equating growth with social progress was again challenged at the second UN Earth Summit in Rio de Janeiro when 170 governments agreed to correct the economists' quantitative view of growth. But it is only recently that new measures of life quality and wellbeing like the previously mentioned *Calvert-Henderson Quality of Life Indicators*, the United Nations' *Human Development Index (HDI)*, the European Commission's *Beyond GDP* initiative and France's President Sarkozy's Commission on the *Measurement of Economic Performance and Social Progress* have started to gain ground.

New initiatives are, however, also pushing the sustainability agenda forward. The United Nations' *Green Economy Initiative*, for example, has been designed to assist governments in 'greening' their economies by reshaping and refocusing policies and investments. The *Green New Deal* initiative from nef (the new economics foundation) includes major structural changes to national as well as international financial systems, including taxation. And the *Global Marshall Plan*, which was originally devised by Former American Vice-President Al Gore, works for a socially just green economy.

Likewise, complementary money systems designed to foster cooperation, community and long-term sustainability like the LETS concept, the RecycleBank and the point system experiments of health insurers (as described in Chapter 1) are also turning the current negative development around by aligning financial and social needs.

Nevertheless, none of the new measures, initiatives or systems have been taken into the mainstream yet. So, as economist Hazel Henderson and systems theorist Fridtjof Capra conclude, the global transition to sustainability is no longer a conceptual nor a technical problem. It is a problem of values and political will.[8] And – one might add – also a problem of short-sightedness.

For national decision-makers are still re-elected on four-year cycles, just like most corporate decisions are still made on the basis of quarterly reports. So when planning for the future, they may not fully weigh the long-term benefits of investing today because they operate with short-term NIMTOF (Not in My Term of Office) horizons. In other words, if a major crisis occurs, everyone hopes it is not on their watch.[9]

In fact, forward-thinking analysts criticize governments for reactively bailing out failing industries and iconic giants of the old world economy, initiating stimulus plans designed to raise consumption and trying to rebuild on old models of the past in an attempt to put things back the way they were, instead of asking fundamental questions about the adequacy of our current systems or investing in new market solutions and infrastructures necessary to meet 21st century needs.

As Alan Webber, co-founder and former editor-in-chief of the fastest growing business magazine in readership ever, *Fast Company*, puts it: 'The general interest is in returning things to the way they were before. The pre-assumption is that the system still works, we just kind of messed it up. Public conversation is much less about what we have to change in terms of the underlying purpose of business or underlying operations of capitalism. The question is much more, "how did we let this thing get out of control – we probably need more regulation". And at every single one of these crunches we end up saying "well it was a bunch of bad guys who did some bad things, but fortunately we're going to make it through and everybody can go back to business as usual".'

And so, many companies are still stuck in maximising shareholder value and economic returns. Just like bankers are going back to their usual ways of rewarding themselves, using the billions of dollars that governments spent bailing out failing banking systems for bonuses and pay structures that are still widely defended by the big banking bosses.[10, 11] Economists are now even starting to warn of a 'green bubble' because of the narrow government and investor focus on cleantech and greentech as the golden gate to renewed growth and wealth.[12]

So the question is whether we will remain in the already familiar boom-and-bust cycle so that, in a decade or two, we can dust off the 1933 speech of Franklin D. Roosevelt again and repeat the warnings of Adam Smith, or whether the current development is just one minor step forward in an evolutionary process – an evolutionary business revolution.

When old and new paradigms meet

Old systems and world views are breaking down and new ones are in the making. But there is no reason why they cannot co-exist. In fact, paradigm shifts are not necessarily a question of either/or but rather of both/and. So even though we have entered a new era with new logics and principles (as the paradigm table in this section illustrates), the tools, skills and mindsets from former eras will continue to exist – but their predominance will change.

As a result, what was acceptable yesterday may no longer be acceptable today. Smoking, for example, which used to be cool and socially accepted, has, in some parts of the world, grown to be increasingly unacceptable, backed by regulations prohibiting it in public transport, restaurants, offices and other public places.

Likewise, we still have hardcore capitalists that work towards one goal only: to get the highest return on their investments irrespective of ethical considerations. And unethical business issues like misleading communications, defective and dangerous products, unsafe working conditions, falsified books and corruption are still on the map, while at the same time there is a growing consensus that ethics and responsibility are necessities and critical strategic competitive parameters to run a business successfully today.

And so, although spiritual values like honesty, integrity, fairness, compassion, personal growth, higher purpose, ethics and service to others are predominant in the new paradigm, they are also meeting the darker sides of our characters like workaholism, foolhardiness, control, resistance to change, narrow focus and manipulation.[13]

But if we take a pragmatic approach in choosing from the new and the old paradigms to address any given problem, we will have more options. During the onset of the dot-com revolution, for example, booksellers feared that their stores would crumble under the onslaught of the mighty Amazon. But instead, the Internet has been integrated into a comprehensive set of channels of a 'call, click or visit' approach. Customers are given a choice of interacting according to the old paradigm, the new or a mix of both.[14]

Similarly, the old model of horse-drawn transportation, supported by blacksmiths, horse dealers and buggy whip makers, has transformed into a new model of automobiles, paved super-highways and petrol stations. Horses have not ceased to exist, but their usage has changed from functional work to recreation – or is mixed with new technologies. In the rugged and hostile terrain of Afghanistan in 2002, US special forces and Afghan allies took to horseback to move along perilous mountain trails, and from their saddles used hand-held computers to help direct the precision-guided munitions of their air force to their targets on the ground.[14]

But just like roads had to be redesigned and rebuilt to accommodate the automobile, new road rules had to be introduced, standardized road signs erected and methods of controlling traffic had to be implemented, so must our current business systems be redesigned, adjusted and adapted to the new economic world order where the mindset of social entrepreneurship prevails.

Symbolic examples of the sustainability shift illustrate how. The former site of British Coal, the Ollerton Colliery, has now been turned into the community-owned Sherwood Environmental Village Ltd. which has challenged perceived conventional wisdom that mining communities would not develop beyond manual trades – let alone deliver in a commercial setting. Today it delivers sustainable development in terms of energy efficiency as well as promotion of renewable energy and biodiversity in a commercial setting, but the profits are reinvested to ensure further development of the site.[15]

Similarly, the former Royal Air Force cruise missile station, Greenham Common in the UK, has now become New Greenham Park, a business park housing over 150 companies, which ensures a sustainable income for the Greenham Common Trust, which distributes funds to local charities and environmental and community projects.

The key is to integrate the new logics and principles of social entrepreneurship into the current system at the level at which it is ready to support them – to include the past and transcend into the future by building on or expanding around the present system in order to leapfrog into a new era.

But, as one of the world's leading authorities on sustainable business development, John Elkington, points out, it will take decades, even generations, for the new paradigm to work its way through, despite the new technologies and innovative business models that are already out there and the huge array of experiments that are underway. 'Nothing guarantees our economies or societies a future, other than our willingness to recognize the emergent realities in good time and take timely and effective action to ensure that we create more sustainable outcomes,' Elkington notes.[16] In short, it is up to us to shape the future we want.

With the dynamic race between modern, material values that are following in the wake of rapid industrialization of developing countries and the postmodern, immaterial values that are gaining a foothold particularly in the Western part of the world, the early decades of the 21st century are, however, likely to be a time of intense confusion and conflict over which paradigm holds the greatest promise for progress.

But, as the Danish Nobel Prize winner physicist Niels Bohr, who made fundamental contributions to understanding atomic structure and quantum mechanics, once said: 'How wonderful we have met with a paradox. Now we have some hope of making progress.'

It is in this field of tension that we find new opportunities to make business and change society. For in between the paradoxes new meanings and logics can lead to innovation and progress that generate both material and immaterial growth. The present space between the two paradigms offers us a golden opportunity to create a new vision for the future.

The paradigm shift as described in *The New Pioneers*

Sections	Old Paradigm	New Paradigm
A business world of disorder	Corporate responsibility is a liability	Corporate responsibility is business
	Greed	Enlightened self-interest
	Either/or	Both/and
The globalization race	Multinational company	Globally integrated company
	Western/national/local	Global/glocal
	Natural resources	Human resources
	Generate knowledge	Apply knowledge in new ways
	Industrial society	Knowledge and innovation society
	Unlimited growth	Sustainable growth
Five planets wanted	Industrial systems	Industrial ecosystems
	Linear processes	Circular processes
	Cradle to grave	Cradle to cradle
	Eco-efficiency	Eco-effectiveness
	High-carbon economy	Low-carbon economy
	Master Nature	Learn from Nature
More wealth and more inequality	Public aid/charity	Aid for trade/private enterprise
	Poor people	Entrepreneurs, customers, partners
	Premium markets	Bottom of the Pyramid markets
	Market growth	Inclusive growth
	Extend distribution	Build shared commitment
The silent killers	Material growth	Immaterial growth
	Wealth and doing well	Health and wellbeing
	Accomplish more by working hard	Accomplish more by working less
Generation MeWe	Work for survival/wealth	Work for self-realization/ wellbeing
	Rational, emotional	Rational, emotional, spiritual
	Human resource management	Human purpose management
	Goal in life is material success	Goal in life is inner/outer balance
The Global Brain	Geographic communities	Online communities
	Organizations	Networks
	Protectionism	Knowledge sharing
	Information	Interaction
	The power of few	The power of many

continued on next page...

The paradigm shift as described in *The New Pioneers* – *Continued*

Sections	Old Paradigm	New Paradigm
Collaborative problem solvers	Stakeholder groups	Social networks
	Centralized problem solving	Collective problem solving
	Mass consumption	Mass participation
	Closed research & development	Open source co-creation
Civil power brokers	National legislation	Global activism
	Institutional power	Grassroots power
	Mainstream media	Citizen-powered media
	On-the-street activists	Online (sl)activists
	Opponents	Alliance partners
Conscious buycotters	Boycotts	Buycotts
	Price/quality-based products	Values-based products
	Luxury consumption	Sustainable consumption
	Big brands	Ethical brands
The new faces of capitalism	Tri-sector welfare model	Fourth sector mindset
	Charities and public institutions	Social enterprises
	Philanthropists	Social venture capitalists
	Altruism	Business opportunity
	Business entrepreneurs	Social (business) entrepreneurs
The value of social entrepreneurship	Society as stakeholder	Society as beneficiary
	Financial value and capital	Blended value and capital
	Problems and deficiencies	Opportunities and resources
	Profit as a goal	Profit as a means
	Return on investment	Social return on investment
	Quantitative growth	Qualitative growth
Responsible business 2.0	Single bottom line	Double/triple bottom line
	Shareholder value creation	Stakeholder value creation
	Compliance and risk management	Business development
	Add-on CSR	Strategic CSR
	Changes to the edges	Changes to the core
	CSR	CSO/CSI/CSE
A business force for good	Competitors	Partners
	Mergers	Buy-ins
	Top-down *or* bottom-up	Top-down *and* bottom-up
	Corporate social responsibility	Social intrapreneurship

Utopias and pessimism
– *about hope and fear*

> 'You see things; and you say, "Why?"
> But I dream things that never were,
> and I say, "Why not?" '
>
> *George Bernard Shaw*

The future is not something that just happens to us or something we predict. It is something humans actively create. This is the main point of one of the founding fathers of futures studies, Dutch futurist, sociologist and former political advisor, Fred Polak.

With his magnum opus *The Image of the Future* (1973) Polak demonstrates the importance that cultural assumptions have had throughout the development of Western civilization based on 1500 years of Western beliefs about the future. He shows that society's image of the future is a self-fulfilling prophecy. One of his examples is the image of the state of Israel, which goes back to the prophecies in the Old Testament.

Based on his historical culture studies, Fred Polak concludes that if a culture lacks a positive vision of the future, its creative power and culture will, in time, stagnate and eventually die out. Negative images and collective pessimism ultimately lead to the very collapse they fear.[17]

A large part of the cultural heritage of the West, however, builds on the conviction that pessimism is realistic and possible, whereas optimism is unrealistic and utopian. The optimist believes that we are living in the best of all worlds and the pessimist is afraid that this may be true. And neither of them do anything about it – the first because nothing needs to be done, the other because nothing can be done.[18]

In fact, the findings of a 2007 global Gallup survey which questioned 61 600 people in 60 countries about the prospects for a safer and more economically prosperous world showed a lack of optimism on both counts, most notably in Western Europe and North America. They do not have faith that the next generation will live in a safer world.[19]

But in a pessimistic world, America would never have been discovered, nor would penicillin. In short, there is no progress without optimism. And this is the reason why we need utopias. For, as Fred Polak puts it, 'we may well ask ourselves if the decline in utopian thinking is not also a decline in social progress itself. ... When man's utopian aspirations to develop his own humanity die out, then man himself dies.'[20]

As the examples in this book have illustrated, a global transition to sustainability is not a utopian quest! And being optimistic is not denying the difficulties and challenges that we face during the course of transforming our businesses and society into a sustainable version. Being optimistic simply means that there is a *will* to overcome these obstacles, no matter how big and enduring they may turn out to be. ⏐

The delicate balance is, in other words, to find a way of navigating between the ideal images of the future and the current tough realities without ending up with fatalistic pessimism or wishing it all away in a wave of utopian optimism. In other words, to be able to act rather than get overwhelmed by the overflow of negative stories and gloomy future scenarios that the current challenges create.

It is easy to become engulfed by the gloomy waves of doom. And no doubt, the threats of the current imbalances are accelerating at an unprecedented pace. So the window of opportunity for addressing these critical issues is narrow and closing fast. Tony Manwaring, CEO of the UK-based think tank, Tomorrow's Company, expresses this concern: 'We are at the frontier of a new era in humanity, and it would be fine if it was like discovering America, but it is not. We do not have the time.' We could, in other words, pass unknown points of no return if effective countermeasures are not found in time.

American futurist John L. Petersen, founder of the renowned Arlington Institute (TAI), which specializes in thinking about global futures, foresees that it can go two ways for mankind: 'It will either mean global instability or global renaissance. This could sound like a doomsday scenario, but it could also be something that is just very different. In any case, everything that we know will be fundamentally changed within the next couple of decades.'

The barriers

One of the reasons why paradigm shifts take a long time is the either/or perception – that you have to choose between two alternatives instead of making the most of them both.

For example, although social and environmental concerns are moving up the corporate agenda, the demands of short-term profit are still paramount, which increases the risk of postponing sustainable innovations relating to the longer-term future. But, as we have seen, investors are also responding to signs of strength by rewarding the companies that try to balance long-term sustainability strategies with short-term margin enhancement approaches.[21]

For pharmaceutical multinational Novo Nordisk, which operates with the earlier-described ideal *Utopian Change*, there is a fine balance between what the company wants to achieve in the long term and what is currently possible. Their experience is that the role of engaged citizen requires both adaptability and persistence – it requires working with a long-term strategy but also being willing to adjust the course along the way to take into account the short-sighted, one-dimensional economic logic that still prevails.

As CEO, Lars Rebien Sorensen, explains: 'It is utopian to think that there will be no unrest in the world and that everyone acts sensibly and rationally. Nevertheless, our work with the ideal Utopian Change has given us a clear picture of the role that we can play now and in the future to push the current development even further.'

Another barrier to change is the power of habits and the fear of the unknown. When it comes to putting ideas into action on an incomplete foundation with many unfamiliar factors, it is tempting to stick to what we know, instead of moving out into the great ocean of the unknown. Microsoft's wariness of open-source software, Polaroid's grudging move into digital cameras and GM's and Ford's reluctance to embrace hybrid cars are just a few of the stories of leaders trapped by conventional thinking.[22]

To provide a sense of security we cling to old mindsets that might include the idea that economic growth should be the primary goal of society or that making species extinct does not matter as long as humans survive.[23]

But the only thing we have to fear is fear itself, to cite one of Franklin D. Roosevelt's well-known quotes from the Great Depression. At that time the American citizens' own fear of losing money reinforced the crisis: because they drew their money from the banks, little money was circulated and companies and private inviduals could not borrow money to start up new activities.

Similarly, the paradox of sustainability, i.e. what appears to have positive effects in the short term may turn out to be unsustainable in the long term, may paralyse many companies rather than move them to action. In other words, too much critical analysis may lead to paralysis. So, on the sustainability journey we also need to arm ourselves with intuition and learning along the way. As British economist John Maynard Keynes said, it is better to be roughly right than precisely wrong.

The fear of the unknown is best friends with resistance to change. Microcredit, for example, has gone through the same stages that every innovative idea undergoes: first, it is ridiculed; second, it is opposed; and third, it is accepted and embraced as self-evident.[24]

A similar reaction pattern is also what American sustainability expert, Bob Willard, has experienced amongst sceptical CEOs when they are presented with the 'social capitalistic' business model. Willard has experienced several variations of the typical defensive reaction to change:

1. Deny that there is a problem or that the organization is contributing to it.
2. Delay by asking for more studies or evidence of a problem.
3. Divide and isolate the heretic(s) who suggest there is a problem or wrongdoing.
4. Discredit the credentials and motives of the proponents of change.[25]

Nevertheless, microcredit is eradicating poverty penny by penny, venture capitalists are pouring money into wind and solar energy and new money systems are creating economic growth as well as social cohesion. An incubation period and proof that the idea works is only natural, but it is on the back of the creative force of social innovators and positive visions for the future that sustainability breakthroughs like these are happening.

The power of positive visions

In 1939–40, during the Great Depression, General Motors created a dynamic and positive vision of what America could be in 1960: a highly car-centred society with automated highways and vast suburbs. The vision was presented on the exhibit Futurama at New York World's Fair to show the world 20 years into the future, and it made such a deep impression that it has shaped urban development in the United States over the past 70 years.

An updated version, Futurama II, was presented at New York World's Fair in 1964–65, this time depicting life 60 years into the future. Scenes included an Antarctic 'Weather Central' climate forecasting centre, a 'Hotel Atlantis' for underseas vacationing, desert irrigation and land reclamation, building roads in the jungle and a City of the Future. The exhibit proved to be the most popular with more than 26 million people attending the show in the two six-month seasons the Fair was open. Once again the exhibit was sponsored by General Motors.[26]

On June 1, 2009 the credit crisis closed General Motors, which is now owned by the United States Treasury and Canadian governments, a symbolic mark of the end of the industrial era.

Today it is time for a new vision. With a positive vision for solving climate change facilitated by William Becker, executive director of the US Presidential Climate Action Project, and supported by a wide range of project partners and advisors leading the field of sustainability and climate change research, a 21st century Futurama – The Future We Want (futurewe-want.org) – is now being formed to show what life will be like in a sustainable society.

The Future We Want will, among other things, offer an interactive exhibit that presents a series of realistic animations and videos of green buildings, renewable energy and sustainable transportation systems; a highly interactive website where visitors can dig deeper into the future and participate in design-ing it; and ongoing educational tools for citizens and planners who want to take action. It will offer us some glimpses of what the future will look like guided by principles of sustainability.

So we have two choices: we can either deny realities and continue doing what we have always done, adopting a wait-and-see-what-the-future-will-bring attitude until we are eventually forced to change our course of direction. Or we can consider whether there could be any other ways of thinking, living, working and interacting and then shape our systems, technologies and skills accordingly.

We must, in other words, dare to think the impossible. Dare to go down new paths and have the patience to experiment, well aware of the fact that with new steps slip-ups may follow, that compromises must be made and that transformation takes time.

But most important of all is that we have a clear vision for the future – that we have a point of direction. Sustainable development is, for an increasing number of people, already that common point, and they are already well on their way to achieving their common goal. To them it is not only a meaningful but also a feasible foundation for renewed growth and welfare in the 21st century. It is not a utopian dream but an absolutely realistic possibility.

Everyone has a role to play
– and the power of YOU!

> 'Never doubt that a small group of thoughtful, committed citizens can change the world. Indeed, it is the only thing that ever has.'
>
> *Margaret Mead*

Addressing 21st century challenges and needs requires the efforts of many. For no one group can address these issues alone. So while governments are expected to take the lead with globally and nationally supported efforts, other stakeholders are just as important to ensure success in solving global problems concerning economic, social and environmental issues. And, as we have seen throughout the book, this requires a combined bottom-up and top-down approach manifested in new coalitions, partnerships and the coordinated actions of many to reach new and sustainable results. In short, we all have an important role to play.

But although sector borders are blurring and sustainability agendas are uniting former enemies, there is still a need for actors in and between society's three sectors to play their designated roles to drive the current transformation forward.

There is a need for a dynamic, commercial market with tough competition and demanding consumers to ensure continuous renewal and pave the way for the adoption and development of ethical products and services. There is a need for a stabilising factor in the shape of public and civil organizations that can work more long-term than corporations. There is a need for passionate, ethically driven social entrepreneurs with the perseverance to carry on, although the results may not show at first instance. And there is a need for persistent grassroots activists who continue to ask critical questions and put continuous pressure on unethical companies and organizations until they eventually understand or no longer have any other choice than to change their unsustainable practices.

The new business opportunities that are emerging as a part of the new world economy will attract many new players, including those who are driven by other motives than responsibility and sustainability. And ethically based companies may lose out to less scrupulous competitors. For there are still serious failures and gaps in the frameworks of law and regulation needed to deal with major global issues. Therefore, there is also a need for consistent regulations that level the playing field across industries and countries.

For example, legislation that levers the use of energy from renewable resources, carbon offset markets and trading systems and legal structures that expand the purpose of companies to include more than profit maximization. Tax systems also need to be restructured so that, for example, environmentally destructive activities are internalized and consequently reflected in market prices.

Governments should also consider incentives and other means of rewarding companies that go beyond the legal requirements for sustainability practices. Their national development strategies should actively encourage steps to find synergies between profit, sustainability and innovation.[21] And their efforts should bridge the gap between what people want and what governments support. When will we, for example, see Ministers for Life Quality and Wellbeing? Offices for Organic Foods? Agencies for Happiness and Social Capital?

We need political pioneers, courageous and visionary nations that will and can take the lead to take the necessary steps towards more sustainable growth. This will not only contribute to a better world, it will also constitute the foundation for renewed competitive strength in the 21st century globalization race.

But politicians and policy-makers are usually not entrepreneurial per se. So they should use their power and skills to find inspiration, support and implement the ideas that are developed in 'society's department for research and development', for example, by local communities, citizens and social (business) entrepreneurs.

As the renowned American economist Jeffrey Sachs put it in an article in *TIME* magazine: 'Great social transformations – the end of slavery, the women's and civil rights movements, the end of colonial rule, the birth of environmentalism – all began with public awareness and engagement. Our political leaders followed rather than led ... If as citizens we vote for war, then war it will be. If instead we support a global commitment to sustainable development, then our leaders will follow.'[27]

The power of YOU!

Søren Hermansen lives on a small Danish island called Samsø with 4300 inhabitants. Until 1997 almost all its power came from oil or coal. But then the island won a contest sponsored by the Danish Ministry of Environment and Energy. This led to a ten-year experiment of becoming energy self-sufficient, although the government initially offered no funding, tax breaks or technical expertise.

But Søren saw an opportunity and believed that it could be realized. So, after showing up at every community meeting to give his 'going-green pitch', he eventually convinced the conservative Samsø islanders to invest in and support the economic and environmental potential of making the island energy independent. And so, oil-burning furnaces were replaced by centralized plants that burned leftover straw or wood chips to produce heat and hot water, shares were bought in new wind turbines and solar thermal panels were placed to create electricity and heating.[28]

Today Søren runs the Energy Academy, an alternative energy research centre, and travels all around the world to tell the story of Sustainable Samsø. In 2008 he was featured in *TIME* magazine as one of its Heroes of the Environment in a special report on the world's eco-pioneers and was, in 2009, awarded the same prize Al Gore received two years earlier, The Göteborg Award for Sustainable Development. Why? Because Samsø is now carbon-neutral, produces 10% more clean electricity than it uses, with the extra power fed back into the grid at a profit, and government officials from all over the world are flocking to the now international showcase of renewable energy to gain inspiration for their own sustainability initiatives.

When one of them, the Egyptian ambassador to Denmark, found out how many people lived on the island, he is said to have exclaimed in surprise,

'That's three city blocks in Cairo!' to which Søren replied, 'That's maybe where you should start, not all of Egypt, take one block at a time.'[29] And this is one of the key messages that Søren conveys – that environmental change can only come from the ground up, provided we have the will as well as the right support to take one local step at a time – and then the rest will follow.[28]

So what can *you* do? The pioneers I have talked to have different approaches. Some have a grand plan, a great vision for humanity. Others take small steps by making a difference where they are – as managers, teachers, speakers, writers, engineers, architects, IT specialists and business owners. In other words, regardless of position or location, you can create change from where you are.

As individuals – as citizens, consumers, employees and managers – we must be conscious of the opportunities we have to affect the current development. As active co-creators of our own future we cannot wait for others to make the decisions for us. We must start with ourselves, by making conscious choices on an everyday level and by trying to live and work in accordance with our values. With the danger of being ridiculed and criticized. With the danger of stepping out of line and being imperfect.

For we can all contribute to a better world. We can all, within our respective spheres, be pioneers who experiment and find new ways of adapting ourselves to current realities. If only we can find the courage to break new ground and make mistakes. If only we can find the will to persist until we succeed. The journey continues and future sustainability maps will be shaped by you and me.

The Avenue Delicatessen
Order #: 1-18835
TBL13
Server: Madeline
Cashier: Noah
Register: Counter (receipt)
2014-04-08 18:22:55

1 Tea Hot	1.50
- Lipton	
1 Arancini	5.50

Subtotal:	7.00
PA Sales Tax (6% of 7.00):	0.42
Total:	7.42
Paid in cash:	10.00
Change:	
Net Paid:	7.42
Amount Due:	0.00

The Avenue Delicatessen
27 N. Lansdowne Ave
Lansdowne, PA 19050, 610-622-3354
** PLEASE PAY AT REGISTER **
http://theavenuedeli.com

REFERENCES

Introduction

1. Ray, P.H. and Anderson, S.R. (2000) *Cultural Creatives*, New York: Three Rivers Press.

2. According to Anderson and Ray, 20 million Americans from the 'Modern' subculture, which in 1999 constituted 93 million Americans, are joining the Cultural Creatives movement. Aburdene, P. (2005) *Megatrends 2010*. Charlottesville: Hampton Roads Publishing Company, Inc.

3. Inglehart, R. (1995) Changing Values, Economic Development, and Political Change, *International Science Journal* No. 145. Cited in Elgin, D. and LeDrew, C. (1997) *Global Consciousness Change: Indicators of an Emerging Paradigm*, www.awakeningearth.org

4. Hawken, P. (2007). *Blessed Unrest: How the Largest Movement in the World Came into Being and Why No One Saw It Coming*. New York: Viking Press.

5. Hakim, C. (2000). *Work-Lifestyle Choices in the 21st Century*. New York: Oxford University Press.

6. Elgin, D. and LeDrew, C. (1997). *Global Consciousness Change: Indicators of an Emerging Paradigm*. www.awakeningearth.org

7. Drucker, P.F. (1993). *Post-capitalist Society*. New York: HarperCollins.

8. http://en.wikipedia.org/wiki/Slow_Food [Accessed March 2010].

9. www.grameen-info.org [Accessed March 2010].

10. http://en.wikipedia.org/wiki/Creative_destruction [Accessed March 2010].

11. Silverthorne, S. (2007) Rediscovering Schumpeter: The power of capitalism, *Harvard Business Working Knowledge*, 7 May.

12. The Entrepreneurial Society, *The Economist*, 14 March 2009.

Chapter 1   Outer globalization

1. BSR Report (2008) *Meeting the Challenge of a Reset World.*
2. http://historymatters.gmu.edu/d/5057/ [Accessed March 2010].
3. McVeigh, T. (2008) The party's over for Iceland, the island that tried to buy the world. *The Observer*, 5th October.
4. Velde, D.W. (2008) *The global financial crisis and developing countries.* Overseas Development Institute, October. Available at: http://www.odi.org.uk/resources/download/2462.pdf
5. Gumble, P. (2009) Rethinking Marx. *TIME*, 2nd February.
6. Dixon, F. (2003) Total Corporate Responsibility – Achieving Sustainability and Real Prosperity. *Ethical Corporation Magazine*, December.
7. Sen, A. (2009) Capitalism beyond the crisis. *The New York Review of Books*, 56(5).
8. Eagleton, J. (2009) What is the significance of the economic crisis? *Spiritual Business Network Journal*, 1, May.
9. Mulgan, G. (2009) After capitalism. *Prospect*, April.
10. Progressive Policy Institute (2008) *The Number of Transnational Companies Grows By 2,500 a Year.* Trade Fact of the Week, 3rd December 2008. Available at: www.ppionline.org
11. Gabel, M.G. and Bruner, H. (2003) *Globalinc. An Atlas of the Multinational Corporation.* New York: The New Press.
12. Hart, S.L. (2005) *Capitalism at the Crossroads – The Unlimited Business Opportunities in Solving the World's Most Difficult Problems.* New Jersey: Wharton School Publishing.
13. KPMG (2005) *International Survey of Corporate Responsibility Reporting 2005.* Available at: www.kpmg.com.
14. Grayson, D., Lemon, M., Slaughter, S., Rodriguez, M.A., Jin, Z. and Tay, S. (2008) *A New Mindset for Corporate Sustainability.* White Paper sponsored by BT and Cisco. Available at: http://www.connect-world.com/PDFs/white_papers/a_new_mindset_wp_en.pdf.
15. Tomorrow's Company (2009) *Tomorrow's Global Talent: How Will Leading Global Companies Create Value through People?*
16. www.mallenbaker.net/csr/against.php [Accessed March 2010].
17. Global Education Research Network (date unknown) *Corporate Citizenship Around the World: How local flavor seasons the global practice.* Available at: www.bccorporatecitizenship.org
18. http://en.wikipedia.org/wiki/Karoshi [Accessed March 2010].

19. World Resources Institute (2005) *Millennium Ecosystem Assessment, 2005. Ecosystems and Human Well-being: Opportunities and Challenges for Business and Industry.* World Resources Institute, Washington, DC.

20. Aburdene, P. (2005) *Megatrends 2010.* Charlottesville: Hampton Roads Publishing Company, Inc.

21. Tomorrow's Company (2007) *Tomorrow's Global Company: Challenges and Choices.*

22. *Report on Progress 2009: A review of signatories progress and guidance on implementation, 2009.* Principles for Responsible Investment (PRI). Available at: www.unpri.org

23. Alboher, M. (2009) A social solution, without going the nonprofit route. *The New York Times,* 4th March.

24. Lenssen, G. and Lazy, P. (2007) Learning to lead. Article in *Business Education Special Report 2007,* Ethical Corporation.

25. Sirkin, H. (2008) New World Disorder. *TIME,* 27th October.

26. The early pioneers. *The Economist,* 26th June 2007.

27. Fremtidens Arbejdsmarked [The Future Labour Market]. Danish report from *Monday Morning,* 2004. Available at: www.mm.dk

28. The United Nations Environment Programme (UNEP) (2007) Global Environment Outlook: Environment for Development (GEO-4). Available at: www.unep.org/geo/geo4/

29. Groshen, E.L., Hobijn, B. and McConnel, M.M. (2006) *U.S. Jobs Shipped Abroad: A New Measure.* University of California, Berkeley, Domestic research function, revision 1, 24th January.

30. Davis, G.F., Whitman, M.V.N. and Zald, M.N. (2008) The responsibility paradox. *Stanford Social Innovation Review.*

31. www.ibm.com/ibm/governmentalprograms/samforeignaffairs.pdf

32. Aguiar, M., Bhattacharya, A., Bradtke, T., Cotte, P., Dertnig, S., Meyer, M., Michael, D.C., and Sirkin, H.L. (2006) *The New Global Challengers: How 100 Top Companies from Rapidly Developing Economies are Changing the World.* The Boston Consulting Group.

33. Goldman Sachs (2003) *Dreaming with BRICs: The path to 2050.* Goldman Sachs Global Economics Paper No. 99, 1st October.

34. Sirkin, H. (2008) Loads of Rivals for America. In New World Disorder, *TIME,* 16th October.

35. Vietor, R.H.K. (2007) *How Countries Compete: Strategy, Structure, and Government in the Global Economy.* Boston, Massachusetts: Harvard Business School Press.

36. The Climate Group (2008) *China unleashes Clean Revolution.* 31st July.

37. Bradsher, K. (2006) The Ascent of Wind Power. *The New York Times,* 28th September.

38. http://www.newint.org/features/2009/06/01/future/ [Accessed March 2010].

39. http://www.whitehouse.gov/issues/energy-and-environment [Accessed March 2010].

40. HM Government (2009) *Building Britain's Future: New Industry, New Jobs.* Available at: http://www.bis.gov.uk/files/file51023.pdf

41. Statistics Denmark (2009) *Statistical Yearbook 2009.*

42. World Business Council for Sustainable Development (2007) *Doing Business with the World – The New Role of Corporate Leadership in Global Development.*

43. Salt, B. (2008) *The Global Skills Convergence.* Study, KPMG.

44. Drucker, P. (1987) Social Innovation: Management's New Dimension. *Long Range Planning,* 20, Issue 6.

45. Green, J. (2007) *Democratizing the Future: Towards a New Era of Creativity and Growth.* Philips Design.

46. Lindgaard Christensen, J., Dalum, B., Gregersen, B., Johnson, B., and Lundvall, B.-A. (2005). *The Danish Innovation System.* Department of Business Studies, Aalborg University, Denmark, DRAFT.

47. Denmark's success built on socially innovative movements. *Monday Morning,* No. 34, 5th October 2009.

48. World Economic Forum (2005) *Nordic countries and East Asian tigers top the rankings in the World Economic Forum's 2005 competitiveness.* Press Release, 28th September.

49. Finnish Wellbeing Center – *An Innovative Landing to Japan.* Available at: www.e.finland.fi, 27 May 2005.

50. http://www.aei.gov.au/AEI/PublicationsAndResearch/Snapshots/50SS09_pdf.pdf

51. The Young Foundation (2009) *Fixing the future: Innovating more effective responses to recession.*

52. Capra, F. and Henderson, H. (2009) *Qualitative growth.* The Institute of Chartered Accountants and Tomorrow's Company.

53. Kamp, J. (2005) Money should work for us, not the other way around. *ODE Magazine,* September.

54. Searching for a sustainable GDP. *Monday Morning,* No. 20, 25th May 2009.

55. The BRICs as drivers of global consumption. *BRICs Monthly,* Issue 09/07, 6th August 2009.

56. http://www.weforum.org/docs/AMNC09/AMNC09_ExecutiveSummary.pdf

57. Tomorrow's Company (2009) *Tomorrow's Climate Beyond Peak Carbon.* Discussion paper, May.

58. Brown, L.R. (2006) *Plan B 2.0: Rescuing a Planet Under Stress and a Civilization in Trouble.* New York: W.W. Norton & Co., Inc.

59. World Business Council for Sustainable Development (2008) *Sustainable Consumption Facts and Trends: From a Business Perspective.*

60. World Watch Institute (2006) *Annual Report 2006.* Available at: http://www. worldwatch.org/system/files/Annual_Report_2006.pdf

61. http://www.actionbioscience.org/environment/worldscientists.html

62. Global Humanitarian Forum (2009) *Human Impact Report: Climate Change – The Anatomy of a Silent Crisis.*

63. The International Bank for Reconstruction and Development/The World Bank (2008) *Global Monitoring Report 2008: MDGs and the Environment:Agenda for Inclusive and Sustainable Development.*

64. http://www.who.int/water_sanitation_health/mdg1/en/index.html

65. UNICEF and The World Health Organization (2008) *Progress on Drinking Water and Sanitation: Special Focus on Sanitation.*

66. Annan, K.A. (2002) Companies must take lead to ensure globalisation benefits many. *Financial Times,* 4th February.

67. Bristow, S. (2007) The future of business environment – the climate factor. In *Sustainable Futures: An Insight into Sustainability Trends in Business,* InterfaceFLOR Europe report 2007. Available at: http://www.taniaellis.dk/ bilag/Sustainable%20Futures%20FINAL.pdf

68. http://www.ge.com/files_citizenship/pdf/reports/ge_2008_citizenship_ report.pdf

69. Fitzpatrick, L. (2009) General Electric, Special report on 25 Responsibility Pioneers. *TIME,* 10th September.

70. Squatrigli, C. (2008) Deutsche Bank Loves Shai Agassi's Plan to Bring Us EVs. *Wired,* 14th April.

71. Interface (2009/2010) Interface Reports Annual Ecometrics, April 2009 with latest amendments from Interface Corporate Communications Director Karen Hall, April 2010.

72. http://en.wikipedia.org/wiki/Industrial_ecology [Accessed March 2010].

73. *Managing with soul: Combining corporate integrity with the bottom line.* Knowledge@Wharton, 19th November 2003.

74. Poverty. *The Economist,* 23rd April 2009.

75. http://en.wikipedia.org/wiki/Measuring_poverty#cite_note-3 [Accessed April 2010].

76. World Bank Group (2008) *Global Financial Crisis: Responding Today, Securing Tomorrow.* Background paper, G20 Summit on Financial Markets and the World Economy. Washington, DC, 15th November.

77. http://www.abc.net.au/news/stories/2009/06/20/2603762.htm

78. See, for example, http://www.unmillenniumproject.org/

79. Kirkup, J. (2009) *G8 leaders announce £12.3 billion package for world's poor.* Telegraph.co.uk, 10th July.

80. Hoffmann, K. (2005). *Aid industry reform and the role of enterprise.* Shell Foundation.

81. Shell Foundation (no date) *Down to Business: New Solutions to Old Problems.* Available at: http://www.shellfoundation.org/download/pdfs/sf_brochure_16pp_aw_2.pdf

82. 25 responsibility pioneers. *TIME*, 21st September 2009.

83. Bornstein, D. (2004) *How to Change the World – Social Entrepreneurs and the Power of New Ideas.* New York: Oxford University Press.

84. http://www.wri.org/stories/2007/03/measuring-base-pyramid

85. http://www.bop-protocol.org/docs/BoPProtocol2ndEdition2008.pdf

86. http://www.unilever.com/images/es_Project_Shakti_tcm13-13297.pdf

87. http://www.unilever.com/sustainability/casestudies/economic-development/creating-rural-entrepreneurs.aspx

88. www.grameen-info.org [Accessed March 2010].

89. World Resources Institute (2007) *The Next 4 Billion: Market Size and Business Strategy at the Base of the Pyramid.*

90. International Business Leaders (2009) *Business Linkages: Enabling access to markets at the base of the pyramid.*

91. http://www.tetrapak.com/Document%20Bank/FfDO/FfDO.pdf

92. Examples from *Newsweek*'s senior editor Rana Foroohar's speech at the annual Confederation of Danish Industry's Business Summit in September 2009.

93. Beyond the green corporation. *BusinessWeek*, 29th January 2007.

94. World Economic Forum (2009) *Global Risks 2009 – A Global Risk Network Report.*

95. www.tobaccoatlas.org

96. WHO (2005) *Preventing Chronic Diseases – A Vital Investment.*

97. World Economic Forum (2008) *Working Toward Wellness: The Business Rationale.*

98. http://www.mckinseyquarterly.com/How_to_control_health_benefit_costs_1394

99. http://www.americanchronicle.com/articles/view/43913

100. Hoel, H., Sparks, K. and Cooper, C.L. (2001). *The Cost of Violence: Stress at Work and the Benefits of a Violence/Stress-Free Working Environment*. Geneva: Report commissioned by the International Labour Organization (ILO).

101. Mental health and working life. EUR/04/5047810/B6, WHO European Ministerial Conference on Mental Health, 17th November 2004.

102. Edahiro, J. and Oda, R. (date unknown) *Japan's Paradigm Shift from Growth to Happiness: Slowing down to Advance Well Being*. Japan for Sustainability. Available at: http://www.bhutanstudies.org.bt/admin/pubFiles/17.conf.doc

103. *France Telecom workers driven to suicide*, NowPublic.com, 6th October 2009 and Wave of staff suicides at France Telecom, *The Guardian*, 9th September 2009.

104. http://www.novonordisk.com/investors/download-centre/reports/annual_review_2003_uk.pdf

105. http://www.idec.org.br/pdf/OMS_companies_commitment_WHO.pdf

106. Forsikringsbranchens nye gulerod: Sund livsstil skal belønnes kontant, *Mandag Morgen*, No. 13, 3rd April 2006. [Danish article]

107. http://en.wikipedia.org/wiki/Karoshi [Accessed March 2010].

108. http://en.wikipedia.org/wiki/Triple_bottom_line [Accessed March 2010].

Chapter 2   Inner globalization

1. http://thinkexist.com/quotation/our_prime_purpose_in_this_life_is_to_help_others/260139.html

2. Elgin, D. and LeDrew, C. (1997) Global Consciousness Change: Indicators of an Emerging Paradigm. www.awakeningearth.org

3. The Harwood Group (1995) *Yearning for Balance: Views of Americans on Consumption, Materialism, and the Environment*. Prepared for the Merck Family Fund by The Harwood Group. Available at: http://www.iisd.ca/consume/harwood.html

4. Gilbert, S.J. (2008) Spending on happiness. *Harvard Business School Working Knowledge*, June.

5. www.causes.com [Accessed March 2010]

6. Taylor, L. (2007) Do good, get a tan. *Fast Company*, 12th March.

7. *Dramatic increase in number of volunteers as recession takes hold*. Press release from Volunteering England, 21st April 2009.

8. Tomorrow's Company (2009) *Tomorrow's Global Talent: How Will Leading Global Companies Create Value through People?*

9. Ellis, T. (2002) *The Era of Compassionate Capitalism: A Vision of Holistic Leadership Development in the 21st Century.* Executive MBA dissertation. London: Henley Management College. Available at: http://www.taniaellis.com/publications/papers/

10. http://sec.online.wsj.com/article/SB122455219391652725.html

11. *Who Wants to Be CEO?: Understanding CEO Capital.* Burson-Marsteller report, 2006.

12. *Reward – seeking the ideal blend of financial compensation and fulfilment.* Egon Zehnder International 6th International Executive Panel, June 2009.

13. *Plateauing: Redefining Success at Work.* Knowledge@Wharton, 4th October 2006.

14. Aburdene, P. (2005) *Megatrends 2010.* Charlottesville: Hampton Roads Publishing Company, Inc.

15. Working for the Earth: Green Companies and Green Jobs Attract Employees. *Sustainability Investment News,* 9th October 2007.

16. Global Education Research Network (date unknown) *Corporate Citizenship Around the World: How local flavour seasons the global practice.* Available at: www.bccorporatecitizenship.org

17. Thompson, D. (2008) Green isn't gold for MBAs, *Business Week,* 15th January. Two-thirds of 523 MBA students at 12 top-ranked international business schools said they would never work for a tobacco firm, and almost half of them said they would not work in the energy or automobile industries.

18. The Rise of the Greenagers. *Xtreme Insight Youth,* 2009.

19. Ethical Corporation (2007) Weaving ethics into business education. In *Business Education Special Report 2007.*

20. http://mbaoath.org/wp-content/uploads/2009/05/mba-oath2.pdf

21. B-schools rethink curricula amid crisis. *The Wall Street Journal,* 26th March 2009.

22. The do-good disconnect. *Business Week,* 21st April 2008.

23. A Hippocratic oath for managers. *The Economist,* 4th June 2009.

24. www.beyondgreypinstripes.org [Accessed March 2010].

25. Roner, L. (2007) Protesting improves your prospects. In *Business Education Special Report 2007,* Ethical Corporation.

26. Cf. findings from study of MBA student attitudes, conducted by Aspen Institute Center for Business Education, 2008. Cited in The do-good disconnect, *BusinessWeek,* 21st April 2008.

27. *Where will they lead? MBA student attitudes about business & society.* Initiative for Social Innovation Through Business: The Aspen Institute. Presentation on Gender Findings of Study at Simmons School of Management, 24th June 2003.

28. *Make Room, Wikipedia: Internet-based Collaboration Could Change the Way We Do Business.* Knowledge@Wharton, 21st February 2007.

29. Internet World Stats, www.internetworldstats.com, June 2009.

30. Prahalad, C.K. and Krishnan, M.S. (2008) *The New Age of Innovation – Driving Co-created Value Through Global Networks.* New York: McGraw Hill.

31. www.creatingcustomerevangelists.com/cm [Accessed March 2010].

32. Green, J. (2007) *Democratizing the Future: Towards a New Era of Creativity and Growth.* Philips Design.

33. Bughin, J., Chui, M. and Johnson B. (2008) The next step in open innovation. *The McKinsey Quarterly*, June.

34. *TIME*'s Person of the Year: You. *TIME*, 13th December 2006.

35. Kelley, K. (2009) The new socialism: Global collectivist society is coming online. *Wired*, 22nd May.

36. Thomas, M. and Brain, D. (2008) *Crowd Surfing – Surviving and Thriving in the Age of Consumer Empowerment.* London: A & C Black Publishers.

37. http://en.wikipedia.org/wiki/Google [Accessed March 2010].

38. http://www.article13.com/A13_ContentList.asp?strAction=GetPublication& PNID=1199

39. Howe, J. (2009) *Crowdsourcing – How the Power of the Crowd is Driving the Future of Business.* London: Random House Business Books.

40. *The Economist* Intelligence Unit's briefing papers The Digital Company 2013: Freedom to Collaborate, September 2008 and The Digital Company 2013: How technology will empower the customer, June 2008.

41. Visscher, M. (2007) The power of many. *ODE Magazine*, May.

42. http://en.wikipedia.org/wiki/Prediction_market#Use_by_corporations [Accessed March 2010].

43. http://cci.mit.edu/about/MaloneLaunchRemarks.html

44. The Obamas on the meaning of public service. Exclusive interview in *TIME*, 10th September 2009.

45. Volans Ventures Ltd (2009) *The Phoenix Economy – 50 Pioneers in the Business of Social Innovation.*

46. Hollender, J. and Fenichell, S. (2004) *What Matters Most – Business, Social Responsibility and the End of the Era of Greed.* London: Random House Business Books.

47. Hart, S.L. (2005) *Capitalism at the Crossroads – The Unlimited Business Opportunities in Solving the World's Most Difficult Problems*. New Jersey: Wharton School Publishing.

48. www.whiteband.org [Accessed March 2010].

49. http://en.wikipedia.org/wiki/World_Social_Forum [Accessed March 2010].

50. Baldwin, T. (2007) Fear and Blogging on the Campaign Trail. *Times Online*, 29th December 2007.

51. IBM Institute for Business Value (2008) IBM Corporate Social Responsibility Study, 2008. *Attaining sustainable growth through corporate social responsibility*.

52. http://mynewsjunkie.com/2009/06/13/twitter-users-shame-cnn-for-not-covering-iran-elections-riots/

53. More examples at http://www.expolink.co.uk/whistleblowing-hotline/PDF/Whistleblowing%20update%20international.pdf

54. Ansatte skal sladre om sidemanden. *Politiken*, 20th August 2009 [Danish article].

55. Poulter, S. (2009) Sharp practice? The razor heads that cost just 5p to make, but sell for £2.43 each. *Daily Mail*, 8th June 2009.

56. http://socialinvesting.about.com/od/srishareholders/a/socialactivism.htm

57. http://socialinvesting.about.com/od/srishareholders/a/SRIEngagement.htm

58. Grayson, D. *et al.* (2008) *A New Mindset for Corporate Sustainability*. White paper sponsored by BT and Cisco.

59. Hoffman, A. (2009) Shades of green. *Stanford Social Innovation Review*, Spring.

60. Brugmann, J. and Prahalad, C.K. (2007) Co-creating Business's New Social Compact. *Harvard Business Review*, February.

61. http://www.quotationspage.com/quote/31607.html

62. World Business Council for Sustainable Development (2008) *Sustainable Consumption Facts and Trends: From a Business Perspective*.

63. Der er kun en gud – bundlinjen. *Børsen*, 27th May 2005 [own translation of quote in Danish article].

64. Co-Operative Bank (2004) *Ethical Consumerism Report 2004*.

65. Co-Operative Bank (2007) *Ethical Consumerism Report 2007*.

66. Caplan, J. (2009) Shoppers, Unite! Carrotmobs Are Cooler than Boycotts. *TIME*, 15th May.

67. Consumer demand for green products is still rising. *Sustainability Investment News*, 18th February 2009.

68. Ray, P.H. and Anderson, S.R. (2000) *Cultural Creatives*. New York: Three Rivers Press and www.lohas.com

69. The good consumer. *The Economist*, 17th January 2008.

70. Grande, C. (2007) Ethical consumption makes mark on branding. *Financial Times*, 20th February.

71. www.lohas.com [Accessed March 2010].

72. BBMG (2007) *The Conscious Consumer Report 2007*.

73. M&S survey referred to in The good consumer, *The Economist*, 17th January 2008.

74. Stengel, R. (2009) The responsibility revolution. *TIME*, 21st September.

75. *Mainstream now the force behind change for business.* LOHAS.com, 3rd July 2008.

76. Survey on consumer perceptions of the role business plays in society. *The McKinsey Quarterly*, September 2007.

77. Derbyshire, D. (2006) McCartney vegetarian brand may be devoured by Nestlé. *telegraph.co.uk*, 19th April.

78. http://www.bitc.org.uk/resources/case_studies/afe1311_innocent.html

79. http://www.wholefoodsmarket.com/company/index.php [Accessed March 2010].

80. Fishman, C. (2004) The supermarket that changed the world. *ODE Magazine*, December.

81. The business of saving the world. *What is Enlightenment*, Issue 28, March–May 2005.

Chapter 3 The routes to sustainable business success

1. Emerson, J. and Bonini, S. (2006) Capitalism 3.0, *Value*, 1(1), Feb/March.

2. http://www.unrisd.org/unrisd/website/document.nsf/0/5F280B19C6125F438 0256B6600448FDB?OpenDocument

3. www.csrgov.dk

4. www.skollfoundation.org/aboutskoll/index.asp [Accessed March 2010].

5. The halo effect. *TIME*, 20th September 2007.

6. UN Global Compact and Dalberg Global Development Advisors (2007) *A business guide to partnering with NGOs and the UN, 2007/8*.

7. http://group.tnt.com/aboutus/partnerships/index.aspx [Accessed March 2010]

8. http://www.ge.com/files_citizenship/pdf/reports/ge_2008_citizenship_report.pdf

9. Kramer, M. and Kania, J. (2006) Changing the Game – Leading Corporations Switch from Defense to Offense in Solving Global Problems. *Stanford Social Innovation Review*, Spring.

10. Phills Jr., J.A., Deiglmeier, K. and Miller, D.T. (2008) Rediscovering social innovation. *Stanford Social Innovation Review*, Fall.

11. Seelos, C. and Mair, J. (2005) What can businesses do for the needy. *IESE Insight*, January.

12. Bosma, N., Levie, J., Bygrave, W.D., Justo, R., Lepoutre, J. and Terjesen, S. (2010) *Global Entrepreneurship Monitor*. 2009 Executive Report.

13. www.fuqua.duke.edu/centers/case/leaders/ [Accessed March 2010].

14. Smallbone, D., Evans, M., Ekanem, I. and Butters, S. (2001) Researching social enterprise. Final report to the Small Business Service Centre for Enterprise and Economic Development Research, Middlesex University, London. In Doherty, B. *et al.* (2009) *Management for Social Enterprise*. London: SAGE Publications Ltd.

15. Doherty, B., Foster, G., Mason, C., Meehan, J., Meehan, K., Rotheroe, N. and Royce, M. (2009) *Management for Social Enterprise*. London: SAGE Publications Ltd.

16. Marti, I. (2006) Introduction to Part I – Setting a Research Agenda for an Emerging Field. In Mair, J., Robinson, J. and Hockerts, K. (eds) (2006) *Social Entrepreneurship*. New York: Palgrave Macmillan.

17. Elkington, J. and Hartigan, P. (2008) *The Power of Unreasonable People*. Boston, Massachusetts: Harvard Business Press. Also see http://www.sustainability. com/downloads_public/skoll_reports/Hot_Spots_of_Social_Enterprise.pdf

18. Harding, R. and Cowling, M. (2005) *Social Entrepreneurship Monitor United Kingdom 2004*. London Business School, 22nd January. Available at: www. gemconsortium.org

19. *Social enterprise generates £18 bn turnover for the UK*. Press release from The Small Business Service (www.sbs.gov.uk) under The Department of Trade and Industry, 11th July 2005.

20. Mair, J. (2004) Social entrepreneurs. *IESE Alumni Magazine*, July–September.

21. Visscher, M. (2004) Miracle in the desert. *ODE Magazine*, November.

22. Grayson, D. *et al.* (2008) *A New Mindset for Corporate Sustainability*. White paper sponsored by BT and Cisco.

23. Kamp, J. (2005) Money should work for us, not the other way around. *ODE Magazine*, September.

24. Lietaer, B. (2001) *The Future of Money*. London: Century.

25. Robertson, C. (2008) *Social entrepreneurs: Green and Good.* BBC News, 6th October.

26. www.roskilde-festival.dk [Accessed March 2010].

27. www.gam3.com [Accessed March 2010].

28. 25 responsibility pioneers. *TIME,* 21st September 2009.

29. 15 minutes: Victoria Hale. *Stanford Social Innovation Review,* Winter 2007.

30. Mair, J. and Noboa, E. (2006) Social Entrepreneurship: How intentions to create a social venture are formed. In Mair, J., Robinson, J. and Hockerts, K. (eds) (2006) *Social Entrepreneurship.* New York: Palgrave Macmillan.

31. Monllor, J. (date unknown) *Social Entrepreneurship: A study on the source and discovery of social opportunities,* University of Illinois at Chicago.

32. *Greyston Bakery: Let 'Em Eat Cake.* www.cbsnews.com, 11th October 2004.

33. Yunus, M. (2007) *Creating a World Without Poverty.* New York: Public Affairs.

34. www.schwabfound.org [Profile description of Aravind Eye Care Hospital].

35. Auerswald, P. (2009) Creating social value. *Stanford Social Innovation Review,* Spring.

36. Dees, G. (2009) Social ventures as learning laboratories, Innovations, Davos-Klosters 2009.

37. Clinton, L. (2009) *The Social and Commercial Two-Step.* www.socialedge.org, 22nd December.

38. Alboher, M. (2009) A social solution, without going the nonprofit route. *The New York Times,* 4th March.

39. Chertok, M., Hamaoui, J. and Jamison, E. (2008) The Funding Gap. *Stanford Social Innovation Review,* Spring.

40. Developed by The Community Development Venture Capital Alliance.

41. Devised by Jed Emerson and the Roberts Enterprise Development Fund (REDF) and, more recently, extended by the new economics foundation (nef).

42. http://www.se100.co.uk/

43. Recent development by The Young Foundation and Social Finance.

44. Mair, J. and Marti, I. (2006) Social entrepreneurship research: a source of explanation, prediction and delight. *Journal of World Business,* 41(1), 36–44.

45. Hartigan, P. and Billimoria, J. (2005) Social entrepreneurship: an overview. *Alliance,* 10(1), March.

46. Austin, J. and Reficco, E. (2009) *Corporate Social Entrepreneurship.* Harvard Business School, Working Paper 09-101.

47. World Business Council for Sustainable Development (2006) *From Challenge to Opportunity: The role of business in tomorrow's society.*

48. The good company. *The Economist*, 20th January 2005.

49. A change in climate. *The Economist*, 17th January 2008.

50. IBM Global Services (2006) *Business model innovation – the new route to competitive advantage*.

51. Willard, B. (2005) *The Next Sustainability Wave*. Canada: New Society Publishers.

52. Ramzy, A. (2009) Coke's recession boomlet. *TIME*, 21st September.

53. KPMG (2008) *KPMG International Survey of Corporate Responsibility Reporting 2008*. Available at: www.kpmg.com

54. http://www.nikebiz.com/crreport/ [Accessed January 2010].

55. Visser, W. (2010) CSR 2.0 – The Evolution and Revolution of Corporate Social Responsibility. In Pohl, M. and Tolhurst, N. (eds) (2010) *Responsible Business: How to Manage a CSR Strategy Successfully*. Chichester: John Wiley & Sons, Ltd.

56. Just good business. *The Economist*, 17th January 2008.

57. Walt, V. (2009) Charity Crunch Time. *TIME*, 19th March.

58. Kanter, R.M. (1999) From Spare Change to Real Change: The Social Sector as a Beta Site for Business Innovation. *Harvard Business Review*, 77, 123–132.

59. Who said CSR and Innovation are not for SME? *IESE Insight*, October 2007.

60. *Deloitte volunteer IMPACT survey reveals link between volunteering and professional success*. CSR News, 6th January 2005.

61. SustainAbility (2008) *The Social Intrapreneurs: A Field Guide for Corporate Changemakers*.

62. http://www.timesonline.co.uk/tol/news/uk/article641494.ece

63. The greening of Walmart. *TIME*, 3rd April 2006.

64. http://socialinvesting.about.com/od/srishareholders/a/SRIEngagement.htm

65. How responsible is socially responsible investing? *ODE Magazine*, March 2005.

66. Demos (2002) *Getting down to business – An agenda for corporate social innovation*.

67. Grayson, D. and Hodges, A. (2004) *Corporate Social Opportunity – 7 Steps to Make Corporate Social Responsibility Work for Your Business*. Sheffield: Greenleaf Publishing.

68. Aburdene, P. (2005) *Megatrends 2010*. Charlottesville: Hampton Roads Publishing Company, Inc.

69. Mahler, D., Barker, J., Belsand, L. and Schulz, O. (2009) *"Green" Winners: The Performance of Sustainability-focused Companies in the Financial Crisis*. A. T. Kearney.

70. Blom, P. (2009) The Upside of the Downturn. In *Social Innovation in a Post-Crisis World, innovations*, Davos-Klosters 2009.

71. http://www.triodos.com/com/whats_new/latest_news/press_releases/share_issue_2009

72. Wittenberg-Cox, A. and Maitland, A. (2008) *Why Women Mean Business.* Chichester: John Wiley & Sons, Ltd.

73. Herrmann, N. (1996) *The Whole Brain Corporation.* McGraw-Hill.

74. Thomas, M. and Brain, D. (2008) *Crowd Surfing – Surviving and Thriving in the Age of Consumer Empowerment.* London: A & C Black Publishers.

75. Gregersen, S. (2009) *Ethical leadership in times of change. A study of leadership with or without the use of ethics as a cornerstone during the financial crisis on Iceland in 2009.* Master of Cultural and Creative Leadership dissertation from University of Portsmouth.

76. http://www.spiegel.de/international/europe/0,1518,620544,00.html

77. A stress test for good intentions. *The Economist,* 14th May 2009.

78. Coined by Jed Emerson, www.blendedvalue.org.

79. Global Education Research Network (date unknown) *Corporate Citizenship Around the World: How local flavor seasons the global practice.* Available at: www.bccorporatecitizenship.org

80. Markides, C. and Geroski. P. (2005) *Fast Second – How Smart Companies Bypass Radical Innovation to Enter and Dominate New Markets.* Hoboken: John Wiley & Sons, Inc.

81. Rangan, V.K., Leonard, H.B. and McDonald, S. (2008) *The future of social enterprise.* Harvard Business School Working Paper, 08-103.

82. Special: Practical lessons for getting into the bottom of the pyramid. *IESE Insight,* 2009.

83. Mair, J. and Seelos, C. (2005) What can companies learn from social entrepreneurs? Executive summary of IESE conference *Social Entrepreneurs as Competitors and Partners in Global Markets,* 19th September.

84. http://insight.iese.edu/doc.aspx?id=565&ar=6&idioma=2 and www.schwabfound.org

85. Black, L. (2009) Pots of Gold. *The Guardian,* 18th February.

86. Gilbert, S.J. (2008) The surprisingly successful marriages of multinationals and social brands. Interview of Austin, J.E. and Leonard, H.B. *Harvard Business School Working Knowledge,* 15th December.

87. Smoothie drink pioneers sell Innocent stake for £30 million. *The Times,* 7th April 2009.

88. www.stonyfield.com [Accessed March 2010].

89. Co-Operative Bank (2007) *The Ethical Consumerism Report 2007.*

90. O'Rourke, D. (2006) Buying in or selling out? *Stanford Social Innovation Review*, Fall.

91. Light, P.C. (2009) Social entrepreneurship revisited. *Stanford Social Innovation Review*, Summer.

Chapter 4　Visions for the future

1. The Skoll World Forum on Social Entrepreneurship (2009) print ad in *TIME*.

2. Elgin, D. (1999) The 2020 Challenge: Evolutionary Bounce or Evolutionary Crash? www.newhorizons.org/future/elgin2020

3. Thomas, M. and Brain, D. (2008) *Crowd Surfing – Surviving and Thriving in the Age of Consumer Empowerment*. London: A & C Black Publishers.

4. Mair, J. (2004) Social entrepreneurs. *IESE Alumni Magazine*, July/Sept.

5. SustainAbility (2007) *Growing opportunity: Entrepreneurial solutions to insoluble Problems*.

6. Volans Ventures Ltd (2009) *The Phoenix Economy – 50 Pioneers in the Business of Social Innovation*.

7. World Resources Institute (2005) *Ecosystems and well-being – opportunities and challenges for business and industry, Millennium Ecosystem Assessment*. World Resources Institute, Washington, DC.

8. Capra, F. and Henderson, H. (2009) *Qualitative growth*. The Institute of Chartered Accountants and Tomorrow's Company.

9. World Economic Forum (2009) *Global Risks: A Global Risk Network Report*.

10. Story, L. and Dash, E. (2009) Bankers reaped lavish bonuses during bailouts. *The New York Times*, 30th July.

11. http://www.dailymail.co.uk/news/worldnews/article-1081624/Goldman-Sachs-ready-hand-7BILLION-salary-bonus-package–6bn-bail-out.html

12. http://articles.moneycentral.msn.com/Investing/Extra/BewareOfAGreenBubble.aspx

13. Read more about spiritual values in business in Ellis, T. (2002) *The Era of Compassionate Capitalism: A Vision of Holistic Leadership Development in the 21st Century*. Executive MBA dissertation. London: Henley Management College. Available at: http://www.taniaellis.com/publications/papers/

14. Wind, Y. and Crook, C. (2005) *The Power of Impossible Thinking: Transform the Business of Your Life and the Life of Your Business*. Wharton School Publishing.

15. www.sev.org.uk [Accessed March 2010].

16. What will rise from the ashes of the credit crisis? *Monday Morning*, No. 20, 25th May 2009.

17. Ray, P.H. and Anderson, S.R. (2000) *Cultural Creatives*. New York: Three Rivers Press.

18. Laszlo, A. (2003) Evolutionary Systems Design: A Praxis for Sustainable Development. *Journal of Organisational Transformation and Social Change (OTASC)*, 1.

19. http://extranet.gallup-international.com/uploads/internet/DAVOS%20 release%20final.pdf

20. Polak, F. (1973) *The Image of the Future*. Amsterdam, New York: Elsevier.

21. Grayson, D. *et al.* (2008) *A New Mindset for Corporate Sustainability*. White paper sponsored by BT and Cisco.

22. Garvin, D.A. and Levesque, L.C. (2006) Meeting the challenge of corporate entrepreneurship. *Harvard Business Review*, October.

23. Dixon, F. (2003) Total corporate responsibility – achieving sustainability and real prosperity. *Ethical Corporation Magazine*, December.

24. Kamp, J. and Visscher, M. (2006) Turning poverty into peace. *ODE Magazine*, December.

25. Willard, B. (2005) *The Next Sustainability Wave*. Canada: New Society Publishers.

26. http://en.wikipedia.org/wiki/Futurama_(New_York_World%27s_Fair) [Accessed March 2010].

27. Sachs, J.D. (2008) Common Wealth. *TIME*, 13th March.

28. Walsh, B. (2008) Soren Hermansen. *TIME*, 24th September in *TIME*'s special report on Heroes of the Environment 2008.

29. Tagliabue, J. (2009) From Turbines and Straw, Danish Self-Sufficiency. *The New York Times*, 29th September.

FURTHER READING

Books

Aburdene, P. (2005) *Megatrends 2010.* Charlottesville: Hampton Roads Publishing Company, Inc.

Bakan, J. (2004) *The Corporation: The Pathological Pursuit of Profit and Power.* New York: Free Press.

Bason, C. (2010) *Leading Public Sector Innovation: Co-creating for a Better Society.* Bristol: Policy Press.

Benyus, J. (2002) *Biomimicry: Innovation Inspired by Nature.* New York: Harper Perennial.

Bishop, M. and Green, M. (2009) *Philanthrocapitalism: How Giving Can Save the World.* A & C Black Publishers Ltd.

Bornstein, D. (2004) *How to Change the World – Social Entrepreneurs and the Power of New Ideas.* New York: Oxford University Press.

Brown, L. R. (2006) *Plan B 2.0: Rescuing a Planet Under Stress and a Civilization in Trouble.* New York: W.W. Norton & Co., Inc.

Bruijn, T. J. N. M. and Tukker, A. (eds.) (2002) *Partnership and Leadership – Building Alliances for a Sustainable Future.* Kluwer Academic Publishers Group.

Chanda, N. (2007) *Bound Together: How Traders, Preachers, Warriors and Adventurers Shaped Globalization.* New Haven: Yale University Press.

Clark, M. (2009). *The Social Entrepreneur Revolution.* Marshall Cavendish.

Doherty, B. *et al.* (2009) *Management for Social Enterprise.* London: SAGE Publications Ltd.

Drucker, P. (1985). *Innovation and Entrepreneurship.* Burlington: HarperCollins.

Elkington, J. (2001) *The Chrysalis Economy: How Citizen CEOs and Corporations Can Fuse Values and Value Creation.* Oxford: Capstone Publishing.

Elkington, J. and Hartigan, P. (2008). *The Power of Unreasonable People.* Boston, Massachusetts: Harvard Business Press.

Fombrun, C. J. and van Riel, C. (2004). *Fame & Fortune, How Successful Companies Build Winning Reputations.* Upper Saddle River: Financial Times Prentice Hall.

Gladwell, M. (2000) *The Tipping Point.* New York: Little, Brown and Company.

Grayson, D. and Hodges, A. (2004) *Corporate Social Opportunity – 7 Steps to Make Corporate Social Responsibility Work for Your Business.* Sheffield: Greenleaf Publishing.

Guillaume, M. (2009). *The Seven Deadly Sins of Capitalism and Some Ways to Reinvent Free Markets for Welfare.* Belgium, www.mikeconomics.net

Hakim, C. (2000) *Work-Lifestyle Choices in the 21st Century.* New York: Oxford University Press.

Handy, C. B. (1998) *The Hungry Spirit.* New York: Broadway Books.

Hart, S. L. (2005) *Capitalism at the Crossroads – The Unlimited Business Opportunities in Solving the World's Most Difficult Problems.* New Jersey: Wharton School Publishing.

Hawken, P. (2007) *Blessed Unrest: How the Largest Movement in the World Came into Being and Why No One Saw It Coming.* New York: Viking Press.

Hawken, P., Lovins, A. and Lovins H.L. (2000) *Natural Capitalism: The Next Industrial Revolution.* London: Earthscan Publications.

Henderson, H. (1999) *Beyond Globalization: Shaping a Sustainable Global Economy.* Kumarian Press.

Herrmann, N. (1996) *The Whole Brain Corporation.* McGraw-Hill.

Hollender, J. and Fenichell, S. (2004) *What Matters Most – Business, Social Responsibility and the End of the Era of Greed.* London: Random House Business Books.

Hollender, J. and Breen, B. (2010) *The Responsibility Revolution: How the Next Generation of Businesses Will Win.* San Francisco: Jossey-Bass.

Howe, J. (2009) *Crowdsourcing – How the Power of the Crowd is Driving the Future of Business.* London: Random House Business Books.

Kanter, R.M. (2009) *SuperCorp: How Vanguard Companies Create Innovation, Profits, Growth, and Social Good.* New York: Crown Business.

Kim, C. W. and Mauborgne, R. (2005) *Blue Ocean Strategy.* Boston: Harvard Business School Press.

Lietaer, B. (2002) *The Future of Money: Creating New Wealth, Work and a Wiser World.* Century.

Mair, J., Robinson, J. and Hockerts, K. (eds.) (2006) *Social Entrepreneurship.* New York: Palgrave Macmillan.

Markides, C. C. (2008) *Game-Changing Strategies.* San Francisco: Jossey-Bass.

McDonough, W. and Braungart, M. (2002) *Cradle to Cradle: Remaking the Way We Make Things.* New York: North Point Press.

Paines, L. S. (2003) *Value Shift: Why Companies Must Merge Social and Financial Imperatives to Achieve Superior Performance*. New York: McGraw Hill.

Pohl, M. and Tolhurst, N. (2010) *Responsible Business: How to Manage a CSR Strategy Successfully*. Chichester: John Wiley & Sons, Ltd.

Polak, F. (1973) *The Image of the Future*. Amsterdam: Elsevier.

Prahalad, C. K. (2004) *The Fortune at the Bottom of the Pyramid*. Wharton School Publishing.

Prahalad, C.K. and Krishnan, M.S. (2008) *The New Age of Innovation – Driving Co-created Value Through Global Networks*. New York: McGraw Hill.

Ray, P. H. and Anderson, S. R. (2000) *Cultural Creatives*. New York: Three Rivers Press.

Robinson, J., Mair, J. and Hockerts, K. (eds.) (2009) *International Perspectives on Social Entrepreneurship Research*. New York: Palgrave Macmillan.

Sirkin, H., Hemerling, J. and Bhattacharya, A. (2008) *Globality: Competing With Everyone from Everywhere for Everything*. New York: Business Plus.

Surowiecki, J. (2004) *The Wisdom of Crowds*. New York: Anchor Books.

Tapscott, D. and Williams, A. D. (2008) *Wikinomics: How Mass Collaboration Changes Everything*. New York: Portfolio.

Temple, N., Darach, J. and Rösch, V. (eds.) (2004) *The Global Ideas Book*. The Institute for Social Inventions.

Thomas, M. and Brain, D. (2008) *Crowd Surfing – Surviving and Thriving in the Age of Consumer Empowerment*. London: A & C Black Publishers Ltd.

Vietor, R.H.K. (2007) *How Countries Compete: Strategy, Structure, and Government in the Global Economy*. Boston, Massachusetts: Harvard Business School Press.

Visser, W. (2010 forthcoming) *The Age of Responsibility*. Chichester: John Wiley & Sons, Ltd.

Visser, W. and Tolhurst, N. (2010) *The World Guide to CSR: A Country-by-Country Analysis of Corporate Sustainability and Responsibility*. Sheffield: Greenleaf Publishing

Watson, T. (2008) *CauseWired: Plugging In, Getting Involved, Changing the World*. New Jersey: John Wiley & Sons, Inc.

Willard, B. (2005) *The Next Sustainability Wave*. Gabriola Island: New Society Publishers.

Wind, Y., Crook, C. and Gunther, R. (2005) *The Power of Impossible Thinking*. New Jersey: Wharton School Publishing.

Wittenberg-Cox, A. and Maitland, A. (2008) *Why Women Mean Business*. Chichester: John Wiley & Sons, Ltd.

Yunus, M. (2007) *Creating a World Without Poverty: Social Business and the Future of Capitalism*. New York: Public Affairs.

Key reports/papers

Bosma, N., Levie, J., Bygrave, W.D., Justo, R., Lepoutre, J. and Terjesen, S. (2010) *Global Entrepreneurship Monitor. 2009* Executive Report.

BSR (2008) *Meeting the Challenge of a Reset World.*

Capra, F. and Henderson, H. (2009) *Qualitative growth.* The Institute of Chartered Accountants and Tomorrow's Company.

Co-Operative Bank (2007) *The Ethical Consumerism Report 2007.*

Dalberg Global Development Advisors (2007/8) *Business Guide to Partnering with NGOs and the United Nations.*

Elgin, D. (1999) *The 2020 Challenge: Evolutionary Bounce or Evolutionary Crash?* www. newhorizons.org/future/elgin2020

Elgin, D. and LeDrew, C. (1997) *Global Consciousness Change: Indicators of an Emerging Paradigm.* www.awakeningearth.org

Ellis, T. (2002) *The Era of Compassionate Capitalism: A Vision of Holistic Leadership Development in the 21st Century.* Executive MBA dissertation. London: Henley Management College. Available at: http://www.taniaellis.com/publications/papers/

Emerson, J. (2003) The Blended Value Proposition: Integrating Social and Financial Returns. *California Management Review,* 45(4), Summer.

Grayson, D. *et al.* (2008) *A New Mindset for Corporate Sustainability.* White Paper sponsored by BT and Cisco.

Green, J. (2007) *Democratizing the Future – Towards a New Era of Creativity and Growth.* Philips.

Hockerts, K. *et al.* (2008) *CSR-Driven Innovation. Toward the Social Purpose Business,* www.csrinnovation.dk

KPMG (2008) *KPMG International Survey of Corporate Responsibility Reporting 2008.* www.kpmg.com

Millennium Ecosystem Assessment (2005) *Ecosystems and Human Well-being: Opportunities and Challenges for Business and Industry.* World Resources Institute, Washington, DC.

Porter, M.E. and Kramer, M.R. (2006) Strategy and Society: The Link Between Competitive Advantage and Corporate Social Responsibility, *Harvard Business Review.*

SustainAbility (2007) *Growing Opportunity: Entrepreneurial Solutions to Insoluble Problems.*

SustainAbility (2008) *The Social Intrapreneurs: A Field Guide for Corporate Changemakers.*

The Economist Intelligence Unit (2008) The Digital Company 2013: How Technology Will Empower the Customer. *The Economist,* June.

The Economist Intelligence Unit (2008) The Digital Company 2013: Freedom to Collaborate. *The Economist,* September.

The Harwood Group (1995) *Yearning for Balance: Views of Americans on Consumption, Materialism, and the Environment.* Prepared for the Merck Family Fund by The Harwood Group. Available at: http://www.iisd.ca/consume/harwood.html

Tomorrow's Company (2007) *Tomorrow's Global Company: Challenges and Choices.*

Tomorrow's Company (2009) *Tomorrow's Climate Beyond Peak Carbon.* Discussion paper.

Tomorrow's Company (2009) *Tomorrow's Global Talent – How Will Leading Global Companies Create Value Through People?*

United Nations Environment Programme (UNEP) (2007) *Global Environment Outlook: Environment for Development (GEO-4).* Available at: www.unep.org/geo/geo4/

Volans (2009) *The Phoenix Economy: 50 Pioneers in the Business of Social Innovation.*

World Business Council for Sustainable Development (2007) *Doing Business with the World: The New Role of Corporate Leadership in Global Development.*

World Business Council for Sustainable Development (2008) *Sustainable Consumption – Facts and Trends From a Business Perspective.*

World Economic Forum (2005) *Partnering for Success: Business Perspectives on Multistakeholder Partnerships,* January.

World Economic Forum (2009) *Global Risks: A Global Risk Network Report,* January.

World Resources Institute (2007) *The Next 4 Billion. Market Size and Business Strategy at the Base of The Pyramid.*

Links

Acumen Fund: www.acumenfund.org

Ashoka: www.ashoka.org

Australian OzIdeas and Innovations: http://home.vicnet.net.au/ ozideas/

Base of the Pyramid (BOP) Learning Laboratory: www.bopnetwork.org

BOP Protocol: www.bop-protocol.org

Boston College Center for Corporate Citizenship: www.bbcorporatecitizenship.org

Center For Advancement of Social Entrepreneurship: www.fuqua.duke.edu

Center For Social Innovation, Stanford University: www.gsb.stanford.edu/csi/

Centre for Social Innovation: www.socialinnovation.ca

Changemakers (an Ashoka programme): www.changemakers.net

CSR-Driven Innovation: www.csrinnovation.dk

CSR International: www.csrinternational.org

Development Marketplace: www.developmentmarketplace.org

Ethicaleconomy: www.ethicaleconomy.com

Ethiscore: www.ethicscore.org

Europan Academy of Business in Society: www.eabis.org

European Foundation for Management: www.efmd.org

European Research Network: www.emes.net

Fair Pages: www.thefairpages.com

Force For Good companies: www.forceforgood.com

Fourth Sector: www.fourthsector.net

Fourth Sector Strategies: www.fourthsectorstrategies.com

Futerra (The Greenwash Guide, Tips for Sustainability Communication): www.futerra.
  co.uk

Global Entrepreneurship Monitor: www.gemconsortium.org

Global Exchange for Social Investment: www.gexsi.org

Global Ideas Bank: www.globalideasbank.org

Growing Inclusive Markets: www.growinginclusivemarkets.org

Ideas Compass: www.ideascompass.dk

i-Genius: www.i-genius.org

Index: www.indexaward.dk

Innocentive: www.innocentive.com

Learning Innovation and Technology Consortium: www.learninginnovation.org

LOHAS: www.lohas.org

NESTA: www.nesta.org.uk

Net Impact: www.netimpact.org

PBS's NOW competition: www.pbs.org/now/enterprisingideas

Pioneers of Change: www.pioneersofchange.net

Sins of Greenwashing (Terrachoice): www.sinsofgreenwashing.org

Skoll Foundation: www.skollfoundation.org

Social Capitalist Awards (Fast Company): www.fastcompany.com/social

Social Edge (a Skoll Foundation programme): www.socialedge.org

Social Enterprise Alliance: www.se-alliance.org

Social Enterprise Coalition: www.socialenterprise.org.uk

Social Enterprise London: www.sel.org.uk

Social Firms: www.socialfirmsuk.co.uk

Social Fusion: www.socialfusion.org

Social Innovation Exchange: www.socialinnovationexchange.org

Social Innovation Japan: www.socialinnovationjapan.org

Social Innovator: www.socialinnovator.info

Stanford Social Innovation Review: www.ssireview.org

TakingITGlobal: www.takingitglobal.org

The Future We Want: www.futurewewant.org

The Hub: www.the-hub.net

The Institute for Social Entrepreneurs: www.socialent.org

The New Pioneers: www.thenewpioneers.biz

The Schwab Foundation for Social Entrepreneurship: www.schwabfound.org

The Skoll Foundation: www.skollfoundation.org

The Stuart C. Dodd Institute For Social Innovation: www.stuartcdoddinstitute.org

The Young Foundation: www.youngfoundation.org

Tomorrow's Company: www.tomorrowscompany.com

United Nations Global Compact: www.unglobalcompact.org

United Nations Millennium Development Goals: www.un.org/millenniumgoals

United Nations Principles for Responsible Investment: www.unpri.org

UnLtd – the Foundation for Social Entrepreneurs: www.unltd.org.uk

Vanno: www.vanno.com

WeCollaborate: www.wecollaborate.org

Wiser Earth Directory: www.wiserearth.org

World Bank's Doing Business: www.doingbusiness.org

World Business Council for Sustainable Development: www.wbcsd.org

World Economic Forum: www.weforum.org

Worldchanging: www.worldchanging.com

X Prize Foundation: www.xprize.org/future-x-prizes

Young Social Enterprise Initiative: www.ysei.org

ACKNOWLEDGEMENTS

This book is the result of the efforts and influence of many. First and foremost, I would like to give a warm thank you to the many practitioners from the sustainable business field for interviews, conversations and correspondence – their input has been an invaluable inspiration for the book:

Founders of The Green Children Foundation and The Green Children, Tom Bevan and Milla Sunde; former Director of Social Enterprise Coalition (SEC), Jonathan Bland; former Head of Fund Development at The Young Foundation, Andrew Brough; Director of Global Values at The Body Shop, Jan Buckingham; Strategic Director at Worn Again, Jamie Burdett; author and green marketing expert, John Grant; researchers at Global Entrepreneurship Monitor, Niels Bosma, Jan Lepoutre, Rachida Justo and Siri Terjesen; Director of the Doughty Centre for Corporate Responsibility at Cranfield School of Management, David Grayson; Associate Professor at the Center for Corporate Social Responsibility at Copenhagen Business School, Kai Hockerts; CEO of INDEX:, Kigge Hvid; CEO and co-founder of MyC4, Mads Kjaer; former marketing director at InterfaceFLOR, Karin Laljani; CEO at Tomorrow's Company, Tony Manwaring; social entrepreneur and consultant, Oliver Maxwell; Head of Social Finance at NESTA, Sarah McGeehan; CEO and President of InterfaceFLOR Europe, Middle East, Africa and India, Lindsey Parnell; Creative Director at Imaginal, James Parr; founder of The Arlington Institute, John L. Petersen; founder of Ethicaleconomy, Nicolai Peitersen; co-founder of The Hub, Jonathan Robinson; Director of the Schwab Foundation for Social Entrepreneurship, Mirjam Schöning; founder of Specialisterne, Thorkil Sonne; CEO of Novo Nordisk, Lars Rebien Sørensen; CEO at Vestergaard Frandsen, Mikkel Vestergaard Frandsen; co-founder and former editor-in-chief of Fast Company, Alan Webber; and founder of Grameen Bank, Muhammad Yunus.

I would also like to thank the individuals, organizations and institutions that have given me permission to quote or use material from their work.

The book has also benefited from the many people in my network and the subscribers to my newsletter, who have contributed with case suggestions, encouragement and practical input. Likewise, I appreciate the assistance provided by Copenhagen Business School students Mette Mikkelsen and Ida Hemmingsen, who assisted me with the initial research. Particularly heartfelt appreciation goes to my assistant Siri Hjelm Jacobsen, who has been an excellent and loyal support throughout the entire process of researching, translating and editing.

A special thanks goes to John Grant for sharing his network of inspiring friends and professional contacts in London and, not least, for introducing me to John Wiley & Sons, Ltd. I am also very grateful to Tony Manwaring from Tomorrow's Company for his constructive comments and help after reading the initial drafts of the book, and for the later reviews and other expert input from: social entrepreneur and consultant Oliver Maxwell; industrial PhD and CSR strategist Christina Berg Johansen; anthropologist and Bottom of the Pyramid specialist, Louise Koch; social media specialist Henriette Weber; and Søren Lyngsgaard and Martin Fluri from the Danish Cradle-to-Cradle team. Also thank you to Liselotte Østerby from Adfairtising for her great input on cover and page design.

My deep appreciation also goes to the whole team at John Wiley & Sons, Ltd, including Senior Marketing Executive Natalie Girach, Marketing Manager Nick Mannion, Project Editor Vivienne Wickham, Content Editor Samantha Hartley, Publishing Assistant Michaela Fay and not least my patient Executive Commissioning Editor, Claire Plimmer, for professionalism, great feedback and continual support. I also thank Helen Heyes for copy-editing the manuscript.

I owe more than I can say to my close friends and dear family, who have engaged themselves in different ways throughout all stages of the book's progress, including proofreading, offering time breaks away from the computer and not least accepting the intrusion of this book into many evenings and weekends. You are the ones who make life worth living – and a book about sustainability worth writing.

Finally, thank you to all the New Pioneers out there. Without you there would be no book. Without you there would be no change and progress.

ABOUT THE AUTHOR

Tania Ellis (b. 1969) is a Danish–British prize-winning writer, speaker and business innovator who specialises in social business trends. She is frequently quoted in a wide range of national and Scandinavian media, who use Tania Ellis as trendspotter, commentator and opinion-leader.

She has over 20 years of work experience from the business sector, 12 of the years in various management positions in the airline and advertising industry, and holds an Executive MBA from Henley Management College in London. In 2003 she founded communications and consulting company Inspiratorium, where she gives advice and inspiration on social business trends to private, public and civil organizations with the purpose of promoting innovative and sustainable practices that generate both social and economic growth.

As one of Scandinavia's leading experts on social business, Tania is a popular speaker and inspirator on topics such as leadership, work–life demands, corporate and employer branding, corporate social responsibility, (corporate) social innovation and social entrepreneurship.

Tania has hosted workshops and spoken to over a hundred companies, trade unions, associations, NGOs, educational institutions, ministries, public institutions, municipalities and think tanks, and has reached more than 7000 participants ranging from opinion-formers, managers, CEOs, politicians and cabinet minsters to employees, activists and private individuals.

Clients include the Danish Association of Lawyers and Economists, multinational healthcare company Coloplast, social business school Kaospilots, the Danish Ministry of Education, Scandinavian telecompany TeliaSonera, the Norwegian state-owned innovation promoting company, Innovation Norway, and one of Northern Europe's leading energy groups, DONG Energy.

As innovation agent and consultant, Tania Ellis is also involved in projects and initiatives that aim to create both economic and social value. These include the pre-stage development of an online CSR-innovation tool (www. ideascompass.dk) that has been initiated by the Danish Commerce and Companies Agency, board work for The Food Bank, which collects and distributes surplus food from the food industry to social service agencies in Denmark, committee work for the Danish Ministry of the Interior and Social Affairs for reorganization of governmental grants to voluntary social organizations, and strategic consulting and project management for the Center for Social Economy, which promotes and supports social entrepreneurship in Denmark.

In addition, she has authored dozens of articles on business trends, and won Danish business magazine *Berlingske Nyhedsmagasin*'s 2004 award for her paper 'A Leadership Model for Future Denmark,' based on her Executive MBA dissertation 'The Era of Compassionate Capitalism' (Henley, 2002/3).

Her book contributions include the first Danish book on social innovation and social entrepreneurship, *De Nye Pionerer* (Jyllands Postens Forlag, 2006), *The CSR World Guide* (Greenleaf Publishing, 2010) and the Danish anthology on social entrepreneurship, *Socialt Entreprenørskab* (Børsens Forlag, 2010). She has also contributed to InterfaceFLOR's Danish 2007 sustainability report, *En Bæredygtig Fremtid* (A Sustainable Future) and to the Confederation of Danish Industry's 2009 Business Summit publication, *Fremtiden er Tæt På* (In the Near Future).

Read more at www.taniaellis.com

INDEX

Index compiled by Annette Musker